Gone to God:
A Civil War Family's Ultimate Sacrifice

by Keith Kehlbeck

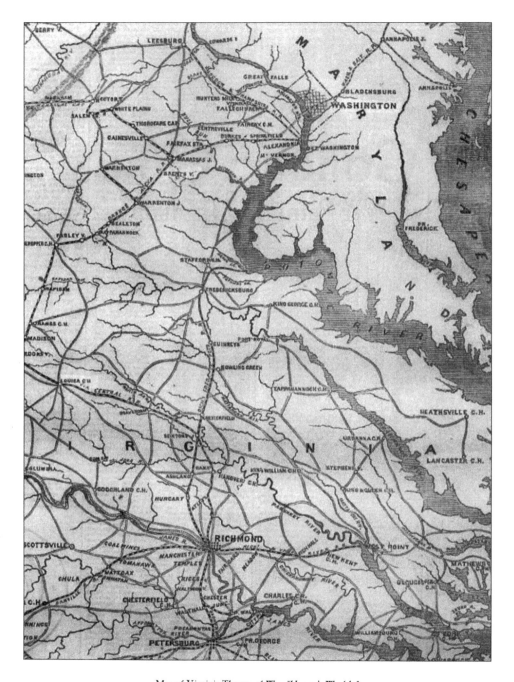

Map of Virginia Theater of War, "Harper's Weekly"

PREFACE

A Civil War Legacy:
Gone to God: One Family's Ultimate Sacrifice

Ever since iconic historian Bell I. Wiley broke proverbial Civil War literary ground with his *The Life of Johnny Reb* (published in 1943), the voices of individual soldiers—and by extension, their families and contemporaries—have played an important role in the historiography of America's formative conflict. Works such as Wiley's do not merely describe the battles and skirmishes, but (as articulated by the publisher) "…provide an intimate picture of a soldier's daily life—the songs he sang, the foods he ate, the hopes and fears he experienced, the reasons he fought."

In 1990, filmmaker Ken Burns helped commemorate and (re-)popularize the American Civil War by telling its story through still images and the words of those involved in the conflict. From Abraham Lincoln to the lowliest private, North and South, we heard about the transformational event of our history told by those who were there. The story of the Towles brothers of the 4th Virginia Cavalry—primarily told in their own words—is in that same tradition.

More recently, Drew Gilpin Faust, in her acclaimed book, *This Republic of Suffering*, charted the impact death and dying had on our nation during and after the war. My book is a microcosm of that study, examining how *one* family dealt with loss and remembrance.

Built on unpublished, original source materials, it tells the story of a family's loss on a personal level. Because of this, the story of the Towles brothers resonates today, 150 years after their deaths.

It goes without saying, of course, that the stories of individuals and families during the Civil War inevitably intertwine with the larger events that shaped the conflict and the times. The voices of combatants, like those of their family members, provide valuable and essential depth, context, and texture to the struggle between North and South. More to the point, the passions of family and friends, as captured in the words of primary source materials, are testament to the intensity of the war. Even today, removed as we are by nearly fifteen decades, echoes of the conflict are present in family anecdotes, and particularly in "what might have been" laments handed down from generation to generation in families that lost entire lines as a result of the war.

We take for granted today that we can often document, sometimes in excruciating detail, how decisions are made, the details of daily life, the sequence of events, and their rationales. The relative paucity of records from only a few generations removed makes the task of storytelling much more challenging, due to time and, in no small part, to the destruction that accompanied war and occupation. What is clear, however, is that the Civil War—or the War Between the States (or even the War of Northern Aggression, depending on your persuasion)—was a monumental event that changed the course of public and private history.

Like many old Virginia families, the Towleses (and their relatives: the Chownings, Chiltons, and Ewells) found their comfortable lives inexorably disrupted in only a few, short years. What had been prosperous antebellum estates, churches, communities, and farms were ravaged—and sometimes ultimately lost—as part of a struggle that changed America in many ways. And of course, there was the human cost, reflected here in the losses suffered by the Towles family.

The Towles story also reminds us how lives often are interconnected. It has been said that all individuals are related with the proverbial "six degrees of separation," and this story does nothing to disprove that old adage. Serendipity managed to draw several more recognizable personalities from the war into the Towles story, individuals such as Belle Boyd, Jeb Stuart, and George Armstrong Custer. Even a Hoosier (and now Michigander) like me has a connection; my wife is the great-granddaughter of the Towles brothers' youngest sister.

My wife's family encouraged me; it is, after all, their story. In this regard, I owe my mother-in-law (who taught history and generously shared her trove of family letters and diaries) a special debt of thanks. With a modest collection of first-person accounts and a great deal of additional secondary-source research, I've set out to place a powerful family story into the context of the war's larger panorama. As part of this effort, I examined the social, military, and community fabric of the Towles brothers' perspective and experience.

The 4th Virginia Cavalry was a Confederate unit that fought respectably and as a discrete unit until Appomattox. Inasmuch as the Towles brothers were a part of Company A of the 4th, this story is also its story.

The Old Capitol Prison, where Robert Towles spent several months during the conflict before escaping, had been a meeting place for the US Congress and would serve as the backdrop for trials and executions after the war. Today, its former footprint overlaps the location of the U.S. Supreme Court building in the nation's capital. Known as "the Bastille of the North" by those who decried its role as a holding place for alleged dissidents, spies, and other threats to the Northern war effort, Old Capitol is seen from the perspective of a Confederate scout, "spy," and "bushwacker," who also happened to be a twenty-year-old son of an Episcopal rector.

Religion plays an important factor in the Towles story. The intricacies of the Virginia Episcopal Diocese serve as a backdrop for the family's experiences, particularly given the overt religiosity of the various family members and inasmuch as Reverend Towles's service to his church and his communities precedes, coincides with, and follows the War.

Then, of course, there is the war itself—the prelude, outbreak, prosecution, finale, and aftermath—all covered extensively in other nonfiction scholarship, including acclaimed seminal works such as Bell Wiley's, as well as through new (and continuing) research and writing being done by a next generation of historians. Several of the latter have been extraordinarily encouraging and gracious in their assistance during this long project.

With *Gone to God,* I don't presume to replace the existing canon of Civil War regimental, battle, and biographical studies, but I do hope to complement it by adding to the growing body of work that examines the war at a personal level.

History certainly can be said to be much more than dates and places. Indeed, individuals—their lives, stories and experiences—comprise much more of the warp and weave of history than the more mundane recitations of statistics. This "personal" aspect to history, and in particular to the Civil War, is what I've loved since my Great-Aunt Elva encouraged me to read Bruce Catton during the Centennial years and since my family took a bus trip to Gettysburg when I was ten years old. I must say that I have found it very satisfying to chronicle the lives of these three young Virginia cavalrymen. After all, my mother always said that I was born on the *south* side of Indianapolis.

In any case, my lifelong interest has been strengthened through the journey I've been privileged to take during the process of writing the story of the Towles brothers. My hope is that the manuscript captures the more human aspects of one family's history—a history that was inexorably altered by circumstances.

Keith Kehlbeck
January 2013

TABLE OF CONTENTS

LIST OF ILLUSTRATIONS

ACKNOWLEDGEMENTS

As with any project that involves family and one's own passion—in this case, Civil War history—this book has been a "labor of love."

Its genesis goes back to an early conversation with my future mother-in-law, Virginia Webb, whose love of history and family—and generous support, both financial and otherwise—made this project possible. Her stewardship of family letters and records was essential to the book and a tribute to her mother, Aileen, the family genealogist, who I wish I'd known. Thanks for being so patient, Virginia, and I hope you and Alfred enjoy the final product.

Thanks, also, to my family; if we Kehlbecks had come to the U.S. in the 1840s, rather than the 1870s, we likely would have fought for the Union, and perhaps I might not have been around to write this book. Thanks for small favors and twists of karma! My parents nurtured my love of history through my formative years, took me to my first battlefield (Gettysburg) when I was ten years old, and have always expressed their pride in my accomplishments and interests. They have loved and supported me unconditionally throughout my life, and I will always be grateful that they encouraged me to explore my love of books and the past. How many other parents would have put up with seemingly endless dioramas of toy soldiers, memberships in the History Book Club, and dinnertime blatherings along the lines of "...and then, the Confederates charged..."? Well, come to think of it, my wife fits that profile, too, but more about that later...

Over the course of the decade or so when I worked intermittently on the book, I was assisted time and again in my research by friends in the Civil War community, who span the spectrum as mentors, fellow enthusiasts, friends, and role models.

Notably, historian Robert K. Krick—friend, avid shuffleboard competitor, wordsmith extraordinaire, cigar aficionado and wine skeptic—graciously provided guidance and access to his incomparable and extensive notes of publications and notations for all things related to the Civil War, and in particular, the 4th Virginia Cavalry. On his tip and with his assistance, I was able to secure through auction an original transcription of Robert Towles' diary. Perhaps more importantly, he was unstinting in his insistence that I complete this task and add to the published canon of original Civil War source materials. Mission accomplished, Robert.

Along the way, others contributed to my efforts: My father-in-law Richard Webb sent "odds and ends" from family storage that included John Pope's wallet. An Episcopal archivist, Julia Randle, helped track the arc of John Towles' career when I was starting this project. Eric Wittenberg graciously walked the battlefield of Trevilian Station with me, lo these many months ago. My old friend Libby Wright plowed through Southern Claims Commission records. Pam Sackett from the Friends of Brentsville Courthouse turned me onto the great little book, *Autobiography of Arab*. Steve Reger, a friend from the Capitol Hill Civil War Roundtable in DC, took me on a tour of Effingham, which was owned by his family at the time. A director at Mary Ball Washington Library and Museum, Cathy Currey, helped photocopy an original diary late one night. Our cousin several times removed, Randy Chowning, showed us Chowning Ferry Farm and the wonderful family cemetery that still exists on the ancestral property. The list goes on and on. It takes a village to make a book!

Other friends who provided encouragement and suggestions along the way included our Northern Neck cousins, David and Anne Cheek, my pals Jackie Hagan and Joe Glatthaar, Sarasota Civil War Education Association friends over the year like Bob Maher, Jack Davis, John Zervas, Craig Morin, the late David Hinze and his wife Mary, Melissa Delcour, Champagne buddy Tom Perry, "Whiskey Jim" Sikorski, Steve Ritchie, and Marge Putnam, who has sat next to me for many of the years at the annual conference.

Needless to say, over the years I've also received inspiration from the legendary historians and authors who've attended Sarasota, such as Charlie Roland and Bud Robertson, to name only a couple. Please forgive me, all whose names I've inadvertently omitted here: I hope you enjoy reading the story of the Towles family as much as I enjoyed researching and writing it.

Special thanks to my editors at Windy City: Chris Nelson, who provided invaluable insight on the flow and content of the manuscript, and Jan Green, who meticulously edited the copy and provided a much-needed ego boost through her encouragement and praise. To the three Windy City principals:

Lise Marinelli, Dawn McGarrahan Wiebe, and Kristyn Friske… thanks for making this project a reality!

Finally, I couldn't have persevered with this project without the love and support of my immediate family, my wife Ali, our daughter Emma (of whom I am very proud!), and our pugnacious Cairn Terrier, Sammy (and his predecessor Willie the Wonder Dog). Ali, in particular, possesses a most wonderful combination of seemingly infinite patience, unconditional love, and extraordinary intelligence. Although the story is of her family, she graciously gave me the space to finish the project in my own way, and always provides valuable feedback and editing when asked. I love you, Ali. This one's for you and all of the Towles women who preceded you…

For Sophronia, Ella, Aileen, Virginia, Ali, and Emma
Six generations of extraordinary women

Dear Departed Children

They're taken from the smiling home
And from the happy hearth,
And gathered up in clustering bands,
Like flowers of the earth.
Their little feet are seen no more,
Where once in joy they trod,
Those children we have fondly loved—
For they are gone to God.
Our lovely, gentle, cherub ones
Bow'd 'neath the chastening rod;
Their voices hushed, their eyes are dimmed
And they are gone to God.

S.E. Towles

Prologue:

"Gone to God"

Losing a child is always tragic, and no more so than when the loss comes while sacrificing for cause and country. War in general, and the American Civil War in particular, is replete with examples of devastated families, whose sons, husbands, and fathers gave what has been called the "last full measure" in defense of their beliefs and their homes.

Abraham Lincoln's poignant 1864 letter to Mrs. Lydia Bixby, a Boston widow who was believed to have lost five sons in the Civil War, is often cited as testimony to the heartbreak and loss attendant to armed conflict. "I feel how weak and fruitless must be any words of mine which should attempt to beguile you from the grief of a loss so overwhelming …I pray that our Heavenly Father may assuage the anguish of your bereavement, and leave you only the cherished memory of the loved and lost, and the solemn pride that must be yours, to have laid so costly a sacrifice upon the altar of Freedom," wrote Lincoln. That subsequent inquiries showed only two of Mrs. Bixby's sons died in battle in no way diminishes the sentiment embodied in the letter. Indeed, the Bixby letter is representative of the pain felt by and for Civil War families on both sides of the Mason-Dixon Line.

During the Civil War—unlike in today's armed forces—most regiments on both sides were recruited and organized from discrete geographic areas. Regiments therefore included local citizenry and often multiple family members. The fervor for the cause—North or South—is apparent from the numerous documented examples of siblings and cousins, sons and fathers on regimental rosters. Daniel Herrin of Wayne County, Georgia, sent seven sons to fight for the Confederacy. On the Union side, a German immigrant family by the name of Finch contributed *sixteen* sons to several Ohio regiments raised at the commencement of the War. The Lynn Family from Virginia's Prince William County had six family members listed on the 4th Virginia Cavalry's regimental roster. These and many other examples demonstrate that the Civil War was a war that produced casualties and that involved families in ways nearly unthinkable by modern military standards.

Statistics tell the story. In raw totals, the number of soldiers who died between 1861 and 1865 is approximately equal to the total American deaths in *all other wars* through the Korean War. Recent scholarship has suggested that the number may have been as high as 750,000. Author Drew Gilpin Faust points out that a similar rate of death—relative to the U.S. population in 1860—would mean upwards of six million fatalities today. During the course of the War, a large percentage of the available white manpower pool in the South served in the Confederate armies; more than 250,000 of them were killed in battle or died of disease. On the Northern side, more than 360,000 young men died. In simpler terms (and relative to their respective populations), historians have estimated that the war claimed ten percent of all Northern males between the ages of twenty and forty-five and a staggering thirty percent of all Southern white males between the ages of eighteen and forty. Clearly, such carnage would devastate many families and communities on both sides of the Mason-Dixon Line.

With the scope of the conflict, it is not surprising that families suffered multiple losses. Georgian James Robinson lost three of his five sons during the war. Three brothers from the southern Indiana Alford family were killed within a year and a half of volunteering for the Union. In the Shenandoah Valley, three of four Hite brothers died while serving in the Stonewall Brigade. The list goes on and on.

Some families lost loved ones on the home front, as well as suffering losses in combat. No more powerful example exists than that of the Towles family of Virginia. Within an eight-month span in 1863–1864, the Rev. John Towles and his wife Sophronia lost four children. Three sons—all of the male family members of arguable enlistment age—died in battle, and a daughter, age fifteen, died of illness while a refugee with her parents.

Such loss often seemed too great to accept, even in religious households. Sophronia Towles became so ill upon hearing of one son's capture and another's death that many family members feared for her life. John Towles had tried to keep the news of her eldest son's death from his wife, but she learned of the tragedy from a letter which came in her husband's absence. An "extreme illness" followed for many days. "Part of the time she was as ill as she could be to be alive," wrote Reverend Towles.

Many such understandably emotional reactions have been documented. "Sad tidings are brought to our cottage this morning…mother and sisters are overwhelmed, while our whole household is shrouded in sorrow," wrote a South Carolina woman upon hearing that a young family friend had been killed in battle. The news of the death of Johnston Pettigrew, a promising officer in the Army of Northern Virginia, prompted a member of his family to write, "Our brightest hope is gone. It is so dreadful. Alas for the young; all hope for the future of this frail life is put out…Surely we are broken up." The plaintive George Frederick Root song, "The Vacant Chair," bemoans the absence of Union sons and husbands gone to the war and to their deaths: "We shall meet but we shall miss him; there will be one vacant chair." Such sentiments were no doubt magnified in families where more than one chair became empty.

On the home front, families experienced a vicious cycle of grief, worry, hope, and despair, often exacerbated by limits of contemporary communication or inaccurate reports. When bad news came, it was followed by anxiety over other sons and husbands who remained in harm's way. "You may be the only one of our soldier boys now left alive to us," wrote John Towles to his youngest son, urging caution only a few months before that boy, too, was killed in battle. The forlorn hopes of bereaved families often were dashed as the casualties mounted in a war that must have seemed interminable and merciless to its participants in the field and to their support networks at home.

Like many families, the Towleses could find some comfort in the survival of three younger children who lived to adulthood. Beloved cousins and family friends survived the conflict. And throughout the ordeal, the family's faith did much to sustain their hopes for the future. Reverend Towles, an Episcopal rector since 1836, no doubt called upon his fervent belief in a better afterlife to rally his family's spirits as they absorbed the enormity of their loss. "Leave vengeance with Heaven," wrote Reverend Towles, when informing his middle son of his older brother's death. "Your brother has taken flight to bright mansions beyond the skies, there to part no more with those who for the present are lost."

We know from the modest surviving cache of Towles family letters and diaries that their sons faced death and loss with an admirable quietude and a certainty that a vastly better life awaited them. Indeed, the boys' concern was more for their parents, for whose emotional and physical wellbeing they feared more than death. "He is now resigned to the Will of the Lord, [and] all he cares to live for is to be a comfort to his parents," wrote a nurse caring for young Robert Towles as he lay dying in June of 1864.

The story of the Towles brothers of the 4th Virginia Cavalry is one of fidelity to duty, love for family and friends, and ultimately, the void left behind when each of these "noble boys" died a "tryumphant" death. Their exploits frame the context within which the Southern Confederacy struggled to secure its independence.

With hindsight, we know that more than 600,000 Americans gave their lives for the causes in which they believed. With that perspective, the loss of three Confederate cavalrymen is merely a small reminder of the suffering caused by war. Their story, from the Towles family's origins to the aftermath of war, provides a glimpse of the personalities and settings—on the battlefield, homefront, and politically—that characterized this transformative period in American history. More importantly, however, it serves as a microcosm of the void left on both sides of a struggle that claimed an entire generation of young people—for many families their best, their brightest hopes for the future.

CHAPTER ONE

A most agreeable and lovable man
A fine, old Virginia family

"For many years now, the Rev. John Towles has been
acceptably serving the needs of Dettingen Parish."

Bishop William Meade
Old Churches of Virginia, Vol. II

Towles

Rev. John Towles

Effingham, home of the Howison family,
neighbors to the Towleses in Prince William County

St. James Church, Brentsville

"Old Dal" Dr. E.A. Dalrymple,
Principal at the Episcopal High School in
Alexandria and Towles family friend

The Towles family of Virginia traces its roots to the earliest days of what is now called the Northern Neck of Virginia—the land between the Potomac and Rappahannock rivers. Henry Towles "the Immigrant" settled in Virginia from Liverpool, England, in 1652, having come to America at twelve years of age. A planter and landowner, Henry served as constable in Accomac County on the eastern shore of Virginia. His extensive landholdings eventually included property further south in Middlesex County and in what is now Lancaster County, Virginia.

In 1711, his son Henry purchased more than three hundred acres on an island between the Rappahannock River and the Corrotoman River from Mr. John Pyne, "gentleman," for the sum of four hundred and six pounds sterling and thirty thousand pounds of tobacco. He called this piece of land Towles Point, and it became the ancestral home for generations of the family. The Immigrant's great-grandson would specify in his will that "the said land not in any case be sold but always remain an inheritance to [Towles] heirs lawfully begotten forevermore."

As with many early American families, the Towles family genealogy includes large numbers of children and exhibits a propensity for the use and re-use of family names. A third generation Towles patriarch sired fourteen children by two wives and managed to incorporate the names of virtually all of his siblings and recorded forbears in various combinations. At a time when many children did not survive beyond childhood, such persistence helped assure the continuation of the family name and fortunes.

Surviving court records from early Virginia reveal the Towles family to have been active in real estate, in politics, and in the defense of hearth and home. As the family grew, so did its holdings in Middlesex, Orange, Madison, and Culpeper counties. Through marriage, the family added property such as the nearby estate of Poplar Neck. A few immigrated to the Carolinas, Louisiana, and Kentucky, where branches of the family prospered. By the turn of the nineteenth century, the Towles name had become a respected and ubiquitous feature of Virginia and southern society.

Several Towleses distinguished themselves in the Colonial Militia and during the Revolutionary War. A fourth generation Henry Towles was a lieutenant in the 5th Virginia Regiment and served as a delegate to Virginia's Constitutional Convention from Lancaster County. Oliver Towles was a lieutenant colonel in the Revolutionary War and later received for his services a parcel of land in the newly-acquired Louisiana Purchase. Henry Hill, a son of a third-generation Towles daughter and himself grandfather to Confederate General A.P. Hill, served under Revolutionary War hero Light Horse Harry Lee.

Fourteen members of the Towles family fought in the War of 1812, and at least one was commissioned an officer. During the war, a British frigate raided the family plantations on the Rappahannock. As the British entered the Corrotoman Creek landing, the mistress of Towles Point threw the mansion's keys into the Rappahannock, rather than give them up to the enemy. She then defied the raiders to open the house; they did not. Perhaps it is appropriate that a surviving wax seal depicts the Towles family coat of arms with a lion prominently featured.

Many members of the Towles family served their community in leadership and professional capacities. Lawyers, architects, and planters are well-represented in the family tree of the early Towles generations. In some cases, jobs seemed nearly a birthright. For example, Henry the Immigrant's great-great-grandson James followed in the footsteps of his father and grandfather and served as clerk of the court in Lancaster County. As would become apparent, however, James's son would not continue this family tradition.

James Towles had married the sister of another prominent Lancaster County citizen, Col. John Chowning. In 1813 James and Felicia Chowning Towles's only son John was born at Towles Point. Presumably, young John Towles could have easily settled into a life of public service and landholding in his home county. A different profession beckoned to this young man, however.

Baptized and confirmed in the local Episcopal Parish of St. Mary's Whitechapel, John Towles—perhaps at the instigation of his father—sought out opportunities that would take him from the security of Towles Point. In 1833 John was enrolled at distant Kenyon College, an Ohio institution that served as a preparatory school for the Episcopal ministry. Although the family was Episcopalian, this was probably intended as a way to open the world to young John or to provide a stimulus for growth, rather than as a conscious nudge towards the church. This path would provide the young man with a lifetime's calling, however.

Kenyon College had been founded in 1825 as an institution of the Episcopal Church, and comprised three separate schools, including a military academy and the Bexley Hall Seminary. Its founders, Philander Chase and Charles P. McIlvane—president of the college during John Towles's matriculation—served as Episcopal bishops for Ohio and were considered leading evangelical Episcopalians.

Throughout the antebellum period in particular, the Protestant Episcopal Church had a very decided split between the High Church and Low Church, or evangelicals. The High Church placed great importance on ritual and ceremony, while the Low Church was simpler and incorporated informal praise and worship, as well as emphasizing biblical revelation over symbolism. Each group had great suspicion of the other, and Episcopalians of each stripe gravitated to the educational institution hailed by their group. Philander Chase and Charles McIlvaine were both evangelicals, and Kenyon College accordingly was a school associated with their movement.

It is interesting to note that a surprising number of young men were sent to the Kenyon schools from southern and mid-Atlantic states in the early 1800s. Virginia was considered one of the primary evangelical dioceses of the time, and the Virginia Theological Seminary the foremost evangelical seminary. It is not surprising, then, that a young Virginian interested in the ministry would pursue an ecclesiastical education that took him from Kenyon College to the seminary.

Upon returning to Virginia in 1835, John married his first cousin, Sophronia Elizabeth Chowning, whose family lived on land adjoining Towles Point. John was three years older than Sophronia, but they had no doubt grown up together, since the families lived in close proximity and were already connected through marriage. For the young, soon-to-be cleric, being married to Sophronia must have been a welcome tie to home and loved ones. Sophronia also came from a well-established Tidewater family.

The Chownings actually pre-dated the Towles family in the New World, with royalist Robert Chowning "the Immigrant" fleeing England in 1649 after the beheading of King Charles I and coming to Virginia. According to family tradition, Robert Chowning's descendants had "in every generation made substantial contributions to the life and history of Lancaster County." As with the Towles family, a number of Chownings served in the Continental Army and during the War of 1812.

Robert Chowning the Immigrant's grandson George purchased land adjacent to Towles Point, and started a plantation known since Revolutionary times as "the Ferry." Sophronia's father, Col. John Chowning, who had inherited the Ferry, no doubt instilled in his daughter the importance of family and the self-confidence derived from generations of successfully laboring to establish a comfortable way of life on the banks of the Rappahannock.

The interconnection of the two families—Sophronia's Aunt Felicia had married her husband-to-be's father—and their close proximity in the Northern Neck led to frequent social and professional collaboration. A surviving receipt for eleven-year-old Sophronia's school tuition, payable to James Towles, indicates that Sophronia's uncle was involved in her education and upbringing. Later, Clerk of the Court James Towles acted as executor for Col. John Chowning's will and was responsible for the disposition of his bequests, including a trust for James's daughter-in-law-to-be. On Sunday, August 2, 1835, at St. Mary's Whitechapel, the Rev. Ephraim Adams further cemented the bonds of two of the area's oldest families by uniting John and Sophronia in marriage. It was to prove a lasting union between two people of formidable family traditions.

Shortly after entering the blessed state of matrimony, John entered the Virginia Theological Seminary in Alexandria to pursue the ministry. "Embosomed deep in lofty woods," the diocesan seminary was initially established in Williamsburg, but had been relocated to Alexandria in 1824 during a period of internal church divisions over the propriety of having a seminary that might compete with the Episcopal General Seminary, then in New Haven. The new seminary was noted as a place where "(God's) spirit worked in the minds of good men in Virginia and Maryland, inspiring them with love for the souls perishing for the bread of life, and with zeal for the sending forth of true ministers of the Word."

The course of study was rigorous. In addition to English, the Junior Class studied the four Gospels and the Acts of the Apostles in Greek, and eighteen chapters of Genesis and thirty Psalms in Hebrew. The Senior Class studied all of the Epistles and twenty chapters of Isaiah in Hebrew, in addition to "Systematic Divinity and Church History, etc." Class members were also required to prepare theses, sermons, and to read services—all in all, quite a complete religious education.

Seminary records show John Towles as a Middle Year student during 1836 and 1837, and alumni records list John Towles of Lancaster County as a graduate of the Class of 1837.

Upon graduation, he was ordained a deacon at the seminary and, later that year, as a priest at St. Paul's, Alexandria. In this, he was initiated into his chosen profession by the Bishop of Virginia, the Rt. Rev. Richard C. Moore. While the young priest acclimated to his duties, he and Sophronia became parents to their first child, Catherine Felicia, who was born in March of 1837. Tragically, the little girl died of illness the following year.

The couple's grief must have been lightened by the birth of their first son, John Vivian, in February of 1839. This healthy boy would be known affectionately as "Viv." Having become a family man, all that remained was a posting for the young cleric; it was not long in coming.

By April of 1839, John Towles was called to become rector of St. James Church, Brentsville, Dettingen Parish, and St. Paul's Church, Haymarket, Leeds Parish, both in Prince William County, Virginia. He would guide the two churches' flocks for the next twenty-three years. "Mr. Towles was a Virginia Seminary man" and inherited his parishes from "a succession of worthy rectors," reported a parishioner some years later. At the time he took over the rectorship, Dettingen Parish extended from Dumfries and Occoquan to the Bull Run Mountains. The parish also included missions throughout the area surrounding what is modern-day Manassas.

The town of Brentsville that greeted Reverend Towles and his family in 1839 had been chartered and had served as the county seat since 1822, when the district court had been moved from Dumfries. Changing navigational patterns on the Potomac resulted in the decline of Dumfries as a thriving, colonial merchant town, and the resulting population shift to the west mandated the relocation of the political center of the county. Brentsville grew rapidly, and an 1835 gazetteer reported that "the Court House, clerk's office and jail are handsomely situated on the main street, in a public square of three acres. Besides them, the village contains 19 dwelling houses, three miscellaneous stores, two handsome taverns, built of brick and stuccoed, one house of entertainment, one house of public worship, free for all denominations, a Bible society, a Sunday school, a temperance and tract society…There is in the vicinity a common school in which the rudiments of English education are taught…population 130 persons."

Nearby Haymarket was originally called Red House, the name being derived from a red brick tavern located at the intersection of the Dumfries Road and the heavily traveled Carolina (or "Rogues") Road. The tavern—a popular watering hole and stopping point for travelers on both roads—was noteworthy enough to be included on Thomas Jefferson's 1787 map of Virginia. The town itself was officially laid out in 1798, and was probably named after the celebrated race course in England. Before shifting to more prominent Dumfries, the district court for the county met briefly in Haymarket during the first decade of the new century.

Of primary importance for the new rector was the care and nurturing of the two churches within the parishes under his direction. St. James, near Brentsville, was one of the first Episcopal churches built after the disestablishment of the Church of England following the Revolutionary War. A solid, brown-stone, single-gable-roof church was constructed in 1847, but the new rector would have been greeted by a modest chapel built in 1822, when Brentsville was founded.

West of Brentsville, Haymarket boasted the county's oldest church, St. Paul's, whose walls dated to the late eighteenth century. During its early years, the structure—designed by noted local architect James Wren—encompassed many uses, including district courthouse, jail, and school. In 1830, it was finally converted into a full-time church, with a square, railed-in chancel in its west end, a high pulpit back of the chancel, and a small table with marble top used for Holy Communion. What had been the jury room was converted into a vestry and rector's study, which opened into a gallery supported by pillars, so that the clergy had a long march down steps and up the aisle to the chancel.

Bishop William Meade of Virginia, the preeminent cleric of the Virginia Diocese prior to the Civil War, noted in his 1831 book, *Old Churches and Families of Virginia*, that the old court house at Haymarket "has been purchased and converted into a handsome and convenient temple of religion. A race course once adjoined the buildings, and in preaching there in former days I have on a Sabbath seen from the court house bench on which I stood the horses in training for the sport which was at hand. Those times have, I trust, passed away forever." Indeed, the town probably owed its name to the lively horse races which occurred there in the early 1800s. Presumably, Bishop Meade was confident that the new rector would guide his flock in a direction more favorable in the eyes of the Lord.

As the dominant church in colonial Virginia, the Anglican Church—and its American successor the Protestant Episcopal Church—served as a center not only for religious services, but also for social and political activities. Parishioners would gather at the church to socialize, to discuss business, politics, and crops.

With the benefit of formal education, clergymen were considered to be part of the upper strata of Virginia society. Incumbent upon the new pillar of society was the establishment of a homestead and livelihood, and John Towles set about this task with determination.

Purchasing a tract of land near Brentsville, the new rector began to add land and property as his means allowed. What no doubt began as a modest farm grew as John and Sophronia added to their holdings. Surviving land records from the 1840s and 1850s show that the Towleses bought and sold tracts of land southwest of Brentsville on Broad, Slate and Cedar Runs. By 1859, property tax records identify the Towles farm as comprising more than 1,000 acres. Like many of his neighbors in antebellum Virginia, John Towles would have planted a wide variety of crops: corn, wheat, rye, and some tobacco and fruits, such as peaches, apples, and cherries. The farm would also have included cows, pigs, and sheep. This diversity (as opposed to strictly focusing on tobacco, a crop that typically exhausts the land) would have helped the farm thrive in the decade prior to the war. While not a "plantation" in the popular sense of the word, the Towles farm appears to have been a quite successful venture, given its growth and as documented in U.S. census records.

The family was growing as well. Although two more babies died in infancy, Sophronia gave birth in 1843 to the couple's second son, Robert, followed by James in 1845, Rosalie in 1847, Ella in 1850, Churchill in 1852, and LeRoy in 1855.

Having himself experienced the benefits of a broad-based Episcopal education, John Towles would see that his own children be given opportunities to learn. Eldest son Vivian, in particular, was encouraged to pursue a higher education, first at the Episcopal High School in Alexandria and then, briefly, at far-away University of Michigan.

The Episcopal High School, founded in 1839 to provide an institution "of Episcopal character," had been the brainchild of the Convention of the Diocese of Virginia, which saw a great need for such a facility. "There is at present no institution of learning under the care of the Episcopal Church in the diocese, and…the sons of our Episcopal families are too often entrusted to local and irresponsible schools, which are either sectarian…or totally unorganized and desultory in their operations," wrote a sponsoring cleric. With the help of Bishop Meade, a tract of land near the Theological Seminary in Alexandria was acquired, and the Rev. William Nelson Pendleton was engaged as its first principal.

As originally envisioned, the school would have no more than thirty boys, and none under the age of fourteen. The standard of scholarship was high, with classes in mathematics, chemistry, astronomy, and engineering. Also included were instructions in "mental and moral philosophy," which must have seemed daunting to the young students.

In the 1840s, Dr. E.A. Dalrymple had been named principal, replacing Reverend Pendleton. Dr. Dalrymple, who would become a lifelong Towles family friend, was, according to a contemporary, "a personality, a fine scholar, an enthusiastic teacher and an unrivalled disciplinarian. His watchword was thoroughness." "Old Dal," as he was known, apparently did not spare the rod, and in consequence, few students were spoiled. Whippings were administered not only for misdemeanors, but also for imperfect recitations. Since Dr. Dalrymple's specialty was Latin, no doubt many a sore backside resulted from less-than-stellar renditions of Caesar's Gallic Wars.

"To make mere scholars, or exact men of business, is not the sole duty of the Christian teacher…He is not only to labor to make them useful men, but so far as in him lies, he is to endeavor to make them Christian gentlemen," wrote Dr. Dalrymple. Listed as a graduate in the class of 1854, Vivian Towles would have no doubt been heavily influenced by these sentiments, in addition to deriving benefit from the high school's rigorous academic program.

By the standards of today, the range of textbooks and studies at the Episcopal High School would make it more of a collegiate school than a secondary school, and it is probable that the institution's contemporary reputation was what drew increasing numbers of young men to its halls. By the time Vivian Towles graduated, the school had grown to nearly one hundred young men.

Viv's experience at Episcopal High School may have broadened his horizons, or perhaps his father saw the benefit to be derived from a Midwestern education such as he himself had received at Kenyon College. In any case, Vivian Towles traveled west after his graduation to attend classes in Ann Arbor, Michigan, at the fledgling University of Michigan. "My connection with your son, Viv dates to our time together at the University of Michigan (circa 1857)," wrote a college friend to Vivian's parents after the war. While not much is known about young Vivian's experience in the Wolverine State, it can be assumed that he soon became anxious to return home. Perhaps the increasingly strident sectional tensions drew him south. Or perhaps he was simply homesick for Virginia and his family. In any case, his tenure at the University of Michigan lasted less than a year.

The Towles family farm to which he returned had grown in his absence. In addition to being the respected rector of a large and active parish, John Towles now operated a prosperous farm, complete with all of the accoutrements such an enterprise required.

In slaveholding-Virginia of the mid-1800s, property and farming would come with the attendant need for slaves. Although most of the farms in Prince William County had slaves, the great majority of farms in the Upper South were owned by men with less than twenty slaves. Throughout the 1840s and 1850s, John Towles would own as many as six slaves, according to surviving tax records. Throughout this period, records also show that he occasionally emancipated individuals and families. A recorded emancipation of 1845 states, "I, John Towles, of the County of Prince William, State of Virginia, have manumitted, emancipated and set free, and by these presents do manumit, emancipate and set free Violet Peachy, and I do hereby declare her...to be entirely liberated from slavery..." On another occasion, a mother and her three children were emancipated by Reverend Towles. An example of an emancipation document, found in a surviving deed book is as follows:

> Deed Book 19, p. 77 – Know all men by these presents that I Jno (*) TOWLES, of the County of Prince William, State of Virginia, have manumitted, emancipated and set free and by these presents do manumit, emancipate and set free **Sylvia JACKSON** and I do hereby declare her the said Sylvia JACKSON, to be entirely liberated from slavery and entitled to all rights privileges of a free person, with which it is in my power to

invest her, the said Sylvia JACKSON, hereby emancipated, is a woman of dark complexion, five feet high. and is between the age of fifty five and sixty. In testimony whereof I have hereunto set my hand and seal, this the 28th day of October in the year of Our Lord, one thousand eight hundred and forty five.

John TOWLES { seal}

In the Clerks office of Prince William County Court October 39, 1845

This deed of Emancipation from TOWLES to Sylvia JACKSON was acknowledged by John TOWLES to be his act & deed and admitted to record.

Teste: J. WILLIAMS CC

(* Jno is an abbreviation for John.)

While we have no surviving rationale for such emancipations, it may have simply been a way of rewarding loyal slaves and their families when age or physical limitations made continued service nonproductive. Another possibility is that—like the ongoing debate within the Episcopal Church at the time—John Towles wrestled with the role of slavery, its place in scripture, and the implications of human bondage in a modern, Christian world. In any case, given the political tensions of the time and the great conflict that was about to engulf the nation with slavery at its core, this practice is a fascinating window into the mind of a man who would later lose three sons fighting for the Confederacy. Whatever the reason for these emancipations, it is clear that a farm the size of the Towles's would require continued help in the form of slaves, and Reverend Towles must have periodically added to his workforce accordingly.

As the rector for Dettingen Parish, John Towles regularly performed the expected number of marriages, baptisms, and presumably, funerals. Dettingen Parish vestry records show a number of local weddings presided over by Reverend Towles, including several for neighbors who had become family friends. For example, in April 1859, Reverend Towles presided over the wedding of Miss Bettie Macrae, daughter of Brentsville neighbor and friend, Dr. John Macrae. The wedding was performed at the Macrae home, "Meadowfarm." The Macraes are listed on property records as having one of the original plots of land in Brentsville when the town was laid out. Dr. Macrae's son Lee would go off to war with the Towles brothers and would be counted among their closest friends.

An intriguing entry in the list of marriages performed by Reverend Towles includes one on October 21, 1851 at Haymarket: "Alexander Mason (colored) to Caroline Milford (colored & free). He was a slave, property of Thomas Henderson." Presumably, Reverend Towles had received special dispensation from Mr. Henderson to marry off his "property."

By the eve of the Civil War, life must have seemed settled and rewarding for John Towles and his family. In terms of physical property, the Towleses were affluent, especially when compared to other residents of Prince William County. By 1859, the tax records show that the farm was being run profitably by "John Towles and sons." The 1860 Census shows his values of personal and real estates to be among the highest in the county.

His churches were prospering, and over twenty years of service to the parish had endeared Reverend Towles to his flock. "According to our elders, he was a most agreeable and lovable man, as well as faithful pastor, and the fact of his being from the Northern Neck, from which many of our people had come, was an added bond."

Events beyond Prince William County would soon conspire to drastically change the good fortunes of Reverend Towles and his family, however.

CHAPTER TWO

A Lincoln Pole and the winds of war
Politics and preparation for war

"We have faith in Abraham…Old Abe is ours."

Wide-Awake Club slogan
circa 1860

"Wide Awake" rally, Library of Congress

A "Wide Awake" member in full regalia,
Library of Congress

John Brown, Library of Congress

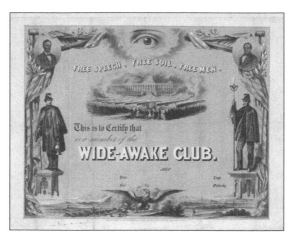

Wide-Awake Club membership certificate, Library of Congress

As antebellum sectional and political tensions spiraled out of control in the late 1850s, the Towles family prospered. The Towles homestead, styled "Vaucluse" by the Reverend Towles, was, by 1860, one of the more prominent houses in Prince William County. Speculation is that John Towles may have named his home as a remembrance of a similarly-named Fairfax County farm near the Episcopal seminary, where seminary students sometimes had Sunday supper.

If there was a more prominent home in antebellum Brentsville, it would have been the nearby Howison family's "Effingham," a substantial structure that survived the war and still stands today. "The house is frame, but of noble proportions with a pair of splendid brick chimneys at each end," wrote an observer many years later. The pride of Effingham was its numerous outbuildings laid out in an elaborate plan, some of which can be traced today. In addition to barns, stables, coach houses, and other buildings necessary for farming, there was a weaver's house, tannery, blacksmith's forge, greenhouse, smoke house, ice house, and an estate office. Slave quarters were numerous, and the 1860 Federal Slave Census for Prince William County noted that the Howisons had more than thirty slaves to tend the farm.

The Howisons were friends and neighbors of the Towles family, with their own distinguished lineage and history in the area. Like the Towleses, the Howisons might well have been in the mind of one nineteenth-century biographer who noted, "In these days when so much that is old and venerable is melting away before the destroying touch of radical philosophy, and when all the tendencies of the times are to teach children that they are better than their ancestors, it may be well, occasionally, to recall the past and to unearth an old family record, which will remind us that our generation is not the first that has lived on the earth." Certainly, families like the Towleses, Chownings, and Howisons had every reason to be proud of their old family records. By 1860, various members of the Howison family had achieved prominence, and the family was well known to their neighbors, the Towleses.

Stephen Howison had been one of the vestrymen at the old Slaty Run Church, which likely was how he would have become acquainted with his neighbor, Reverend Towles. According to his contemporaries, Stephen Howison was "a man of prominence in the community," with a family to match. One of his sons was a United States naval officer who rose to a command in the Pacific, but who had died in 1848. Another son, John, inherited the ancestral fondness for agriculture, and contemporary accounts noted that, under his guidance, Effingham was "beautiful and productive before the war." Effingham's location—like that of Vaucluse—would prove to be problematic during the coming conflict, however.

Prince William County, Virginia, simply was destined to be in the vortex of major military operations in the Eastern Theater of the Civil War.

For the moment, however, life went on in Brentsville and the surrounding area.

Dealing, as ever, with great energy in matters of the spirit, Reverend Towles had expanded his ministry as well as the size of his steadhold. In addition to serving his churches in Haymarket and Brentsville, records show that Reverend Towles found time during the period of 1852 to 1854 to serve as rector in another nearby place of worship, Aquia Church, in the northern part of neighboring Stafford County. Under his supervision, the long-established church underwent repairs, and the vestry was reorganized.

On the political front, however, storm clouds were brewing. A westerner, Abraham Lincoln, had come to national prominence during the 1858 Illinois senatorial campaign, and his rise as a national political figure was strengthened by eloquent and convincing speechmaking at places such as Cooper Union, New York. Lincoln's political philosophy and positions—like many others, north and south—had been influenced by a significant debate and legislation involving new territories, particularly the Kansas-Nebraska Act of 1854. Passed by the U.S. Congress in May of that year, the Act divided the Nebraska Territory into two units—Kansas and Nebraska—and provided for popular sovereignty, empowering voters to decide for themselves whether or not to allow slavery within their borders. The Act served to repeal the long-standing Missouri Compromise of 1820, which had prohibited slavery north of the latitude line below that state. The new legislation affected territories west and north of Missouri, and this enraged slavery opponents and energized its supporters. As a result, proponents of both factions flocked to Kansas in order to influence the voting that would determine the territory's slavery status. What followed were electoral controversies and factional violence, which gave the territory the nickname "Bleeding Kansas." One particularly colorful anti-slavery activist was "Osawatomie" John Brown, who with his sons would gain notoriety by murdering five pro-slavery farmers with a broadsword.

In many ways, the Kansas-Nebraska Act divided the nation and pointed it towards civil war. It also provided a topic around which several notable political careers evolved. For example, one of the founders of the anti-Kansas-Nebraska Act faction was Salmon P. Chase, nephew of the Episcopal cleric, Philander Chase, and later a candidate for president and ultimately secretary of the treasury. Perhaps more importantly, a somewhat unknown western politician (and one-term Congressman) Abraham Lincoln aired his differences over the Act with Illinois Senator Stephen A. Douglas in public speeches and debates; the Lincoln-

Douglas debates served to increase his national political stature and eventually led to his nomination for president.

As Lincoln's political fortunes improved, the fortunes of the nascent Republican Party strengthened; so, too, did the vehemence of Southerners and others who viewed "Old Abe" as a "Black Republican," intent on interfering with their rights and in particular with the status of the "peculiar institution" of slavery.

Electoral politics of the time gave rise to many forms of mass participation, including politically oriented, disciplined social clubs, such as the Republican Rocky Mountain Club, Freedom Club, Bear Club, Lincoln Rail Maulers, and most importantly, the Wide-Awakes. These clubs, usually made up of young, unmarried men, marched in support of candidates in communities throughout the North.

By 1860, hundreds of Wide-Awakes clubs had sprung into existence. Dressed in capes and carrying lighted oil lamps mounted atop four-foot poles—easily converted to cudgels, as one observer noted—they marched, monitored polling places on election day, and added "zest, excitement, and [according to some non-Republicans] bitterness to what was already a crucial and harrowing political campaign."

While the Wide-Awakes marched only in the North, their influence and potential concerned many Southerners. Pro-slavery, extremist, "Fire-Eater" politician, and future Confederate senator Louis T. Wigfall decried Lincoln's candidacy, and with it the elevation of groups like the Wide-Awakes, which he compared to a "Praetorian guard." "No man who has looked upon them…and heard their regular military tramp, does or can doubt [that they are military in nature]," argued Wigfall. By 1860, the *New York Herald* estimated there were more than 400,000 drilled and uniformed Wide-Awakes nationwide.

With the noted military discipline and fervor of the participants, it would come as no surprise that, when war broke out, many Wide-Awakes volunteered immediately to fight for the Union. In the meantime, they were an embodiment of the South's greatest fear—an oppressive force presumably bent on marching to the South, liberating the slaves, pushing aside the Southern way of life, or as one commentator noted, "parading at midnight, carrying rails to break open our doors, torches to fire our dwellings, and beneath their long black capes the knife to cut our throats."

The phenomenon of marching clubs went hand in hand with other political activities. In many communities, demonstrations of all forms came to be flashpoints for political and philosophical differences. Such gatherings were often quite the spectacle, and rallies, processions, picnics, and barbecues were the order of the day. One documented event involved staging wagons drawn by thirty-two yoke of oxen on which were men splitting rails (presumably a reference to that old "railsplitter" Abe Lincoln).

Another favorite event during the 1860 presidential campaign was pole raising. During the campaign, it was a common practice to raise poles, as much as 150 feet high, on which political parties and supporters hung flags and effigies of the candidates they supported or opposed. So-called "Lincoln Poles" were erected in many towns, and the raising of one was occasion for supporters to rally and for ladies to grace such an event "with their presence, good looks, and smiles of approval."

The raising of a pole in Henry County, Iowa, in 1860 was described as follows:

> Four perfectly straight trees of different sizes were selected so as to form a strong, uniformly tapering pole when spliced. The ends of the trees were then hewn at a long angle and laid together. Through the splices two-inch auger holes were bored into which wooden pins were driven. Strong iron bands of the proper sizes were then slipped over the small end of the pole and pounded down over the tapering splices. A heavy log, about twelve or fifteen feet in length, was used for the base, into which the lower section of the pole was mortised and firmly braced laterally. When the pole was finished, a trench, long and wide enough to admit the base log, was dug to the depth of about eight feet. This contrivance was designed to prevent the pole from swinging sideways or over-balancing as it was being raised.
>
> Long pikes with iron spikes in the end were provided for the men who were to do the actual work of raising the pole. Ropes were attached to the top of the pole for the purpose of steadying it in the course of erection. A heavy, forked pole was also ready to be used for steering the flagpole and holding it in place between hoists.
>
> When all was in readiness a captain was chosen and the work of raising began. The small end of the pole was lifted from the ground, the pikes were jabbed in, the ropes were manned, and the guide pole put in place. "Heave, O heave!" cried the captain. All together the pike men heaved with all their might. The great pole raised a few feet, the guide pole was slid farther down to bear the weight, and the men rested from their strenuous efforts. Again and again this process was repeated. Gradually the base log slipped into the trench and at last the pole stood erect with the earth tamped firmly around the base.

How the eager throng cheered when the work was done! From the top, a hundred feet above the ground, floated a large American flag about eight by fifteen feet in dimensions. Inscribed on the banner in large letters were the names of Lincoln and Hamlin.

As with many occasions—and after the boisterous celebration that accompanied the event had been completed—vandals or those of opposing political persuasion razed the Lincoln Pole to the ground. In this instance, the desecration was attributed to "some miscreant," a "villainous Douglasite" or other such ne'er-do-wells or political opponents. The locals, undeterred, shortly raised another pole, "fully eighteen inches in diameter at the base," and that extended a hundred and twenty feet in the air "as straight as an arrow."

Coincidentally, a Lincoln Pole in Prince William County elicited an equally strong counter-reaction and was to play a role in the first "active operation" of a group of young Southern militiamen known as the Prince William Cavalry.

The Prince William Cavalry—later Company A of the 4th Virginia Cavalry—had been organized in the winter of 1858–1859, during what locals called "the John Brown excitement." Under the militia law, the unit drilled monthly at Brentsville under the supervision of William G. Brawner.

Brawner, a local Manassas boy who studied law at the University of Virginia and later set up practice in Brentsville, served as a Prince William County delegate to the convention in Richmond that was to decide the issue of whether Virginia was to secede or remain in the Union. Brawner represented Prince William in all of the sessions of the convention and, after the passage of the ordinance of secession, returned to his home and took command of the 36th regiment of Virginia Militia, which ultimately was called into the field shortly before the battle of First Manassas. During a raid with Confederate partisan John Mosby in June of 1863, Brawner would die while commanding Company H of the 15th Virginia Cavalry—another unit of local boys known as the Prince William Partisan Rangers.

During the 1860 campaign, an active local Republican, John Underwood, with a following of approximately twenty other supporters, had "raised a handsome pole and flag" in the interest of their candidate, Abraham Lincoln, in the nearby town of Occoquan in eastern Prince William County. The local militia—at the time commanded by Eppa Hunton and including the eldest Towles son, Vivian, in civilian clothes—had conflicting motivations: to cut the offending pole down or to protect private property, as instructed by Governor Letcher of Virginia. Their initial inclinations seem to have won out, since the militia, convening as a citizens' meeting, elected a captain and an ax man and proceeded to cut the pole "into convenient lengths…to be divided and later made into walking sticks."

Ultimately, the various tensions brought on by current events and by political confrontations began to manifest themselves in more formally-organized paramilitary organizations. A parallel to the popularity of marching clubs in the North were organizations called the "Minute Men," which were formed throughout the South. Like their Northern counterparts, they, too, held torch rallies and wore uniforms, complete with an official badge of "a blue rosette…to be worn upon the side of the hat."

State militias in the South (with troops such as the Prince William Cavalry) gained impetus from the notoriety of abolitionist John Brown's raid on Harpers Ferry in 1859. The state militia had been revived by action of the General Assembly in March of 1858, but its rate of growth was, by all accounts, accelerated by the John Brown crisis.

Madman or martyr, John Brown had declared his own personal crusade for the abolition of slavery after the Kansas-Nebraska Act of 1854. Five of Brown's sons, all abolitionists, had settled in "Bleeding Kansas" and fought against pro-slavery vigilantes who had come from Missouri. His ill-fated attempt to commandeer the Federal arsenal at Harpers Ferry, Virginia, in 1859—and thereby facilitate and arm a slave uprising—ended in his capture and execution, an event that many saw as the first battle of the Civil War.

The impact John Brown's raid had on many Southern communities was substantial. "After the raid, there was intense excitement throughout the County, as well as all over the state," wrote Woodford Hackley, grandson of a member of the Little Fork Rangers from Culpeper County. "Patrols were increased, mass meetings were held, military companies were raised and equipped, and everything was done to put the State in readiness for war." If others like Brown were successful, "the bucolic, rural life of the South would be gone, as young men in every community geared themselves, if not for war, at least for one cataclysmic battle in which the minions of the evil Federal empire would be driven away, so the South could be left alone," warned another observer.

In the Towles home area near Brentsville, the Prince William Cavalry was not the only company that was formed as a bulwark against rampant abolitionists. In 1859, in a direct response to John Brown and the perceived threats to Southern sovereignty, the Prince William Rifles were assembled in Haymarket under the leadership of a local physician. The company drilled on a regular basis and soon was equipped with Springfield muskets and "neat gray uniforms topped with a tall cap decorated with a pompom."

Militias in other nearby counties were also organizing. In Fauquier County, attorney William Henry Fitzhugh Payne had attended Virginia Military Institute and settled in Warrenton to practice law. At a dinner in 1855, Payne asked fellow Warrenton native Robert Eden Scott whether Scott would like to command a squadron of cavalry. When asked by Scott why he would say such a thing, Payne replied, "the Union will certainly be dissolved in a few years and it ought to be prepared for." Scott assented, and the Black Horse Troop was organized. The name of the troop was based on the idea that the boys from Warrenton, Virginia, were descendants of cavaliers. The horse was considered representative of Virginia, and since the members of the troop were pro-slavery men, the troop was named the Black Horse Troop.

They would defend Virginia, which they called their "beloved country."

In November of 1860, concern for Virginia's preparedness for war led militia authorities to hold a cavalry encampment in Richmond. Approximately 650 troopers comprising fifteen companies of state cavalry converged on the city for drilling. Never had so many militia cavalry been assembled in Virginia. The fifteen companies bivouacked in a place they dubbed "Camp Lee," in honor of Henry "Light Horse Harry" Lee, Virginia's famed cavalryman of the American Revolution—and Robert E. Lee's father. Routine for the encampment included reveille, stable call, watering the horses, breakfast, guard mount, drill, dinner, inspection, supper, and tattoo. The camp also had what was termed a "refreshment saloon," to which "the strictest police regulation" was applied.

The units provided their own uniforms and horses, and the state furnished the men's weapons. While units could presumably choose their own style of uniform, many adopted the dark-blue uniform prescribed by Virginia's militia regulations of the day—similar to the dark-blue United States Army Cavalry uniforms, but adorned with the Virginia state seal on buttons and the belt plate.

While the Prince William Cavalry members were not among the participants in the "Grand Encampment," several future commanders and companies that would comprise the 4th Virginia Cavalry were present, including the Hanover Light Dragoons, commanded by Williams C. Wickham (later colonel of the 4th Virginia Cavalry), and Capt. Lucien Davis and the Powhatan Troop. Col. William J. Hardee of the U.S. Army (previously superintendent of West Point and later corps commander in the Confederate Army of Tennessee) was invited to give advice on cavalry drill instruction.

At the culmination of the encampment, Virginia Gov. John Letcher and other dignitaries witnessed a review that was described as "a magnificent spectacle." At its conclusion, the participating troopers rolled up their tents, exchanged farewells, and "dashed out of the gates, cheering and flourishing their sabers" to the sound of a Scottish piper's "shrill notes." The Grand Encampment was over, but hard service for many of its participants would follow.

By the time Lincoln had been elected, prominent Prince William locals like Eppa Hunton observed that "excitement sometime before had begun to run very high between the North and the South," and the questions of slavery and local self-determination seemed to be the exciting causes. In 1861, the Virginia legislature passed a law calling for a convention to determine the course of Virginia in the debate over secession. Hunton declared himself a candidate for the convention. His opponent was Towles's neighbor (and sibling of John Howison of Effingham), Allen Howison, whom Hunton described as "a Whig gentleman of the county." "I was for immediate secession. Mr. Howison was unconditionally for the Union," noted Hunton in his memoirs. Perhaps reflecting the states-rights fervor of the local populace, Hunton was elected by a large majority over Howison.

The Virginia secession convention assembled in Richmond on February 13, 1861. Called for by a special session of the General Assembly, the delegates convened to determine whether Virginia should follow the example of the seven states in the Deep South that had previously seceded from the Union. Because of its size, industrial capacity, and proximity to the nation's capital, Virginia would be critical to the developing rebellion. Initially, sentiment among the majority of delegates favored staying in the Union. A preliminary vote for secession in February failed, and debate continued through President Lincoln's inaugural address in early March 1861, when the president promised not to interfere with slavery in the states where it existed. As late as early April, another test vote for secession failed by a two-to-one margin. Soon thereafter, however, Confederate troops fired on Ft. Sumter in Charleston, South Carolina, and a Federal response was prompt. When Richmond newspapers reported President Lincoln's call for 75,000 troops to suppress the uprising, the tables were turned. Unwilling to contribute troops to pacify their fellow Southerners, the convention delegates reversed their previous votes and sent the issue to the voters for ratification. On May 23, Virginia ratified the ordinance of secession by an overwhelming margin of 132,201 to 37,451. The die was now cast.

In hindsight, some recognized that events were quickly moving to a point of crisis. "Who that is now falling into the…yellow leaf of even middle life does not distinctly remember the spring of 1861? Not for the beauty of the season…but for the cloud…which began to loom up in the political horizon and the distant mutterings of the storm so soon to burst upon our land?" wrote one Brentsville citizen after the war.

Some already saw the handwriting on the wall. As sectional conflict seemed increasingly likely, the Towles family had a decision to make. For the older boys, continued service in the militia and eventual enlistment in the Rebel forces to defend their "country"—Virginia—was a foregone conclusion. According to family chronicles, even young Jimmie, fifteen years of age, seemed determined to join his older brothers in defending Virginia from the "Yankeys."

For Reverend Towles and the rest of the family, there were other options, however. Earlier than most, John Towles saw that, in the event of conflict, Prince William County was nearly certain to be at the crux of the fighting. With its transecting railroads and central transit route, the area would undoubtedly see significant civil disruption and destruction. For families such as the Towles, with well-established, extended families further south, the decision was inevitable— they would have to "refugee" (in the parlance of the time and as it was called in family records). In early September 1860, with discretion perhaps being the better part of valor, Reverend Towles informed the Episcopalian diocesan authorities and his local vestry of his decision:

> In formally resigning into your hands and into the hands of the ecclesiastical authority of the diocese the charge of this parish which, for the period of 21 years, I have held as your pastor, and hereby dissolving the relation between us which has so long subsisted to our mutual satisfaction, permit me to say, with all sincerity, that I do so with much regret, and not without an honest and earnest conviction after much prayer for Divine guidance that duty calls me elsewhere.

> I shall carry with me the most grateful recollections of your friendship and affection which have never wavered during all the time I have lived among you. My heart was never more stressed by such recollections than at this moment, nor more oppressed by the doubt whether I shall ever again find personal friends so warm and so true in the land of the stranger wither, in the good providence of God, I go, in reliance on His blessing…you have my prayers and best wishes for the welfare of you and yours for time and for eternity. Believe me, Gentlemen, as ever With the highest regard & esteem, Your sincere friend, John Towles.

Shortly thereafter, Reverend Towles, his wife Sophronia, and their youngest children—Rosalie, Ella, Leroy, and Churchill—headed further south, first to New Market, and ultimately to Lancaster County. Later, young Ella would recall that her family left suddenly with only a carriage, house servants, and "a few things in a wagon from Vaucluse."

The Towles family's decision to relocate proved prescient. After hostilities commenced, Vaucluse would soon be taken as a headquarters for a Union general, and early action revolved around nearby Manassas Junction.

During the early months of the war, there were dislocations of the populace on both sides of the Mason-Dixon Line. Union sympathizers headed north, and Confederates caught in Federal territories moved southward. As the war progressed and Federal troops advanced, occupants of border areas sympathetic to the South followed families like the Towleses, seeking refuge in what was hoped would be safe areas. The result was what one historian has called a "virtual flood" of homeless Southerners.

Many factors influenced this refugee migration. Some families were forced to watch helplessly as their homes were confiscated for officers' quarters. As one observer noted, "A certain Yankee general made his headquarters at [a Mrs. Bowman's]; he said, he went there out of kindness, to protect her property; but [he] rather gave it the protection *the wolf gives the lamb*." Mrs. Bowman soon fled.

Other homes and even hospitals were maliciously torched in retaliation for real or imagined offenses, and many citizens were left with no option but to leave. To stay would often result in dire circumstances. One remaining citizen noted that "occupying Union troops…brazenly carry off poultry and produce. During encampments, the soldiers leveled the woods, depleted the orchards and gardens, and even made off with…bees and beehives." Another noted the contrast to their antebellum property once the Federals arrived:

> And now, what a contrast, our beautiful home laid-waste and destroyed, every thing swept off and gone, all the out houses, barns, cattle sheds, fences, hedges, all our beautiful, valuable timber, every tree gone, all our orchards, every thing—only desolation remains—and we almost in a state of starvation and beggary.
>
> The front field is literally filled with wagons and horses, all standing thickly together in rows, with streets in between. There seems to be more wagons and horses than soldiers, and more officers than men, and as many run away negroes as both, and women innumerable…in one regiment alone, the 6th New Jersey of 150 men, there are twenty seven women.

...the feeling of utter hopelessness, and sinking of heart that comes over one at the thought of being surrounded, and imprisoned and exposed to all the insults and annoyances for months of these detestable abominable people.

By 1862, Eppa Hunton's "comfortable and beautiful home" in Prince Williams was destroyed by Union soldiers. By the spring of 1862, the Confederate troops having evacuated Northern Virginia, General Hunton's family, including his sister, Miss Bettie Weir and Eppa Hunton, Jr., a small boy, fled from their home early in the morning, leaving behind most of their possessions. Mrs. Hunton was ill, and had to be removed on a feather bed. When the Federals reached the Hunton home, they dismantled it of its furnishings, and, after destroying the same with axes, they had what they termed a "Rebel mahogany bonfire."

General Hunton's autobiography tells of the evacuation of Centreville and Manassas. "It was very sad to me and to all of us from that county, to give it up to the invaders, but we had to do it. I was at home sick. I could not make preparations to give up my home, or to save any of my property. I moved my wife and son to Bristow—the nearest station—my wife on a bed in a wagon...I left behind me my slaves, household and kitchen furniture and a crop of wheat which I had just threshed, a pair of fine horses and a buggy. Of course all of this property was soon swept away by the Federal army and my horses carried away. The next morning we took the train—the last train that went out. My wife suffered intensely on the way." The Huntons' journey encountered various impediments such as train blockades and, at one point, necessitated boarding the family for a time with a sister of a soldier in Hunton's command.

While the Huntons and others made their way to destinations such as Lynchburg and Charlottesville, the Towles family headed towards the Northern Neck and their ancestral home on the Rapphannock. There, they took up residence at their cousin's house on Greenvale Creek. Reverend Towles was welcomed to his boyhood home and was asked to assume the duties of rector at the church where he and Sophronia had been married more than two decades before. The younger Towles children—Rosalie, Ella, Churchill, and LeRoy—settled into a life far behind the front lines of battle, but not without its hardships and dangers.

For the older Towles siblings, the adventure was just beginning. The rigors of serving in an actual army would soon replace the excitement of serving in a militia cavalry troop. Real fighting, marching—and dying—lay ahead.

CHAPTER THREE

The most insignificant must look his best
War's outbreak, first blood, and a "Sitzkrieg"

"…a fine and soldierly-looking lot of men…"

History of the Prince William Cavalry

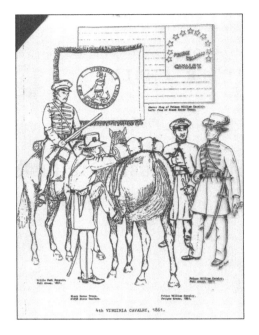

Uniforms of the
Prince William Cavalry,
Uniforms of the Confederacy, Field

William Willis Thornton, Prince William
Cavalry, Courtesy of the Manassas Museum
System, Manassas, Virginia

Maj. Gen William
"Extra Billy" Smith

Cavalry

Amos Benson, Prince William Cavalry, Courtesy of
the Manassas Museum System, Manassas, Virginia

Robert Cushing, Prince William Cavalry,
Courtesy of the Manassas Museum System,
Manassas, Virginia

Robert Holland, Prince William Cavalry,
Courtesy of the Manassas Museum System,
Manassas, Virginia

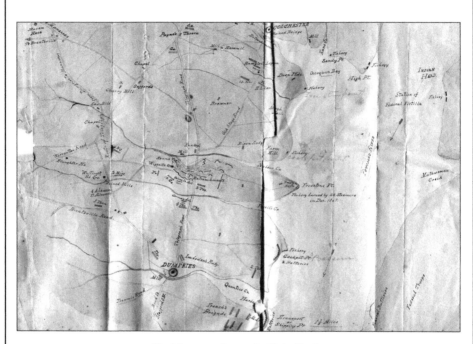

Hand-drawn scouting map by Vivian Towles

Alocal observer captured the significant events in which Virginians were soon caught up. "In April 1861, the storm so long threatened burst upon us. The land was alive with men hurrying to the front. It is scarcely a figure of speech to say that the plow was left in the furrow, and the bride at the altar, by those eager to be in place when the curtain was rung up on the greatest tragedy of ancient or modern times." Leading the response from Southern partisans were the local militias.

The Prince William Cavalry, the pre-war militia troop of Brentsville boys that had been drilling for nearly two years, was officially ordered into Confederate service on April 17, 1861, less than a week after the firing on Ft. Sumter that heralded the beginning of the Civil War.

According to a local observer, the troop "was a fine and soldierly-looking lot of men, numbering some sixty to seventy members." Their uniforms consisted of a frock coat with one row of buttons up the front and one on each side, connecting at the top with a gold-lace V. Pants with yellow stripes, black hats with black plumes on the left side held up with crossed sabers, and a shield with the letters "P.W.C." in front constituted what one observer called "a plain but neat uniform in which the most insignificant must look his best."

Other units were not so finely accoutered. The Little Fork Rangers, for example, were "a fine looking lot of men," but their appearance was far from uniform. "Those who had shotguns carried them strapped on their backs; those who had horse pistols carried them across their saddles in front, as they had no holsters. Many of these horse-pistols were single-barrelled and were of dubious value," said Lieutenant Holtzman of the Rangers. Holtzman opined that the Little Fork Rangers were the "poorest armed body of men in or around Manassas."

The Prince William troop might also have claimed that distinction, but they certainly cut a fine martial picture as they marched off to war. With "the fine-looking and genial Captain William Willis Thornton and his kinsmen at their head," the young men trotted off by fours. Thornton was a 36-year-old, Brentsville farmer, who had been chosen as the captain of the troop after William Brawner had moved on to form another unit of Prince William men. "There were none but admiring eyes and but few dry ones in the old town, which had known and loved most of them from childhood to manhood." Among the officers and non-coms serving under Captain Thornton were Lts. P.D. Williams, J.M. Barbee, and Demetrious Rowe, Orderly Sgt. Thomas Thornton (one of the Captain's "kinsmen"), and Cpls. J. Taylor Williams and Robert Towles—Reverend Towles's second oldest son. Robert Towles's muster records show that he was initially rejected as a recruit, "not being 18 years of age," but persistence apparently bred success, as the young volunteer soon joined the company and rose quickly to the rank of corporal.

The first flag of the Prince William Cavalry had been bestowed upon the unit by "the ladies of Prince William County" at a picnic and cotillion party given on a farm near Bristow Station. The date was Thursday, August 23, 1860, and invitations called locals to attend the boys and to witness presentation of a company flag, which was described as having red-and-white, silk stripes "that so much resembled the Federal flag" that it was subsequently changed, and the white silk used in the alteration was later made a part of a wedding dress.

The seamstresses were Misses Emma and Summer Williams, cousins, who fashioned the white portions of the flag from an evening dress of the latter. Their role in fashioning the banner may have not gone unnoticed. Emma Williams, later Mrs. Captain Davis, suffered the indignity of being the only woman in her county arrested by Federal forces, detained for several weeks in Alexandria, though never charged with anything more serious than "holding communication with the enemy"—said enemy being her husband.

Fully-accoutered and bannered, if not (as subsequent events would demonstrate) adequately armed, the company prepared to join other Virginia units concentrating in the area. Manassas, Virginia was an early point of concentration for units rallying to the cause. A company of infantry from Fauquier County, a Rappahannock cavalry company, and the Prince William Cavalry under Captain Thornton all gathered near Manassas and in the area up to an advanced post at Fairfax Courthouse. "Such was the beginning of the Army of Northern Virginia. Drawn from all ranks and employments in life, it represented every social phase, condition, and occupation, fused and welded by the seismic force of that tremendous upheaval into an organization whose deeds were predestined soon to make all the world wonder."

Like many militia units, the Prince William Cavalry set off for war with great expectations and unbounded optimism. "There was glory and enthusiasm about the new order of things in the waving banners, the glittering uniforms, and nodding plumes that led captive the imagination and silenced reason…youth and gaiety was everywhere apparent," wrote the biographer of the Prince William Cavalry. The Prince William boys' eagerness was mirrored in other cavalry units. Upon being presented with their own flag, the troopers of the Little Fork Rangers were exhorted by their captain as follows, "Boys, will you follow this banner into the face of the enemy, defending it with the last drop of your blood?" They all answered, "Yes, yes!"

Perhaps the *esprit de corps* of the cavalry is best captured by a popular song that would later describe the enthusiasm that seemed to embody this arm of the service, "Jine the Cavalry."

> If you want to have a good time, jine the cavalry!
> Jine the cavalry! Jine the cavalry!
> If you want to catch the Devil, if you want to have fun
> If you want to smell Hell,
> Jine the cavalry!

Subsequent choruses of the song would chronicle various exploits of the Confederate cavalry under its commander Gen. James Ewell Brown "Jeb" Stuart, including a ride around Union General McClellan, confronting Joe Hooker in the Wilderness, and the invasion of Pennsylvania that culminated in the Battle of Gettysburg. Whatever the ultimate glamour of being part of Stuart's cavalry, however, the troops first had to be further trained and incorporated into larger organizational units. Drilling, marching, and first blood awaited the new cavalrymen.

The Prince William Cavalry's first camp after it was ordered out was on a farm called Saffolds, near Occoquan in eastern Prince William County. From there, it went to the Northern Neck for several weeks, which must have seemed ironic to the Towles brothers, whose family was at the time living with relatives in that area. The company's pre-war training must have shown through, as officers organizing the Confederate forces complimented the company highly for its "promptitude and efficiency."

In May, the unit had returned to Brentsville with orders to march again to Occoquan, where it picketed landings on the Potomac and guarded roads in expectation of an attack from the Federal forces in Alexandria.

On May 24, the cavalry burned the bridge over the Occoquan and the troopers were ordered to report to Manassas Junction, where a fight was rumored to be imminent. As this proved to be a false alarm, the men were subsequently ordered to Fairfax Courthouse, where in late May 1861, one of the first skirmishes of the war occurred.

In command of the Rebel forces at Fairfax Courthouse was Lt. Col. Richard S. Ewell, Virginia Militia, subsequently famous as division and corps commander in the Army of Northern Virginia. Lieutenant Colonel Ewell had only been in charge of the small force at Fairfax for two weeks, having recently left the Federal army to serve as a Confederate officer.

Fairfax Courthouse was a small village of some 300 inhabitants, and was the county seat. The village was built principally on the Little River Turnpike and was located at a point roughly 14 miles from the city of Alexandria. The turnpike served as the main street of the village, which included a hotel where Lieutenant Colonel Ewell made his headquarters.

Captain Thornton's Prince William County men—approximately sixty strong—were positioned on the same side of the street as the hotel, with their horses stabled there. The men themselves had bivouacked in a nearby Methodist church. Another cavalry unit, the Rappahannock Cavalry under Captain Green, was also nearby, as were the ninety or so members of an infantry unit, the Warrenton Rifles, under Capt. John Quincy Marr. The Warrenton unit was one of those formed after the John Brown raid, and, as a local observer noted, had been "drilled with indefatigable industry and instructed in the art of war."

Indications of aggressive Union activity following Virginia's passage of the ordinance of secession led Captain Marr and his troops to march towards the Potomac River, where the danger seemed most threatening. Joining the cavalry companies in Fairfax, the Rifles made the Rebels a significant force.

On the morning of Saturday, June 1, 1861, Union troops moved towards Fairfax. At this juncture, former Virginia Gov. William Smith, recently commissioned as a general in the new Confederate army, was visiting Fairfax Courthouse and found himself involved in the skirmish.

A lawyer, congressman, two-time governor of Virginia, and one of the oldest Confederate generals in the American Civil War, William Smith was known in the North and the South as "Extra Billy Smith" because of his ability early in life to acquire bonuses while operating an overland mail business. He was elected governor of Virginia in 1846 and was serving in Congress when the Civil War began. Although at the beginning of the war he would characterize himself as "wholly ignorant of drill and tactics," he would discover that he enjoyed the experience of combat. Over the course of the next two years, Smith served in various field command capacities and was wounded several times, including at Antietam, where Stuart noted his "conspicuously brave and self-possessed" performance. He must have been a very visible commander, since he often affected an unorthodox field uniform, including a tall beaver hat and a blue cotton umbrella. After an indifferent performance at Gettysburg in 1863, Extra Billy would resign his commission after being elected (again) as governor, in which capacity he served through the end of the war. At Fairfax, his would be a critical role for the untested Confederates.

The commander of the Union forces advancing on Fairfax Courthouse, Lieutenant Charles Tompkins of Company B, 2nd U.S. Cavalry, took his force—which he later estimated to be fifty men—to reconnoiter the country in the vicinity of Fairfax Courthouse. After capturing some Confederate pickets, Tompkins advanced on the town, where he reported engaging "two companies of cavalry and one rifle company," supported by nearby Rebel reinforcements, which brought the size of the defending force to what he alleged was "upwards of 1,000 men."

Tompkins reported receiving fire from Confederates in windows and on the rooftops of the town. Despite what he portrayed as a fierce resistance, Tompkins drove the Rebel cavalry before him before finally retreating in the face of what he took to be overwhelming odds against his force.

Although General Smith and Colonel Ewell confirmed some aspects of the engagement, their reports took issue with much of what Lieutenant Tompkins reported to his superiors. They did note, however, that the Rebel cavalry, being "entirely unfit for effectual service" due to their lack of armaments, retreated before completely forming.

Perhaps more importantly, the Warrenton Rifles had been handicapped by the disappearance of their commander, Captain Marr, who had been struck earlier by a random shot that "suspended the machinery of the heart…necessarily produc[ing] instant death," as the post-action report succinctly noted. Later, one member of his command reported that, as he attempted to organize a defense in the field, Marr had looked at the oncoming Union troopers and asked, "What cavalry is that?" The Union bullet that killed him answered the question and also made him the first Confederate soldier killed in the war. The majority of his command found it difficult to ascertain their commander's location, however, since the unfortunate captain had fallen amongst "rank and tall clover [that] completely enveloped his person."

In Marr's absence, General Smith took the initiative and rallied the infantry in defense of the town. Colonel Ewell, who had sustained a flesh wound in his shoulder during the initial fighting, came up "bare and baldheaded, in his shirt sleeves and bleeding," according to General Smith, and the colonel, with the general, helped organize the Warrenton riflemen, quickly repulsing the Federal troops. "Boys, you know me, follow me," Extra Billy had exhorted the men. "Without hesitation, they jumped the fence…and when [the enemy was] within range of us I gave the command 'fire,'" reported Smith. "It was admirably executed…[and] the enemy fell back."

The Prince William Cavalry's baptism of fire in this engagement was not particularly propitious. Four of its company had been captured during the

Federal advance, and all after-battle reports refer to them as being "driven'" before the Union advance. Certainly at this stage of the war, the lack of weapons made standing before a Federal attack of uncertain numbers problematic. Their commander, Captain Thornton, did perform valuable service, it seems, in riding to summon other cavalry companies camped at Fairfax Station. In his report, General Smith noted wryly, however, that "[n]either man, nor beast, that I could ascertain, sustained the slightest injury."

In his after-report of the incident, Colonel Ewell noted that the cavalry companies (Rappahannock and Prince William) had seen no service and were, in his opinion, "entirely undisciplined." Perhaps more importantly, the cavalry also had very few firearms and no ammunition, which may have contributed to disciplinary issues when confronted with an armed force of Federals. Others described the cavalry as "raw levies and imperfectly armed, [and] misinformed as to the force of the enemy." In any case, Ewell noted that the cavalry played essentially "no part" in the subsequent affair.

The Fairfax Courthouse skirmish resulted in little loss on the Confederate side, other than the unfortunate Captain Marr, and General Smith and Lieutenant Colonel Ewell vigorously disputed the Federal claim of twenty-five Confederates killed and wounded, calling such claims (and the exaggeration of the defending Confederate forces) "the most inexcusable mendacity." Instead, said the general, the Warrenton Rifles had inflicted considerable damage on the enemy and had "forced him to see safety by retiring from the contest, through the fields of an adjoining farm." Most importantly, the Rebels had turned the Union men away from Fairfax, and the negligible intelligence gathered as a result inflated the Confederates in the vicinity, causing the overall Federal commander, Irwin McDowell, to err on the side of caution as he prepared to engage the larger Confederate army assembling near Manassas. In any case, what General Smith termed "this little affair" would pale in comparison with future battles—including the first major battle of the war, which would soon occur near the Manassas railroad junction.

Now that blood had been shed, however, the patriotic rhetoric began to intensify. On June 5, 1861, Gen. P.G.T. Beauregard, the hero of Ft. Sumter, addressed "the good People of the Counties of Loudoun, Fairfax, and Prince William" regarding Union operations in the Northern Virginia area:

> A reckless and unprincipled tyrant has invaded your soil.
> Abraham Lincoln, regardless of all moral, legal, and constitutional
> restraints, has thrown his abolition hosts among you, who are

murdering and imprisoning your citizens, confiscating and destroying your property, and committing other acts of violence and outrage too shocking and revolting to humanity to be enumerated. All rules of civilized warfare are abandoned, and they proclaim by their acts, if not on their banners, that their war-cry is "Beauty and booty." All that is dear to man, your honor, and that of your wives and daughters, your fortunes, and your lives, are involved in this momentous contest…[I] enjoy you by every consideration dear to the hearts of freemen and patriots, by the name and memory of your revolutionary fathers, and by the purity and sanctity of your domestic firesides, to rally to the standard of your State and country, and by every means in your power compatible with honorable warfare to drive back and expel the invaders from your land.

As the long, hot days of summer began in earnest, Virginia cavalry companies scouted the Potomac River frontier and performed picket duty while waiting for the expected Union advance. It came in mid-July, when Federal forces under Gen. Irvin McDowell engaged Confederate forces near Manassas Junction. Depending on your persuasion, naming conventions have designated the battle as the First Battle of Bull Run (North) or the First Battle of Manassas (South). By either name, it was the first major ground battle of the war, involving a total of approximately 40,000 men and resulted in roughly 5,000 combined casualties (killed, wounded, and captured). The battle, though small by comparison to later battles such as Antietam or Gettysburg, would have important psychological consequences in the South and particularly in the North, where the result—a resounding and unexpected Union defeat—would shake the confidence of many. What some had expected to be a "ninety days war" would prove much more lengthy and deadly.

When the Union attack began, Captain Thornton and the Prince William Cavalry were positioned on the extreme Confederate right and, due to the location of the fighting, remained basically inactive during the battle. Other cavalry units would play important roles in the engagement, however.

The Hanover Light Dragoons under Williams C. Wickham, were held in reserve until very late in the day, when the men were ordered to press the Federal retreat. In a letter written the day after the battle, Lieutenant William B. Newton described the action:

The time for us to act had arrived. Our whole body of cavalry...now rushed like the wind to the front. It was indeed a brilliant spectacle...The whole line resounded with a continued cheering. Our company was in the front, and I was in front of my platoon, when, after crossing the swamp, we came suddenly on a detachment of the enemy concealed in the bushes, with their pieces leveled. The Colonel ordered the charge, and the boys rushed on.

Other units, such as the Black Horse Troop, also contributed to the unexpected Union defeat. As a regimental historian noted, at Manassas, the companies that were to comprise the 4th Virginia Cavalry "proved their worth with superb performance under fire throughout the day. They acted as guides and couriers, escorted both the commanding general and the President of the Confederacy and helped to drive the Federals from the field, making their withdrawal a confused and hasty retreat."

After the battle of First Manassas, the Prince William Cavalry camped at various places in the vicinity of Fairfax Courthouse, and connected with other units, such as the Albemarle Troup and the Black Horse Cavalry. The cavalry spent the remainder of the year at various places in Fairfax and lower Prince William County, reconnoitering and screening the Confederate line, but seeing very little, if any, combat—a sign of things to come in the near future, at least.

Many of the cavalry units wintered at a place called Round Top, where one observer described the scene as follows: "The merry fellows that I found in camp at Round Top are merry fellows, indeed. They have not yet felt the pinch of hunger, and but few of the other ills consequent upon the life of the soldier. Within an easy distance of their own homes, with plentiful rations for man and beast, they spend their days in hard riding and scouting, their nights in games and revelry, and doubtless think it is a fine thing. But they will waken ere long to its stern realities, I very much fear."

What followed during the winter of 1861 and 1862 has been called a "Sitzkrieg" by some (from the German "stationary war"), and a phony war by others. When pressed regarding the Union army's inactivity during this time, President Lincoln replied, "If I were sure of victory, we would have one at once, but we cannot stand defeat, and we must be certain of victory before we strike."

Union commanders, including new General-in-Chief George B. McClellan, frantically gathered information and speculated—often with wildly inaccurate results—on the size and scope of Confederate arms. McClellan had enlisted detective Allan Pinkerton to provide intelligence concerning Southern intentions following Manassas, and Pinkerton's gross over-estimation of Confederate strength colored the commanding general's thinking. One report, submitted by McClellan to Union Secretary of War Simon Cameron, stated that "all the information we have from spies, prisoners, &c, agrees in showing that the enemy have a force on the Potomac not less than 150,000 strong, well-drilled and equipped, ably commanded, and strongly entrenched." If he were provided with significant reinforcements, McClellan would attack. Privately, "Little Mac" (as the troops affectionately called him) admitted that the Union Army of the Potomac was probably "condemned to a winter of inactivity."

While Union intelligence was proving to be notoriously ineffective, Confederate troopers such as Vivian Towles and his brothers provided accurate and valuable information as to troop and battery placements and the relative positions of units in the Northern Virginia theater of war. A surviving, color map, hand-drawn by Vivian, shows the area from Occoquan to Dumfries during this time of relative inactivity on this front. Such was the task of Virginia cavalrymen during the so-called "Sitzkrieg."

On September 4, 1861, with the striking of Special Order Number 248, the 4th Virginia Cavalry was officially born. Camped at Sangster's Crossroads in Fairfax County, the young men from Prince William County were chosen to comprise a portion of the new regiment, which was under the command of Col. Beverly H. Robertson. Ranking as Company A, the Prince William Cavalry formed a squadron with the Governor's Guards. The other companies of the 4th included troops from various nearby Northern Virginia counties (Fauquier, Culpeper, Madison) and some from mid-Virginia (Goochland, Hanover, Powhatan, Buckingham, and Chesterfield).

After the success at First Manassas and given the lack of aggressive Northern military action since the battle, Southern morale was high, and a sense of optimism and confidence regarding their cause was apparent. "I wish you could hear the band and see the soldiers parade, it is a grand and imposing sight," said a trooper in the 4th Virginia's Black Horse Cavalry. "Yankeedom is a doomed land, for in every engagement we have had I can see the hand of Providence on our side...I believe we are engaged in one of the noblest causes on earth, namely the defense of our country, our liberty, and the protection of our parents, wives, and children, and all that is dear to man." The assembled troops were called upon for four drills of one hour each day and also had a dress parade each evening.

"Between times, we have to cook, wash, go after provisions, sweep and clean up in front of our bunks and (last but not least) we have to stand guard, having often to shoulder our muskets and march at least 5 miles to stand guard…so you see we are kept pretty busy."

After the Confederate army eventually retired strategically from Manassas in 1862, a reorganization of the company took place, pursuant to an act of the Virginia legislature, which allowed all volunteer companies to elect their own officers. The new officers were: Capt. P.D. Williams, Lts. Lucien Davis, B.D. Merchant, and George Colvin, Orderly Sgt. P.T. Weedon, and other Sgts. J. Taylor Williams and Robert Towles. When George Colvin died shortly thereafter, other non-commissioned officers were elected, including Absolom Lynn and Robert's older brother, Vivian.

Thus organized and flush from the initial excitement of battles small and large, the men of the 4th Virginia Cavalry awaited the next stages of the conflict.

CHAPTER FOUR

Pope's wallet
A treasured memento lost and found

"…one of the most remarkable rides and raids…during the War."

J. Churchill Cooke
Co. G, 4th Virginia Cavalry

the wallet

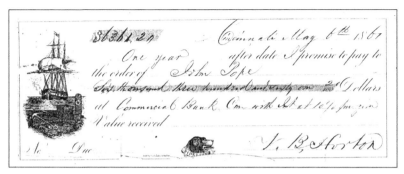

Valentine B. Horton Promissory Note

Gen. John Pope, Library of Congress

Catlett's Station Photo,
Library of Congress

Catlett's Station Sketch, Library of Congress

General Robert E. Lee had taken command of Confederate forces in Virginia during the early summer of 1862, re-christening those forces as "the Army of Northern Virginia," and quickly transforming the strategic picture during an aggressive campaign that came to be known as the Seven Days. Driving Union forces away from the Confederate capital of Richmond, Virginia, Lee seized the initiative in the Eastern Theater. He would not relinquish that initiative for the next two years.

As Confederate cavalrymen, the Towles brothers would see action across the landscape of the War. Under Confederate Cavalry commander Maj. Gen. J.E.B. Stuart, cavalry served two roles. Organized for combat purposes in regiments, brigades and divisions, the Southern horsemen were also renowned for their reconnaissance, and the Towles brothers performed that role admirably when called upon to do so. In the meantime, Towles brothers Viv, Robert, and James served as troopers in the 4th Virginia Cavalry, part of Gen. Fitzhugh Lee's brigade. 'Fitz' Lee was Robert E. Lee's nephew and a trusted subordinate of General Stuart.

In August of 1862, the Army of Northern Virginia faced a threat in the form of Union General John Pope and his newly-formed Army of Virginia. Pope had served in the Western Theater of the War and had been brought east by President Lincoln in an attempt to pressure the Confederates subsequent to Gen. George McClellan's failed Peninsular Campaign earlier in the year. Among Pope's directives to his new army was to hold citizens of his district responsible for the acts of "bushwackers" and requiring citizens to take the oath of allegiance to the United States government and move out of his lines or be treated as spies.

Over the first few weeks of August, General Pope's army jockeyed for position with Confederate commander Robert E. Lee's army. Lee looked—initially in vain—for a way to, as he called it, suppress Pope, who Lee considered a "miscreant" due to the aggressive way that Pope's troops had dealt with Southern civilians. Throughout early August, maneuver and counter-maneuver occurred northwest along the Rapidan and Rappahannock rivers.

On August 17, Lee was informed by General Stuart that Pope's army was in an exposed position between the Rapidan and Rappahannock. The evening before Lee proposed to strike, Union cavalry scouting across the Rapidan advanced into Confederate lines, surprised and nearly captured Stuart at Verdiersville, a hamlet where Stuart and his staff had halted to rest and await scattered units for the next day's advance. James Ewell Brown Stuart was a colorful personality, who "led from the front" and epitomized the dashing Southern cavalier in his impeccable uniform and ebullient personality. Barely escaping the Union horsemen at Verdiersville, Stuart lost a new hat and plume. More importantly, saddlebags captured by the Yankees contained Lee's operational plans for the coming day. Forewarned of this threat, Pope promptly withdrew his troops from their exposed position to one safely behind the Rappahannock River. The episode was a rude surprise for Stuart, who greatly valued vigilance. Moreover, the loss of his famous hat and plume must have caused him considerable chagrin.

With Pope safely behind the river, General Lee looked to regain the initiative against his elusive foe. On August 21, Stuart proposed to do just that. Word had come that John Pope's headquarters trains were exposed at nearby Catlett's Station on the Orange and Alexandria Railroad, and the Bold Dragoon suggested that a column of 1,500 men could cross the Rappahannock, ride to the Union rear, and cut Pope's supply line along the railroad. Stuart hoped that the raid would force the Union army to retreat from the Rappahannock and into the open where the Army of Northern Virginia could strike it. The nominal goal of the expedition would be the destruction of Cedar Run Bridge in Pope's rear.

General Lee agreed to the plan, and Stuart set off with his column, consisting primarily of men from Fitzhugh Lee's brigade, including the 4th Virginia Cavalry under Col. Williams C. Wickham. At least two of the three Towles brothers were with the 4th Virginia at the time—the oldest, Vivian, and middle brother, Robert. Robert—a sandy-haired youth of eighteen—set off on the raid with his horse, Bones. The young Rebel was eager to teach the "yankeys" a lesson.

On the morning of August 22, Stuart crossed the Rappahannock at Waterloo Bridge and Hart's Ford, accompanied by two pieces of artillery. Passing through Warrenton, the Rebel cavalry was eagerly welcomed by the local citizens, who greeted the column with apple pies and smoked fish as the soldiers rested in a field outside of town.

Heavy rain slowed the advance, and by evening, when the troops arrived in the vicinity of Catlett's Station, they were so drenched that some of the men had to stand on their hands in order to get water out of their boots. "We were as wet as water could make us," wrote one trooper. The downpour might have made Vivian Towles regret his wish in a letter home for relief from the "concentrated column of heat pouring down" upon his regiment in the days prior to the raid.

Around midnight, Stuart's cavalry found itself just outside of Pope's encampments. According to one trooper, the scene presented a "vast assemblage of wagons and a city of tents, laid out in regular order and occupied by the luxuriously equipped quartermasters and commissaries, and countless hangers-on and stragglers of the army, but no appearance of any large organized body of troops." Though Pope later claimed that the army train at Catlett's was guarded by 1,500 men and was "within easy reach of the whole army," two regiments of cavalry detailed to protect the station had yet to arrive, and all that stood in Stuart's way were a handful of invalids and 160 men of the 13th Pennsylvania Reserves. Known as the "Bucktails" for the distinguishing deer tails attached to their caps, these unsuspecting troops provided little protection against the Confederate column.

The few Union pickets were quickly captured, and the Rebel cavalrymen prepared to attack the vulnerable quartermasters and teamsters, who huddled around their campfires and in their tents. At that moment, the daylong rain intensified into a torrential rainstorm. General Stuart called it the "darkest night I ever knew," and several troopers noted that the rain seemed like "a solid mass of water." During the deluge, the Confederates charged into the camp, giving their 'wildest Rebel Yell,'" which was nearly drowned out by the storm. In seconds, pandemonium reigned.

Because of the rain, efforts to burn the large collection of wagons resulted in little damage, but the wagons, packed and ready to move out, provided a tempting smorgasbord of items for the rampaging Southern cavalry. Tents and tables were overturned, and troopers scattered throughout the camp to forage. Boxes, trunks, stores, desks, and even safes were rifled, and the Confederates made off with everything from "fine, fat horses" to fatigue jackets with epaulets and "underwear of every description." One 9th Virginia cavalryman found a pair of field glasses, which he soon lost when a pocket of Union resistance briefly scattered the pillaging Rebel horsemen.

There also apparently was time for more gustatory pleasures. An officer later noted, "I saw a soldier trying to get the cork out of a bottle. He got impatient with the obstinate cork, so he struck the neck of the bottle on the wagon wheel. There was an explosion and he dropped the bottle like a hot cake. I yelled to him that he was a fool…that it was champagne. He said there was plenty of it in the wagon." Indeed, there was some uneasiness among the officers that the men would become intoxicated, "for there was plenty of liquor in every tent." In fact, the temptation to overindulge amid the bountiful Union stores must have been great, but the importance of restraint was observed, and "none took more than they could carry," according to a member of Stuart's staff.

A number of Union prisoners were taken by the rebels, including an armed woman in a man's uniform. Federals scattered and hid in the darkness, some seeking shelter in wagons or tents. A few were found squatting down under a small bush or sapling for concealment. A Confederate noted that the Yankees were "perfectly frantic with fear."

The Confederates were nearly as disorganized as the Federals. "The command was very much scattered," wrote an officer in the 9th Virginia Cavalry. "Officers and privates alike were engaged in searching wagons and stores." The darkness and storm did nothing to alleviate the incredible confusion. Company K of the 9th Virginia loosed a volley at a line of mysterious lights, which turned out to be a train fleeing the depot.

The intelligence that General Pope's headquarters train was at Catlett's had been one incentive for the raid, but the storm and darkness made it difficult to determine exactly where Pope's tent lay. Fortunately for the Confederates, an escaped slave from Blakely County, who had known Stuart prior to the war, recognized the general and agreeably offered to lead him to the wagons and tents belonging to General Pope's headquarters. The "contraband" (as escaped slaves were known), had been in the service of a member of Pope's staff, and was mounted behind a Rebel trooper "to insure his fidelity." With his help, the Confederates, including Robert Towles, soon found themselves among Pope's personal wagons, baggage, and tents.

Notwithstanding a rumor that Pope's cloak and hat were in one tent and that he had only just walked down through the woods to visit another officer, the Union general was in fact several miles away at Rappahannock Station, but his personal trains and belongings were among those left at Catlett's when the Confederates attacked. In his absence, Pope's trunks and wagons were ransacked along with everything else, and Confederates came away with the Union commander's dispatch book, headquarters papers, personal baggage, and payroll chest, which contained a substantial amount of greenbacks (U.S. paper scrip) and $20,000 in gold.

As soldiers rummaged through the tents and wagons surrounding Pope's headquarters, Robert Towles picked up a leather wallet that he would later determine belonged to the Union commander. Other troopers entered a tent where they found a flask of brandy and several notebooks, including one with battle orders, and cipher dispatches signed by General Pope and his adjutant-general. The morning reports of Pope's army up to the previous day provided valuable knowledge about the condition of his command and the forces present for duty. Correspondence also suggested that Gen. George B. McClellan's troops were on their way from the Peninsula to reinforce Pope.

Despite their success at disrupting the supply depot and the intelligence found among Pope's headquarters tents, the Confederate cavalry chieftain knew that another, more important duty remained. A number of the 4th Virginia Cavalry were sent with engineers and Capt. William Blackford of Stuart's staff to accomplish the primary mission of the raid—the destruction of the bridge at Cedar Run. If the bridge could be destroyed, Pope and his army would be left without supplies for a day or two and might be forced to retreat from their defensive position on the Rappahannock.

The downpour prevented the destruction of the bridge, however. Captain Blackford noted that the rain continued to fall "not in drops but in streams, as if poured from buckets." The men of the 4th Virginia Cavalry did their best to ignite the wooden bridge supports, and failing that due to rain "driven almost horizontally" by a vicious wind, they attempted to chop the bridge down with axes. Neither technique worked, however, and rising creek waters and approaching Union reinforcements soon forced them to abandon the mission. Months later, as he was being sent to captivity in Washington's Old Capitol Prison, Robert Towles would note wistfully that the train was "whirlling across Cedar Run Bridge, and I call to mind one morning [when] I worked so hard to destroy it."

While the raid failed in its primary goal of cutting Pope's supply line at Cedar Run, the capture of Pope's dispatch book was considered by Stuart to be significant. The added satisfaction of acquiring personal belongings of Pope, including "a fine dress uniform," must have pleased Jeb Stuart greatly. Shortly after the raid, Stuart sent a message to Pope through the lines, proposing a "cartel for the exchange of the prisoners," namely Stuart's hat and plume for Pope's uniform. General Pope did not respond to the offer. With much hilarity, Pope's large uniform coat was worn in Stuart's camp by Fitz Lee, and it was eventually forwarded to Virginia Gov. John Letcher for safekeeping. For several months afterwards, the uniform was displayed in a shop front window in downtown Richmond.

For his part, John Pope denigrated what he termed a "small, trifling cavalry raid that produced no loss worth mentioning." Pope sarcastically noted that the raiders "destroyed altogether four or five wagons out of some thousands [and]…a great shout and hurrah were made over this wonderful achievement, out of which the enemy possessed themselves of some private letters having no relation to the war and a few other papers equally unimportant, and also some two or three suits of clothing more or less worn. It was therefore quite a brilliant affair and reflected great credit on all concerned…"

Pope's sarcasm notwithstanding, to the troopers involved the raid had been a great adventure. A member of the 4th Virginia Cavalry, reporting much later to the *Richmond Dispatch*, called it "one of the most remarkable rides that it was my good fortune to be in during the war." And while Robert E. Lee learned little that he did not already know prior to the raid, the events of August 22 showed in dramatic fashion that the Confederate cavalrymen were able and willing to confound their Yankee counterparts at this juncture of the war. The ensuing battle of Second Manassas, the loss of which sent John Pope into exile in the West, was testament to the hard marching and initiative achieved by the Army of Northern Virginia with the help of its incomparable cavalry chief, Jeb Stuart, and his troopers.

John Pope's wallet would later play a personal role for Robert Towles in the aftermath of an important cavalry battle. Ultimately, as a treasured memento kept by Robert's younger sister, Ella, the wallet would survive an 1864 gunboat raid into the Northern Neck, when many of the family's personal possessions were burned by Union marines. Eventually, the keepsake would pass down through Robert's family.

In 1999, it turned up in family records. Among a box of "odds and ends" kept for many years in a filing cabinet, was a small foldover wallet. Inside the well-worn leather pocketbook was a promissory note, payable to and endorsed by John Pope, in the amount of $6,000. Dated May 6, 1861, the note had been executed by V.B. Horton.

Valentine B. Horton was John Pope's father-in-law. His daughter, Clara, had married then-Captain Pope in 1859. A member of the Ohio Congressional delegation, a prominent Republican Party activist and confidant of U.S. Treasury Secretary Salmon Chase, Horton was wealthy, with significant holdings in mining and manufacturing. Largely credited with having done much to develop the coal, salt, and iron industries of the region, he was frequently referred to as John Pope's "rich father-in-law." His patronage and his connections with powerful Republican politicians were largely credited for securing Pope's initial command in the Western Theater and may have influenced Lincoln in bringing the Illinois-born Pope east in 1862.

Ironically, financial reverses marred his declining years, and Valentine Horton eventually died with considerable debts, though "much beloved and respected" by the people of Ohio. Rich father-in-law or not, Horton must have come to need a loan from his new son-in-law, although no specific records exist to explain the debt. In any case, the promissory note validates the wallet as having belonged to the general.

From the diary later kept by Robert and from family letters, it is clear that the Pope wallet was a prized possession of the young cavalryman.

Much later, a handwritten note from Robert's niece, unborn at the time of his death, is attached to the wallet. "This pocketbook was found on the field at Catlett's Station during the War Between the States by Robt. C. Towles. It had been robbed of its contents with exception of a pair of kid gloves (ladies) and what it now contains." The original promissory note, payable "to the order of John Pope" with interest at ten percent, was folded and in an inside pocket of the wallet.

Years later, another Towles family member wrote, "My great uncle was killed, (and) this pocketbook was sent back to Lancaster with his effects. It is my intention to return it (especially the note) to the heirs of Gen. Pope." Perhaps a finder's fee, with interest, would be in order for the much-traveled souvenir of one of Stuart's most celebrated raids.

Chapter Five

Poor darling Rosa
The loss of a younger sister

"All that's bright must fade, the brightest, still the fleetest,
all that's sweet was made…but to be lost while sweetest."

Obituary
November 1862

Chowning Ferry Farm family graveyard

Chowning Ferry Farm family graveyard

sacred ground

Chowning Ferry Farm family graveyard

Rosalie Towles grave

While Robert and his comrades were harassing General Pope, his family had settled into their new lives away from war-torn Prince William County.

After leaving Brentsville, the Towles family had sought refuge in the Northern Neck of Virginia, the narrow, picturesque peninsula that comprises approximately 800 square miles between the Potomac River on the north and the Rappahannock River on the south. Family roots for the Towles and Chowning families run deep in this area, and prior to the war, John and Sophronia's relatives had prospered. The 1850 and 1860 Lancaster County censuses show numerous Chownings, Towleses, Chiltons, and Ewells—all kinsmen of Reverend Towles and his wife— listed as prosperous farmers and landholders.

By the 1850s, the Northern Neck had grown to be a prosperous area of farms and fisheries. Local oysters had become extremely popular and were noted for their taste and size. Prior to the war, even more money had been made by farming, particularly potatoes, and in livestock.

Poet James Allen has perhaps captured the character of the region best with the following:

> Between the yellow Rappahannock
> And the broad Potomac blue,
> There's a lovely bit of country
> Down in old Virginia true.
> Just a narrow strip of inland,
> On the map it's scarce a speck,
> But it's Home to everybody
> In the good old Northern Neck.
>
> The folks have got a charming way
> Of saying, "Come right in."
> There's smoked cured ham and batter-bread,
> With potatoes in the bin.
> The people still believe in God,
> And home is not a wreck.
> And everybody's "Kith and Kin"
> In the good old Northern Neck.

The outbreak of war would dramatically change the dynamics of the area, however.

Because of its geographical position, the Northern Neck was in a vital position—close to both Washington and Richmond and to the state of Maryland. It served as a supply line and spy route to Richmond from points north, an entry point for Confederate blockade runners, and a source of local provender that might supply Rebel troops in the field. For all of these reasons, while the Northern Neck saw no major battles during the Civil War, the area was far from forgotten by the Federal authorities and became a prime focus for Union naval power, as well as occasional land-based raids.

Union Commander-in-Chief Winfield Scott's "Anaconda Plan," devised at the beginning of the war, envisioned a blockade to stop the flow of supplies to the South. As instruments of that blockade, hundreds of Union gunboats became active in the Chesapeake Bay. As a result, Yankee gunboats, "coiled like vipers," prowled the rivers and creeks surrounding the Northern Neck, particularly after the spring of 1861 when the Federal Potomac Flotilla was created.

Ten days after the war began, Cdr. James H. Ward had suggested the creation of a "flying flotilla" to be used on the Chesapeake Bay and its tributaries. Secretary of the Navy Gideon Welles recognized that such a squadron would be ideal for blockade duty on the Potomac. As a consequence, the Potomac Flotilla was assembled and began operations on the Potomac and Rappahannock rivers and on the Chesapeake Bay. The Flotilla consisted of twenty or more gunboats and their launches and cutters and was based at Piney Point, Maryland, across the Potomac from the Neck (not far from the Federal prison camp of Point Lookout, Maryland). The vessels in the Flotilla were of various types—paddle wheel, screw, and schooner—and carried from one to six guns each and were manned by crews ranging from sixteen to fifty-six men.

The Flotilla's main objectives were to keep the Potomac open to Union commercial and war vessels and to prevent the Confederates in Virginia from trading with the lower counties of Maryland. Confiscation of materials and vessels that would support Confederate war efforts and preventing blockade-running were also major concerns of the Flotilla. To many Southerners, the Flotilla's objectives also came to include harassment of "secessionists" in the area, either by bombardment or offloading marines to "investigate" homes along the rivers and tributaries.

Union commanders were careful to indicate that they would respect the rights of those who lived in the area. "I have to inform you that the property of unoffending citizens on the rivers blockaded by the squadron under my command will continue to be respected by me in the future as it has in the past," wrote Foxhall A. Parker, commander of the Potomac Flotilla. What constituted "unoffending citizens" apparently covered a wide range of discretion, however, and in addition to ordinary confiscations, plunder was common. The ships constantly scoured the inlets and creeks in search of boats "or anything they could confiscate or destroy," said one local.

With the embargo in place and because of frequent Federal raids, Lancaster County had become "entirely destitute" by 1862, with crops and livestock either stolen by Union raiders or eaten by starving local citizens. One Federal officer would report proudly that an operation in the Northern Neck had resulted in the destruction of "50 boats and goods in transit worth $30,000, and in the taking of 800 slaves, 40 or 50 prisoners, and many mules and horses."

Reports of the raiders' cruelty and disrespect were commonplace. Contrary to assurances, it seemed to some that anything of any value was taken. In one account, Union cavalry took horses, a man servant, and a "blue pig"—according to locals, probably a mix between a black and a white pig. Livestock certainly would have been eagerly sought after by Union troops as a supplement to standard hardtack and salt pork common in their wartime diets. Raiders seemed not to discriminate in their plunder, however; even household furniture was sometimes carried away by the marauders.

In some cases, confiscations took an almost humorous tone in the Official Records. One such report documented the correspondence to and from the Department of the Navy over the status of a piano that had been taken from a local home by marines from a Potomac Flotilla vessel. Apparently, word of the piano's fate reached all the way up to Secretary of the Navy Gideon Welles, who inquired as to the circumstances of the confiscation. The officer responsible noted that the piano came from what he insisted was an abandoned plantation. "Feeling assured that it would, together with the other articles, be destroyed, I gave orders to have it taken on board," reported William Tell Street, acting master.

"I believe acting Master Street took the piano from the best motives," wrote Foxhall A. Parker, commander of the Potomac Flotilla, responding to Secretary Welles. "But I have ordered that in the future no furniture be taken from private houses under any circumstances." The Secretary agreed. "It is to be regretted that the piano is taken. Now better be turned over for confiscation, or to be retained by proper authority for proper disposition hereafter," wrote Welles. Clearly, household furniture and musical instruments had come to merit special handling by the men of the Potomac Flotilla.

Other activities were not so benign. In his book of local Northern Neck stories about the Civil War, Larry S. Chowning (a distant relative of the Towleses) writes that Union gunboats were seen frequently on the Rappahannock River, and locals were constantly afraid the Yankees might attack their homes. Family lore tells of Federal cavalry riding up to the front of houses, dragging women into the yard and demanding, "Where are all your men?" When told that the men had gone to war, the soldiers proceeded to search for themselves to "find us some Johnny Rebs." Such searches would often include ransacking the surrounding property, outbuildings, barns, and houses themselves. One young boy evaded the Yankees by hiding under the voluminous skirt of a loyal slave woman, who calmly snapped beans throughout the search, not giving away her young charge to the Federal troops.

Federal cavalry also made frequent raids into the area, sometimes remaining for a considerable time. Such raids were conducted on area farms and plantations to disrupt commerce and to punish "secessionists" and were a matter of great consternation among the local populace. In the spring of 1861, a Confederate report had noted: "Much agitation prevails along the Potomac coast from apprehension that the enemy will land in large and small numbers to devastate and plunder."

Amidst all of this chaos and uncertainty, the Towles family sought a semblance of normality in their new home.

In the spring of 1862, with the three eldest boys either with their comrades in the 4th Virginia Cavalry or detached as scouts, Reverend Towles and his wife had with them the younger children, Rosalie, Ella, Churchill, and LeRoy (at six, the youngest). One family friend noted that the Towleses had been "driven from the comforts of home, [and had] sought refuge from the ruthless invaders of our soil, among kind and affectionate relatives in the county of Lancaster." Upon arriving in the Northern Neck, the Towles family had gone to live at Greenvale, a family property near Chowning Ferry Farm, Sophronia's ancestral home.

Originally known as Fairweather Neck (until the late eighteenth century), Greenvale was located on twelve tranquil acres on the Rappahannock River and Greenvale Creek. The history of the land where Greenvale Manor still stands dates back to 1654 when the land was patented to Anthony Stephens as part of a 500-acre parcel. Over the years, it would be owned by a number of prominent Virginia families, with names including Travers, Chichester, Ewell, Ball, Gilmour, Downman, and Chilton, and it was, even at the time, a well-known plantation or farm. Although his name doesn't appear on existing deeds, family tradition has it that Sophronia Towles's father, Col. John Chowning, gave the plantation to his daughter Anna (Sophronia's sister) as a wedding present. Anna married twice, both times to men named Chilton. John Robert Chilton—her first husband—was father of her only issue, two children also named John Robert and Anna.

The Main House, built on earlier foundations, dated back to 1840, and was constructed of cypress with oak joists and beams and had a brick, "English" basement. To the right of the house, facing the Rappahannock, an ice house, well, or root cellar appears to have existed.

At the time of the Civil War, the property belonged to the Chiltons, of which Anna (Chowning) Chilton was the matriarch. Nearby relatives included Myra (Chowning) Ewell of Bona Vista and Chowning cousins at the nearby Chowning's Ferry Farm. The McCarty family maintained the property for Anna, and helped the Towles family settle into their new surroundings.

Many years later, Ella Towles would return to Greenvale, renting it from her cousin Carrie (Cornelia) Carter Chilton, who had inherited it from Anna Chilton's son, John Robert Chilton. In Ella's youth, however, the property must have presented a daunting reality for the young Virginia girl.

Normally, Ella and the other younger members of the family might have inferred that living with relatives, even as a refugee from war-torn Northern Virginia, would be an adventure. After all, the Towles family roots were from Lancaster County, and they remained close to their aunts, uncles, and cousins in the Neck. It was a logical place in which John Towles and his family might take refuge. The area was, however, subject to many of the same privations afflicting the South generally, particularly given its blockade by water and its relative isolation by land due to the large rivers that bordered the area on the north and south. With increasingly scarce resources and the constant threat of Union raids, sharing quarters (even with family) must have been extremely traumatizing, particularly for young children.

In the midst of struggling to feed loved ones and to protect hearth and home, the Towleses, like others, looked to family for love and support. They also were understandably eager to obtain information about their sons who were away fighting in the war.

During the family's relocation to Lancaster County, young Ella would begin a regular and lively correspondence with her soldier brothers that would eventually survive as the primary original source material for her brothers' wartime stories. Understandably, Ella was also particularly close to her older sister, Rosalie, who took her under her wing as the two young women struggled with the realities of their new lives.

Before the war began, Rosalie had been sent to school in Alexandria, Virginia, not far from the Episcopal High School where her older brother, Vivian, had attended classes. The Belle Haven Institute, on Queen Street in Alexandria, provided a proper setting for the education of the daughter of an Episcopal cleric.

A Virginia yearbook of education from the 1870s identifies the institute as "a first-class School for the thorough training of Young Ladies...so long and favorably known to the people of Virginia." The school pre-dated the war and continued to operate after the conflict ended, providing both education and appropriate exposure to local society. "[I]n full view of the Capitol Building at Washington, D.C., and only six miles distant therefrom, its proximity to Washington affords advantages that, under proper restrictions, can be successfully utilized and made auxiliary to the instructions received in the classroom," noted the yearbook.

An advertisement of the time from J.H. Chataigne's Directory of Alexandria and Fredericksburg ranked the Belle Haven Institute as "among the finest and best in the state...[t]his institution is under the personal care and supervision of Prof. N. Penick and lady, assisted by a full corps of competent and proficient professors."

As the Directory explained, "The Principals will seek to educate Young Ladies in the broadest sense of the term...to give them a culture of mind and heart, which will fit them for the social circle and the sphere of domestic duties, and prepare them for that highest position, the office of teaching and training the young."

The course of study was divided into five departments: Primary, Intermediate, Collegiate, Ornamental, and Normal. "Young Ladies may, with the advice and consent of their friends and the Principals, pursue such studies as may seem best adapted to their tastes and capacities," touted the listing for the school.

No doubt a major portion of the curriculum would have centered on the arts, as surviving contemporary snippets about the school indicate that young women from across Virginia completed courses of such studies. Reporting on graduation ceremonies at "the Belle Haven Institute in Alexandria," for example, a Shenandoah Valley newspaper of the time observed that "Miss A.V. Mason of Staunton was awarded a medal in music." The oldest Towles daughter would certainly have been in good company as she began her education.

Rosalie did not take to life away from the family, however. In one pre-war letter home, she wrote her younger sister, saying she would rather be home "now with those I love than to be poring over Schoolbooks."

And by early 1862, those days of school were finished, and Rosalie had joined her parents and younger siblings as they made their way south. As the oldest child with the John Towles family at Greenvale, she would have undoubtedly played an important role in maintaining a sort of normalcy within the family structure, and she must have given her parents and younger siblings a great deal of comfort and support.

In the fall of 1862, however, Rosa—as Rosalie was fondly called by her family— would fall prey to a common enemy of civilians and soldiers of the time...disease.

"As fugitives packed the roads and crowded in with friends and relatives or endured cheerless boardinghouses in towns and cities, they taxed the South's ever-decreasing resources and added to the uncounted deaths of white and black civilians from disease and malnutrition," noted one source. Although with a few exceptions there were no serious epidemics during the American Civil War, suffering and death were nevertheless widespread, and a fair estimate of war-related civilian deaths might total 50,000. Such was the overflowing cup of sorrow the Southern populace had to endure, in addition to combat and disease-related deaths of their soldiers in the field.

In late October, Rosa fell ill with "a severe illness" and fever. Eleven days later, she passed away, leaving a grieving family that would soon suffer additional losses.

Soon thereafter, a family friend wrote, "We heard nothing of dear Rosa's death until last Sunday…while we can offer you no consolation, we <u>sympathize</u> in the loss of your lovely and gifted daughter. I do not know of ever meeting with a young Lady whose engaging and affectionate manners and sprightly mind could have prepossessed me more than your daughter did…I hope while God has sent this heavy affliction upon you and your family, He will give you the strength to bear up under it. He will, I am sure, for He never leaves us comfortless however severe the stroke."

What the actual nature of Rosa's illness was, we will never know. The lexicon of "fevers" in Civil War-era medicine includes a wide variety of types with various causes and symptoms: rheumatic fever; typhoid fever; "bilious remittent fever" (an archaic term for relapsing fever characterized by bilious vomiting and diarrhea); and the collective "camp fever," a term used for all of the continuing fevers experienced by the army, whether typhoid, malarial, or a hybrid of the two. Rosalie's illness may have been one of several common ailments of the time, for example pleurisy, diphtheria, or rubeola (measles), which was often reported among soldiers (a notation on one muster card for Robert Towles indicated that he had suffered from this illness). Perhaps Rosalie may have had what today would be a relatively simple case of strep throat (sometimes called the croup or scarlet fever in Civil War times). With penicillin and rest, we routinely cure this illness today; in 1862, it could be fatal.

The severity of her illness and her relatively swift death may have been exacerbated by the general conditions in the blockaded Northern Neck. Certainly, like much of the South, the local populace endured a general lack of supplies and medicines during the war. In any case, the outpouring of grief from family and friends was immediate and heartfelt.

Cousin J.L. Ewell, like Rosa's brothers a Virginia cavalryman, tried to console her parents, calling her an "interesting daughter just budding into woman hood snatched away from earthly friends and winged her flight to join the Immortal choir in that bright world of eternal bliss. Shurely this was hard to be borne, but God is just and with peaceful submission we should bear his visitations."

Older brother Vivian Towles wrote his parents in mid-November:

>Alpine Nov 16th 1862
>
>My dear Mother,
>
>At last I am able to write you and to mention my dear sister's death. I can trust myself to say but little. Most deeply do I sympathize with my dear parents in this great distress. I can only forget the load of my sorrow which burdens my own soul when I think of what must be your distress. That she is in a state of glorious and happy existence is my only comfort. Of this I am assured. Had I ever thought of her dying I would have pictured her death scene as it occurred, except that suffering. May I live so as to win her approbation could she look down upon me.
>
>My long silence has been unavoidable on account of my injury. I hope Bob has reached you ere this and informed you of how we have been getting along. Tho sad the visit most gladly would I have come also if my horse were able to bring me. I am trying to get him ready for duty by the time I am. I am well all to soreness in the bones and joints of my hand wh[ich] hangs on a long time. I write with diff[iculty].
>
>I have met with much kindness since [I was] hurt from Mrs. Page and daughters at Markam and from Mr. Paine and family at Culpepper. I arrived here on yesterday. Miss Frances & Miss Nancy send much love to you. Miss Frances wishes very much to write to you but is prevented by a boil on her forefinger. The ladies are very kind to me.
>
>Tell my dear sister Ella that she has my deepest sympathy and love and I must earnestly hope that her brothers will be everything to her they should be. Much love to Jimmie, Churchill & Leroy, may they grow up as Dear Rosa would wish to see them.
>
>My love to Aunt Anna, Aunt & Uncle Ewell and my cousins. Tell them that the boys in the 9th are all well. Jno. Chilton in better health than I ever saw him, I think. And now, my dear parents I must bid you adieu.
>
>Your affectionate son
>
>Jno. V. Towles

Nor was the recognition of a death in Reverend Towles's family limited to family members. An obituary in a Richmond newspaper noted:

> DIED, at Green Vale, in the County of Lancaster, Oct. 31st, 1862, after a severe illness of eleven days, Miss Rosalie C. Towles, daughter of the Rev. John Towles, of Prince William, in the 15th year of her age.
>
> Driven from the comforts of home early in the spring of the present year, her parents sought refuge for themselves and family, from the ruthless invaders of our soil, among kind and affectionate relatives in the county of Lancaster. Here, it was hoped, they might enjoy that peaceful domestic happiness, which could not be enjoyed in their deserted home! But alas! For some wise purpose, which futurity will doubtless disclose, that family circle was entered and with the falling of the Autumn leaves, this beautiful girl fell asleep, from all the sorrows, disappointments, and battles of life! To record her death, is truly a melancholy duty, whether it devolves upon relative or friend! By what slender tissue life is held! How little the cord which connects "the here" and "the hereafter". Life and death, time and eternity! To witness thus early the decay of one, just bursting into womanhood, buoyed with hopes of a bright and happy future, was a shock, which fell heavily on *all*! Lively and gentle in her manners, and affectionate in her disposition, she not only doubly endeared herself to those around her, but made all her friends, who were ever associated with her! Not only in the bereaved family circle will the joyous beaming of her bright brown eyes, and the music of her merry voice be missed, — but by all who have ever known her, her loss will be deeply deplored! Yet had her years been prolonged, storms might have arisen, which would have marred the serenity of that soul, which was so willing even in its last hours of early probation that "God's will should be done!" Now these are over. She has finished her earthly pilgrimage—and "after life's fitful fever, she sleeps well!" Though snatched away just on the verge of the summer of her years—she is now reaping the rich harvest of a well spent spring time! She has only entered early, the haven of Eternal Rest!
>
> "Mourn not thy daughter's fading, It is the common lot, That those we love, should come and go, And leave us in this world of woe, *So murmur not!*"

Another obituary placed Rosalie's death in the context of life's transient nature:

> DIED, at Green Vale, in the county of Lancaster, 31st October, 1862, after a severe illness of eleven days, Miss ROSALIE C. TOWLES, daughter of the Rev. John Towles, of Prince William, in the 15th year of her age. Thus early has been snatched away from earth, this beautiful flower, ere its leaves could be touched by the chilling blasts of life's trials and sufferings. Many are the tears of pity and affection, which will involuntarily fall from the friends of this lovely girl, when they connect the above sad lines with the memory of her, whom so short a time ago moved among us, in all the sunshine of her nature.
>
> "All that's bright must fade, The *brightest*, still the *fleetest*, All that's sweet was made, *But to be lost while sweetest.*"

Recent scholarship dealing with death, dying, and mourning during the American Civil War suggests that such obituaries were the rule, rather than the exception. Civil War families on both sides of the Mason-Dixon Line sought solace in the face of great personal loss and often invoked the concept of a glorious afterlife that follows a short, brutish sojourn on Earth.

Nearby Chowning Ferry Farm contains the remnants of a family cemetery, where Rosalie Towles was laid to rest. Others buried there include: Capt. John Chowning and his wife Catherine, as well as various other Chownings, Towleses, and Chiltons (including J.R. Chilton).

Some families lived at such a distance from the parish church that loved ones were buried on the home plantation instead. The earliest recorded stones in a family cemetery in Lancaster County date back to the 1730s, although these stones had been removed from their original location many years previously and were discarded. Fortunately, the Chowning family cemetery remains intact on the Chowning Ferry Farm property, which remains in the Chowning family.

Here, under a small canopy of trees surrounded by other graves and enclosed by a wrought iron fence, "Poor Darling Rosa" rests. Her tombstone reads simply, "Rosalie Towles, 30 December 1847 – 31 October 1862. Daughter of Rev. John & S.E. Towles."

With three other children in harm's way, her family undoubtedly braced for further trials to come.

Chapter Six

Family matters
Letters to a younger sister

"I was much pleased at the receipt of your really very nice, sensible and well written letter."

Letter to Ella Towles from Vivian Towles
August 1862

greetings

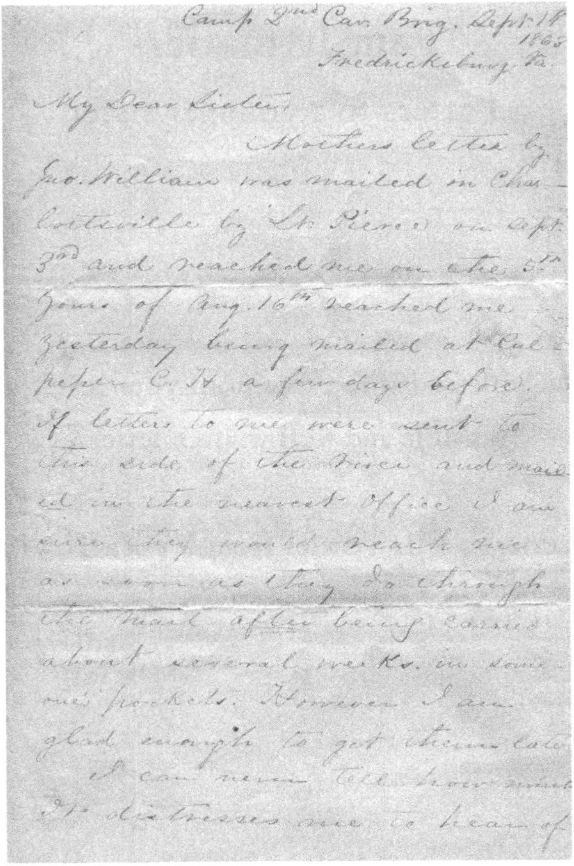

Camp 2nd Cav. Brig. Sept. 14
1863
Fredricksburg Va.

My Dear Sister,

Mothers letter by Geo. Williams was mailed in Charlottsville by Lt. Pierce on Sept. 3rd and reached me on the 5th. Yours of Aug. 16th reached me yesterday being mailed at Culpeper C. H. a few days before. If letters to me were sent to this side of the river and mailed in the nearest Office I am sure they would reach me as soon as they do through the mail after being carried about several weeks in some one's pockets. However I am glad enough to get them late.

I can never tell how much it distresses me to hear of

Letter from Vivian Towles to sister Ella Towles

With family tragedy so fresh in their minds, exactly how did the Towles brothers-in-arms deal with the extended ties that bound them to their exiled family? From the small, but poignant surviving cache of letters addressed to their parents and, in particular, to their younger sister, we get a glimpse of how soldiers in the field were able to remain connected to their loved ones during the war.

Ella Towles—in the fall of 1862, a girl of twelve—was likely the apple of her older brothers' eyes. It is clear that the brothers relished telling her of the "doings" in Prince William that they observed on scouts or other duty. In turn, they solicited status reports from Ella concerning her studies and life in Lancaster County, where the family resided with relatives.

An August 1862 letter to Ella from Vivian is typical of the combination of reports from the front and developments concerning friends and neighbors that the Towles family left behind in Brentsville. "I was much pleased at the rec[eipt] of your really very nice and sensible letter," wrote Viv. "You have no idea how much the prospect of a long absence is lightened by the knowledge that even my youngest Sister is able to contribute so much to my happiness."

The 4th Virginia Cavalry was still close to the front and to the area where the Towles homestead had been in Prince William County. As in letters to follow, her older brother filled in his sibling regarding developments in the family's old neighborhood. In the second year of the war, Prince William County had already seen more than its share of conflict and occupation, including the two battles near Manassas, only a few miles from Brentsville. Firmly along the lines of advance, the area was blanketed with Union patrols and cavalry, which protected the railroads and attempted to root out scouts, partisans, and perceived treasonous citizens who remained behind Union lines. Vivian voiced concerns about the Federal "confiscators," and related that neighbors like the Howisons had "lost all in the way of worldly goods." Some individuals, Viv noted, had been treated "roughly" by the Yankees; others, like Michael Roseberry—a Union man before the war—were, according to Vivian at least, becoming "warm secessionists" because of the occupation.

In *The Years of Anguish,* a chronicle of the war in nearby Fauquier County, one observer reported that "[We] hear every day of outrages perpetrated on our poor people by the Federal soldiers in this vicinity. Houses robbed and burned, bread and meat taken to the last morsel. The last cent of money taken from the pockets of defenseless people." From the tenor of Vivian's letters home, much the same had happened in Prince William.

The desolation of war was readily apparent to the thoughtful young cavalryman.

> In front of us in Stafford we can see the desolate looking farmhouses whose inmates have so long been prisoners and who the yankees say they feed. Behind us on the hills we can see the blackened chimneys of residences burned by a wanton or careless foe during the late engagement while here and there a house still stands but so stripped and defiled that one almost wishes them burned too. The people who lived in all these houses are scattered and gone, even tender ladies and children were dragged with the yankees in their retreat to the North bank, through all the horrors of the battle with pittiless storm and deep mud. I never think of you dear Ella without a feeling of deep gratitude that you have been spared actual contact with the horror of War.

The destruction wrought on pre-war friends and family homesteads was never far from the boys' thoughts. Wrote Vivian, "I have written in Mother's letter an account of the late misdoings of the Enemy in Prince William in which some of our best friends ladies distinguished for piety, virtue, and all goodness have been made to taste almost the last dregs of the bitter cup of War's horrors."

Saying that he was tired of seeing nothing but "men, men, men," Vivian encouraged young Ella to tell him about her life and her "expatriation" in Lancaster County. "I know your exile is much more endurable than that of some others, but I suspect you all and Mother particularly are anxious to again take possession of our own home, however impoverished it may be," wrote Viv.

While Lancaster County was much further south from the frontier between the two armies, it nevertheless was also vulnerable to incursions from Union troops. In one of his letters, Vivian spoke at length about a Yankee cavalry raid into Lancaster and Northumberland counties in the Northern Neck. Having heard about the raid through captured Union newspapers, he surmised that the object of the incursion was to break up blockade-running in the Tidewater area. "Doubtless the invasion caused a very great panic among the good people of the Northern Neck," he wrote his sister. "If the enemy invades the County again however it is too far from their main body for them to stay long or to penetrate into the out of the way place you live in." As events would demonstrate later in the war, this optimism would prove misplaced, however.

The raid into the Northern Neck referred to by Vivian likely was a major cavalry incursion in the early summer of 1863 that was led by Union Gen. Judson Kilpatrick. Contemporary accounts reported that "the enemy burned King & Queen Courthouse and several private residences…Kilpatrick transported his forces up the Bay, landing in Lancaster, and moved a motley crowd of negro men, women and children in wagons, carts, carriages and buggies up through the counties between the Rappahannock and Potomac."

The extent of the plunder was reported as being "nearly 600 horses and mules, about 400 negroes, and a few carriages." The official report for the operation described an even more impressive haul: 800 contrabands (slaves), "innumerable mules, horses, etc.," and between forty and fifty prisoners, including a Confederate captain and lieutenant. The amount of damage done to the Rebels was estimated at nearly $1,000,000—a staggering figure, conservatively equivalent to more than $25 million in today's dollars. The raid's success came at a loss of one man severely wounded and two slightly wounded. "Considering the force engaged and the results obtained, this is the greatest raid of the war," wrote Union Cavalry Chief Alfred Pleasonton to the commander of the Army of the Potomac, Maj. Gen. Joseph Hooker.

One goal was clearly paramount for the Union troopers—finding and securing horseflesh. Three columns reputedly took different routes intended "to sweep every horse and mule out of the Northern Neck," wrote one observer. The Yankees' interest in horses was confirmed by Vivian Towles's letter home.

"I think you all came out much better than I expected particularly in the way of servants. The loss of horses and mules was the most serious," he said. Vivian noted that he, himself, currently had "a tough yankee horse," which must have been captured during one engagement or another. "He has a most delightful gallop and would be of great service to you when at home. I think I will send him home if I can get…another horse to ride. The yankee took me into Maryland and back [during the Antietam campaign] and looks well yet."

Federal raids into the somewhat remote Northern Neck were relatively infrequent, but no less terrifying for their infrequency. Yankee patrols and incursions increased, once most of the local men had gone off to fight in the army. Local citizens eventually became used to the depredations that often accompanied such raids. "They [the Union soldiers] stole at night and in the day came to buy cakes or pies," said one woman. "Times had become very hard with all the people about here, so the ladies were glad to make pies and cakes to sell them."

Locals soon learned to hide valuables, including livestock, when the soldiers were in the area, however. "As soon as the War began, my father took all [our] valuables and packed them carefully in a box, then dug a deep hold in his plant-bed in the garden and put the box in. Then he made the bed again and planted his seed. Soon there were cabbage, lettuce and tomato plants growing on it, and no one would ever imagine a box of valuables was snugly stored away beneath," wrote a grandmother in her war reminiscences to her grandchildren. Another woman kept her silver spoons ready in bags and when she heard the cry of "the Yanks are coming," she would attach the bags around her waist beneath her large hoop-skirt to safeguard the family silver. Presumably, Southern virtue was to be respected, even by the Yankees.

Sometimes, local children were able to dissuade the Union soldiers from taking family possessions. As one soldier headed to the hen house, a young girl wailed, "O, he is going to take our hens!" Perhaps having pity on the child, the man said, "If it is going to distress a little girl, we will not take them." The Yankee soon left, but it likely was a good thing that the family then quickly hid the hens, because the soldier later returned with his mates, and the family poultry may not have been so fortunate on a second try. Vivian must have seen some parallels to this type of activity in his observations in Northern Virginia. "The people in Prince William have the yankees among them again but surely they will not treat them as badly as before for the old men are nearly all either in prison or exiled and the ladies have nothing left worth their taking," he wrote to his sister.

Notwithstanding privations faced by friends and family—in Prince William and far afield in Lancaster County and the Northern Neck—the Towles brothers remained focused on their roles in the family. This was particularly true for the eldest brother, Vivian, who, if he survived, would someday be expected to head the family. Part of that responsibility would be to ensure the proper education and development of his younger siblings.

In a November 1862 letter to his mother after Rosalie Towles's untimely death, Vivian had spoken of what he perceived to be his duty towards his remaining sister Ella. "I most earnestly hope that her brothers will be everything to her they should be," wrote the grieving older brother. In a tribute to his lost sister, Viv expressed the sentiment that the younger children should all grow up as "Dear Rosa" would wish to see them.

By early 1863, Vivian's letters to Ella had taken an even more wistful tone. "I think a great deal about you my dear and only sister, and it is a very great pleasure for me to get a letter from you," he wrote. "You write good news of yourself—that you are well and going to school. I am very glad to hear it indeed and hope your advantages will be many and of long continuance. If I survive this war I intend to make it a part of my business to see that your advantages are abundant."

While the brothers no doubt edited their comments regarding the war in their letters to their sister, some correspondence touched on military matters. A rare letter to Ella from the youngest Towles brother in the service, Jimmie, was addressed to "My Dear Sister" and complained of his having chills and fevers. Reporting that both of his older brothers were fine, Jimmie also noted that "some of Hampton's men caught some Yankee spies and hung them all to the same tree and left them for the Yanks to find." High drama, indeed, for a fifteen-year-old... and even more so for a younger sister!

With the war intensifying in the Eastern Theater, some letters mentioned significant battles and their aftermath. In early May 1863, for example, the armies once again faced off across the Rapidan River frontier, and Vivian was part of the cavalry screen that formed a picket line along the river. Writing from U.S. Ford on May 20, 1863, Vivian told his sister of the stalemate after the recent battle of Chancellorsville, where the legendary Confederate Gen. Thomas J. "Stonewall" Jackson had been mortally wounded.

> I am sitting in a shady grove on a hill where our picket 'reserve' is kept just above the Rappahannock and in what nature formed a most lovely spot. But the desolating and polluting touch of War has been even here in this place and destroyed its fairest charms. It is only here out of sight of the trampled fields and crumbling earthworks, reclining in the shade and in sound of the music of the water the birds and the gentle breezes, that I am able to forget that only a fortnight ago a mighty host of our enemies was marching down these slopes to the river which separated them from safety. [They] trampled the green fields into a waste of mud mixed with all the wreck of war...broken vehicles and weapons, dead animals and ammunition sunk in a common mire and the blue clothing and decayed provisions scattered about as far as the eye can see.
>
> Not far below me is the now famous crossing place where they had their pontoon bridges, three in number. The bridges are gone now but the ropes and anchors which the yankees cut loose in their haste still remain. We have a little band of riflemen here to guard the place and while 'on post' we are face to face with our enemies on the opposite bank of the river and in speaking distance. We are apparently at perfect peace, it being against orders on either side to shoot at each other.

> I suppose it is best to refrain from a kind of fighting which
> cannot be decisive but I must confess that there is at times a strong
> desire to send a bullet into the blue coated wretch who confronts me.

Notwithstanding such instincts, however, picket duty sometimes involved fraternization with the enemy. "While our boys were in the river bathing, I being on post a yankee swam to our bank and spent a half hour in conversation. He was communicative and hoped we would all be home soon and that neither of us would get hurt," wrote Vivian.

Often, the setting must have seemed somewhat surreal, with moments of calm before the coming storm of conflict.

> We are here on picket and the intense heat has driven me
> into a cool and shady sawmill where the splash of cool water over
> the useless machinery and my letter to you has kept my thoughts
> away from what is around me, even the yankees on the other
> bank, and now suddenly I find that It is near my time to go to the
> rifle pits and the black sky and muttering thunder indicate that I
> will get a wetting. So goodbye my dear sister.
> Your affectionate Bro.
> Vivian

Occasionally, the relative familiarity of picket duty was disturbed by high-strung emotions on both sides. "Yesterday there was a most graceless set of fellows down on the other side. They were abusive and insulting and spoke derisively of the glorious Jackson's death. We had to threaten them to make them stop. Today a more respectable set is down. They say little and that is said respectfully," noted Vivian. Stonewall was gone, but apparently not forgotten by either side.

Gettysburg, the great battle in early July between the Union Army of the Potomac and General Lee's Army of Northern Virginia, was also a topic of letters home. Lee's invasion of the North in the summer of 1863 ended with a dramatic defeat in a three-day battle in Pennsylvania, followed by the Confederate retreat to Virginia. In late July 1863, Vivian wrote his sister regarding the aftermath of the battle. "The determined fight we gave the Enemy the other day seems to have procured us a season of rest and plenty but it may end at any moment."

Vivian was proud of the sacrifice made by the 4th Virginia Cavalry. "Our regiment was distinguished by success in every engagement throughout the

Penna. campaign and lost out of 300 men who went in 107 killed and wounded and some few prisoners," he wrote. The much-traveled flag presented so long ago to the regiment had, by this time, seen much better days. "We still carry our old flag…It is now nothing more than a torn and bullet ridden piece of bunting the beautiful painting of Virginia [with the Latin Virginia state motto *sic semper tyrannis*] having faded almost away and portions of the flag being entirely gone. Our Battle Flag is also torn and tattered, our Col. never allowing it to be laid aside for a new one as most regiments have done occasionally," said Vivian.

Vivian's letter went on to speak of some of the Confederate losses at Gettysburg, including family friends wounded and killed. "All of the 8th Va. Infantry…was badly cut to pieces, as was all of Pickett's Virginia Division. J. Lattimer, now the distinguished Major Lattimer of the Artillery, lost his right arm entire and is now at Jordan Springs getting well and will be in the field again soon. He is a noble fellow, so much unlike his fellows." Nineteen-year-old Joseph W. Latimer, the "Boy Major," had learned artillery tactics from Prof. Thomas Jackson ("Stonewall") at the Virginia Military Institute. At Gettysburg, Latimer had performed meritoriously, directing his guns while firing more than 1,100 rounds against the Union artillery. He was wounded by a shell fragment and, despite Vivian's optimism, died a month later.

Perhaps realizing that the horror of war was not the proper topic for his young sister, Vivian conceded that she must "doubtless [be] tired of 'War' and 'Yankees' and indeed I very much regret that there is so little else a soldier can talk or write about. I think you will have to introduce new subjects for here with us we have only two things to talk about viz War, and all the comforts and joys we used to have."

Indeed, many letters included family and domestic themes—quotidian, but to be expected in missives to a younger sister. In one such letter, Vivian passed along the good news that brother Jimmie, who had been captured at the end of March 1863, had been exchanged and had "arrived in Dixie safe and sound." Jimmie's experience included a brief stint in a place his brother Robert would come to know, Old Capitol Prison, before being sent to Point Lookout, where he was eventually exchanged. Upon Jimmie's release, Vivian expected him to again take his place in the ranks, despite his age.

In some cases, social dynamics and conventions of the time were topics of discussion. Engagements, rumored marriages, relocations, and the like were eagerly passed along for family consumption in far away Lancaster County. Sometimes, editorial comments were offered. "At Catlett's two of the young ladies married Yankees much to the indignation of the others," wrote Vivian in one such letter. The Catletts were pre-war neighbors of the Towles, and Catlett's Station an important railroad terminus, as well as the scene of Robert's derring-do during the raid that netted General Pope's wallet.

On the other hand, the boys in the army had only a distant sense of what was happening on the home front with the family in the Northern Neck. "I am sadly ignorant of the state of affairs at home," wrote Vivian. "Once or twice I have had vague and entirely unsatisfactory rumors from the 9th [Va. Cavalry] and after we recrossed the Potomac into Virginia I learned from Cousin Jimmie [Ewell] that you were 'all well.' This is all I have heard since my visit in May. How much I would give to be able to pay you a flying visit, but that cannot be for a long time," wrote the homesick cavalryman.

Occasionally, an unexpected visitor merited a comment in letters home:

> The morning after our late fight, while we were lying in the rain and mud, tired and hungry, I was agreeably surprised and reminded of what now seems olden times by a visit, if I may call it such to walk from one part of a muddy field to another, from James McVeigh [an acquaintance from Prince William]. He called on Bob, never having seen me, but Bob being absent he called for me. He had gotten a transfer from Infantry to Cavalry and was in the Black Horse. He had been with the regiment only a few days and in the gallop we had to the scene of action sprained one of his horses legs, I am afraid, permanently—He says he joined the Cav. in a bad time. I am of the same opinion for independent of the quantity of fighting we have had to do, we have suffered very much from exposure, scarcity and insufficiency of food and our horses subsist entirely upon what grass they can be allowed to graize and a little half ripe wheat…

While the content of letters from Ella *to* her brothers has not survived, she must have expressed a certain amount of feistiness that, in later life, manifested itself in her strongly held beliefs about the North. "Your letter gave me much pleasure," wrote Vivian, apparently in response to one such letter. "I am glad my sister has such brave thoughts about the yankees. Never cringe before them. Young ladies and even little children have found it profitable to be as spunky as possible when the yankees are around. But I sincerely hope your resolutions will never be put to the test," said the protective older brother.

Occasionally, news from home came through somewhat unexpected sources. Vivian often heard from "the boys in the 9th [Virginia Cavalry]"—Vivian's cousins from Lancaster County in the Northern Neck who served in a different regiment that was sometimes in the same brigade as the 4th. On one day in August 1863, one of the cousins would bring news about the family to Vivian.

> On day before yesterday I was very agreeably surprised to see [cousin] John William [Chowning] ride into Camp. He had been sick four or five days at Loyd's and had given a letter which he had for me to Lieut Pierce not thinking that he would see me first. We are camped in the river road about two miles down the river from Town and John rode right into Co. A, it being the first on the road. He remained with me that night and the next day and night and I enjoyed his talk about you all very much. I first learned from him that you had been sick since your vacation. It did not last long and I suppose you have entirely recovered.

John William was also able to provide some details about how the exiled Towles family was living in Lancaster County. "Jno. told me about the fine fish you are eating every day in Lancaster. Small cat fish at $1.00 is the amount of my fish eating this year. I went out and got some extras while Jno. was with me and tried to make him as comfortable as possible," wrote Vivian, who understandably missed his friends and family. "Poor Lee Macrae my best friend is either at home or in a yankee prison. I don't know which. I feel so lonely sometimes that I wished John could stay with me longer and was very sorry when he left which he did this morning."

Ultimately, the distance weighed heavily on the literate young man, as did his helplessness when it came to family matters. Writing his sister, Vivian noted, "I can never tell how much it distresses me to hear of our Dear Mother's ill health and to know that the remedy she so much desires, mountain air, is denied her. I am much consoled by Father's assurance that she is better than of late and that he has much confidence in some new remedies. How I wish this cruel War was over so that I might devote myself to you all."

In Vivian's heart—as with so many young soldiers—home was tantalizingly close…and yet so far away. "Just this little distance this side of Fredericksburg makes me feel as if I was much nearer to you all and causes a longing to go on down the road until I am opposite Greenvale," he wrote. "Give my love to everybody…"

CHAPTER SEVEN

Back with the boys in old Prince William
'Iron Scouts' and a brush with capture

"I only want men on fast horses."

Autobiography of Arab

Col. Elon J. Farnsworth, Library of Congress

Frank Stringfellow, Confederate Scout

uniformed

Jack Shoolbred, "Iron Scout"

Gen. J.E.B. Stuart, Library of Congress

Following the battle of Gettysburg in July, the Army of the Potomac under Gen. George Gordon Meade had been slow to pursue Lee's bloodied but unbowed troops. On July 9, 1863, the Army of Northern Virginia with its wagons, artillery, and wounded had crossed back into Virginia, generally unmolested by the Union army. An exasperated President Lincoln, sensing a lost opportunity, gently berated General Meade, "Would it not have been better to strike a blow, when the enemy was vulnerable?"

From the perspective of a man in the ranks of Lee's army, however, Vivian Towles was perplexed that General Lee had re-crossed the Potomac. He speculated that only a direct order from Confederate President Davis would have made such a retreat necessary, and he echoed the sentiments of other Confederate soldiers who seemed convinced that they would prevail when they next met their Union counterparts. Such was still the confidence of the Army of Northern Virginia in the late summer of 1863.

Indeed, many of the Confederates felt that they had inflicted as much damage as they had received on the ridges and hills of Pennsylvania. The 4th Virginia Cavalry had been part of the invasion. In a late July letter home, Vivian asserted that, "[O]ur army is in fine plight, confident and eager to pay the yankees back for Gettysburg…we lay in line of battle three days in sight of the yankee Army, the whole army anxious for them to make their threatened attack but they retired." This aggressive sentiment mirrored other assessments of the battle's aftermath. In his *Sketches of Hampton's Cavalry,* for example, U.R. Brooks noted, "Our troops, wearied by continual watchings and fighting, but not dispirited, lay all day still expecting again to hear the onward command given. And why was it not given?" Brooks cited the lack of ammunition and supplies as the reason why the Army of Northern Virginia had to retreat beyond the Potomac.

In July and August 1863, after several weeks of maneuvering, the opposing lines stabilized, roughly along the line of the Rapidan River and Mine Run, where General Lee's troops held an imposing defensive position. During the coming months, an uneasy stalemate ensued, and both sides would rest, refit, and prepare for the next round of hostilities—presumably another thrust by the Union armies towards the Confederate capital in Richmond. In the meantime, the northern Virginia counties of Prince William, Stafford, and Fauquier remained staging areas for Mr. Lincoln's army.

As he awaited the anticipated Federal movement, Robert E. Lee continued to rely on Major General Stuart's peerless intelligence gathering. From the earliest days of the conflict, Confederate cavalrymen had been detached as scouts. General

Stuart believed that the South's deficiencies in men and material meant that they had to wage war as never before, bolstered by what Stuart called "complete knowledge of the enemy's strength and plans at all times." Indeed, Stuart, himself, might be called Lee's greatest scout. Certainly, "Marse Robert" valued Stuart's reconnaissance skills as much as his prowess in battle. "He never brought me a piece of false information," Lee lamented after Stuart's death in 1864.

To obtain such knowledge meant that Stuart needed to use a variety of methods, including scouts. In addition to groups of partisan rangers, such as those under the command of Col. John S. Mosby, Stuart and his subordinates regularly detached cavalry scouts, singly or in squads, to determine the enemy's whereabouts and activities.

From the very beginning of the war, Lee and other Confederate commanders saw the value of scouting and employed cavalrymen to accomplish important tasks. Scouts were the real eyes and ears of the army, and Confederate cavalry was much used for this purpose, even at a time when Federal commanders were still chiefly dependent upon civilian spies, detectives, and deserters for information on Confederate strength and movement. Because "spies" and "scouts" were often used interchangeably, it was sometimes difficult to sort out espionage (the work of spies) from "reconnaissance," which is the work of trained observers, such as cavalry scouts. One thing, however, remained constant. If you were caught in your army's uniform, you could expect to be treated as a prisoner of war; if you were in disguise, you were a spy and could be hanged.

One of the most famous of Stuart's personal scouts was Capt. Frank Stringfellow, from Company E of the 4th Virginia Cavalry. Recounting his recruitment as a scout, Stringfellow described how the cavalry chieftain perceived his duties:

> I would be sent often on secret missions, entirely on (my) own, with no one around to make decisions and to give orders. I would have to depend on myself alone—on the quickness of my eye, my hand, and my wits. I would have to learn every road and path in the country in which I operated, (and) it would be my job to flank enemy pickets, penetrate to the very heart of their camps, capture stragglers on the road and high officers in their tents, and learn the Federal strength, positions, and plans…if I could not make my way through the picket lines by stealth, I would have to charge them and fight my way through. And I would have to get back with my information even if a Federal cavalry brigade was on my trail.

Stuart was noted to have said that he would be greatly saddened by the loss of a scout's life in the depths of the forest, but that he would mourn the loss of the scout's information even more.

In John Esten Cooke's *Wearing of the Gray*," Gen. Stuart's former staff member further articulated the attributes of a scout:

> The scout has a thorough knowledge of the country, and is even acquainted with 'every hog path.' He travels in the woods, and often in crossing a sandy highway dismounts, and backs his horse across the road, to mislead the enemy, on the watch for 'guerillas'…Thus lurking and prowling around the enemy's camps, by night and day, the scout never relaxes his exertions until he discovers what he wishes (the strength, situation, and probable designs of the enemy). If he cannot 'flank the enemy's pickets, he charges them. If he cannot glide through, he fights through. If he meets a straggling enemy or enemies not in too great number, he puts his pistol to his or their heads and brings him or them along—pleasantly chatting with them as he goes along, but keeping his eye and his pistol muzzle upon them.
>
> When he relates his adventures, he does so with a laugh—noting the humorous side of things. He has extricated himself from deadly peril safely, 'fooled' his foe, and is chatting after the occurrence with his friends by the camp fire. Could anything be more satisfactory? Thus toiling, watching, and fighting, enduring hardship, risking liberty and life hourly, the scout passes his life. He is not a paid spy—not a spy at all, for he goes uniformed and armed and the work is his reward.

Cooke could very easily have been speaking about Robert Towles, as subsequent events would demonstrate.

The men who served as personal cavalry scouts and aides to General Stuart were an unusual and diverse group. Throughout the war, men such as Stringfellow, Redmond Burke, and Will Farley—in addition to partisans under John S. Mosby—would spend many days behind Union lines on scouting duty, and they risked daily capture. Fearless, energetic, and intimately familiar with Prince William County and his pre-war neighbors, Robert Towles was admirably suited for reconnaissance work in the occupied county, and he would make a lively addition to the scouts operating in the area.

An existing muster card for April and May 1863 shows that Robert was detached as a "Scout for General Stuart." A picture of Robert, likely taken during his detached service, shows a sandy-haired, rakish young man. His weapons suggest that he emulated John S. Mosby's partisans, who traveled lightly and were armed unconventionally for cavalry. "We carried no sabers, being in no manner familiar with the weapon's use," wrote one ranger. Nor did the partisans carry carbines, contrary to popular impression. Instead, each of Mosby's men was armed with two muzzle-loading Colt's 44-caliber army revolvers, worn in belt holsters. "These weapons were extremely deadly and effective in hand-to-hand engagements in which our men indulged."

As occupied territory, with a population sympathetic to the Southern cause, Prince William provided fertile ground for intelligence gathering. The county was familiar territory for the Towles brothers. Having grown up in Brentsville, they knew the county's topography, its landmarks, and its hiding places. Although John Towles, Eppa Hunton, and others had fled the county at the outbreak of hostilities, a number of families remained in the area despite the hard hand of war, and the brothers were familiar to many of these Prince William citizens. In fact, despite the nearly constant presence of Union troops, scouts were often welcomed into local homes and hidden when the occupying soldiers came searching.

One such hiding place was a local mill. "Teneriffe" is mentioned frequently in Robert Towles's letters home, and a careful examination of period maps show why. Teneriff Mills is shown on a map of adjacent Fauquier County, "compiled from various sources, including a reconnaissance by Capt. J. Keith Boswell, Chief Engineer of the Army of Northern Virginia's 2nd Corps, surveys of the O. & A. [Orange & Alexandria Railroad] and the M.G. [Manassas Gap] railroads, state maps, etc."

Teneriffe was the site of one of the oldest mills to be established in Fauquier County and also one of the last to operate in approximately the same location on Cedar Run near Catlett's Station. The first known mill on the site dated back to 1762 and lasted over one hundred years before it was torn down about 1896. At that time, the stone from the old mill was used as a foundation for the mill that still stands, which was in operation until 1952. The house on the site is a two-story, three-bay, stone structure. Teneriffe supposedly was built by an old sea captain, who named the property after the Teneriffe Islands where he was once shipwrecked. Cactus, said to have been imported from these islands, thrives on the rocky terrain of the farm that still overlooks Cedar Run.

The family that operated the mill was named Foulk (or 'Fowke' in a surviving local deed); the 1860 Federal Census shows a household with several daughters.

Perhaps for that reason alone, Teneriffe seems to have been a favorite stopping point for Robert during his "scouts," or trips behind enemy lines.

In addition to partisans and individual detached scouts, other units were also assigned to scouting duty in the area. After the battle of Chancellorsville in May 1863, the cavalry brigade of General Wade Hampton was posted near Brandy Station on the Orange and Alexandria Railroad. The O. and R. was used for transportation of supplies for the Union army and, as a consequence, was heavily guarded at weak points and by roving patrols along the line. The railroad, which ran northeast towards the Federal capital of Washington, cut across Prince William County near the property owned by the Rev. John Towles. A scout from Hampton's 2nd South Carolina Cavalry reported that Prince William County was "the principal scouting ground for the regiment." Company B, the Beaufort District Troop, was the most notable of the units detailed for such duty.

Sgt. W.A. Mickler of the Beaufort Troop led the first group of Carolina scouts in the area. Mickler took as his headquarters the home of Mr. John Cooper, which the South Carolinians identified as the "old Towles mansion." As he came to know the South Carolina scouts in Prince William, Robert Towles would feel right at home, since Mr. Cooper's home was literally the antebellum Towles house. After the Towles family had fled Prince William County at the outbreak of the war, its home had been commandeered as a headquarters for a Union general. Once the front lines and military action had moved elsewhere, a friend of the family, Mr. Cooper, occupied the house and attempted to farm the land, even amidst the chaos of war and occupation in the county.

"If you want to see where we are," wrote one South Carolinian trooper, "get Mitchell's Atlas, look for the County of Prince William, then you will see a little village of Brentsville, draw a line from that to the junction, put a dab just midway, and you have us exactly. The river on which is Brentsville is Broad Run, and flows into Occoquan, near which the [Hampton's] Legion is now encamped, about nine miles from Fairfax C.H. [Courthouse]. We can hear the drums beating plainly at Manassas, and sometimes distinguish the tune the band is playing."

Including details from other companies, Mickler's small force amounted to nearly twenty men. The exploits of these troopers, behind Union lines and in disputed territory, would soon earn them the nickname of Hampton's Iron Scouts. A chronicler of the South Carolinian cavalry explained why the unit was called by that name. "The Yankees called these boys the 'Iron Scouts' because they recovered so quickly after being wounded and seemed to be free from capture."

In author Manly Wade Wellman's semi-fictional stories, based on slender available facts, the Iron Scouts devised their own campfire song:

The Iron Scouts are riding out,
So the Yankee rumor tells,
But when they come to look for us
We're always somewhere else.

We're scouts for the Rebel Army,
Our fame goes far and wide—
When the Yankees hear us coming,
They fling down their guns and hide.

The advance patrol of Iron Scouts was reinforced by comrades, experienced trailers, and enemy watchers, as well as fighters. Among those who joined the South Carolinians was Robert Towles, who, with two other members of the Prince William Cavalry, had been assigned to scouting duty in the area. "A son of Mr. Towles, Bob, a member of the Prince William Cavalry, 4th Virginia regiment, with two others from the same command, Dick and Joe Sheppard, all three regular scouts for Gen. Fitz Lee, voluntarily attached themselves," wrote one of the Iron Scouts.

Another South Carolinian, George D. Shadburne would eventually take command as Hampton's chief of scouts. Late in 1863 Shadburne was assigned to Hampton's 2nd South Carolina Cavalry. When Hampton took command of the Army of Northern Virginia's cavalry corps, he ignored Shadburne's low rank of sergeant and made him chief of his scouts (after Jeb Stuart's death).

In a description that may well have fit any of the Iron Scouts (and Robert Towles), Hampton said of Shadburne, "as soon as a fight began he was instantly transformed into the dashing cavalryman, his whole soul seemed to be in the battle…Armed with at least two pistols and often three, he would dash against the enemy firing with a rapidity and precision not surpassed by even Mosby who was very handy with his pistol."

Some of the South Carolinians were none too thrilled to be stationed so far away from home. The Civil War correspondence of Henry Woodbury Moore and James Washington Moore of the Beaufort District Troop recognized that Union troops were threatening Charleston and its coastal defenses, and the brothers noted ruefully that they were anxious to defend their homes, but were "chained to Virginia while Carolina bleeds." An application to return to South Carolina proved unsuccessful. "Col. Hampton saw the Gen [Lee], and he came back and told us there was no chance for us to go back home. So now we are determined to take our spite out on the Yankees," said one.

In between scouts behind Union lines, the cavalry endured camp life. Distractions in Camp Butler included a fiddler nicknamed "Ole Bull" who "shakes the house to the tune of 'Sally Won't your dog bite.'" Since that name also belonged to Ole Bornemann Bull—a famous, nineteenth-century, Norwegian violinist and composer—it may be that some cultured soldier in the camp jokingly bestowed the same moniker on his enthusiastic comrade. Presumably, the Norwegian virtuoso wasn't known for songs involving Sally and her dog, however.

Others noted the sartorial challenges of a Confederate scout. "We are getting to be a ragged set, so that I am sometimes ashamed of their appearance. We are getting long tailed coats next time, so as not to show the holes in our pants," said a chagrined cavalryman in a letter home.

Sometimes the duty became tedious. "[The] boys are getting tired of scouting with its hard riding and little glory…nightly patrols and acting as couriers is tough work for man and beast," noted James Washington Moore of the 2nd South Carolina. Like others in his unit, he found the local farmers to be quite opportunistic when it came to what they charged the South Carolinians for hay and corn. "Virginians know how to feather their own nests," wrote James. "I have found them in this part [in their talk and actions], more like Yankees than Southerners."

With what today we might call a "target-rich environment," the cavalry and its scouts proved quite effective in their efforts to disrupt Union operations. "We have a scout of 15 men across the river near Bacon Race who are a terror to the Yankees," wrote a captain in Hampton's Legion. "They have brought in some 30 or 40 Yankee [prisoners] today."

For their part, Union troops did their best to deal with the problems caused by the pesky Confederates in the area. Robert's older brother, Vivian, reported in a letter to his young sister that "Yankee Cavalry swept through our old neighborhood last week and ran the scouts out. They caught three of our Co. in bed at Effingham and took horses from Mr. Howison the third or fourth time. How much I hope that that Country will be relieved of its despoilers very soon, and forever."

By 1863, the Iron Scouts had become such a problem for the Union forces that the 8th Illinois Cavalry, a crack regiment in the Army of the Potomac, was detailed to "break up, capture, and drive the scouts out" of Prince William County. Under the command of Elon J. Farnsworth, the 8th Illinois was formed in St. Charles, Illinois in August 1861 and was made up of men from northern Illinois. The unit served the duration of the war, and was the only cavalry regiment to serve the entire war in the Army of the Potomac. Lincoln had given them the nickname of "Farnsworth's Abolitionist Regiment" when he watched them march past the White House. Their battle cry was "Tally-Ho," and their bugle call was the first six notes of the tune "A Hunting We Will Go."

One exchange with the 8th Illinois in the spring of 1863 at Warrenton, Virginia, led to the death of a "beardless youth," Billy Dulin, a sixteen-year-old attached to the scouts. Dulin was wounded and trapped under his horse, when Union Col. Farnsworth allegedly shot the helpless young man. Dulin's compatriots swore revenge, with members of the 4th Virginia's Black Horse company going so far as to engrave Farnsworth's name on their cartridge boxes. Later that year, at Gettysburg, now-General Farnsworth was said to have committed suicide when wounded and incapacitated during a charge, rather than experience retribution by surrendering to the Confederate cavalry. Some historians doubt the story, but it does illustrate how personal the conflict could become.

Traveling with near impunity back and forth across the buffer zone between the armies, the Iron Scouts and their companions routinely brought useful information to Robert E. Lee and Jeb Stuart. The work was not without danger. Men such as Iron Scouts Mickler, Jim Dulin, Dick Hogan, Sim Miller, and Jack Shoolbred, as well as the Towles brothers and other Virginian cavalrymen assigned to scouting, risked death or capture daily, although early in the war the latter often meant being paroled for exchange and reporting back for duty.

Young James Towles apparently followed in his older brothers' footsteps and took his turn scouting in Prince William. His capture in March 1863 caused great consternation among his family before his release. Writing from prison in early 1863, young Jimmie explained his predicament. "There were seven of us captured in Prince William, after a half hour fight with 50 of the 8th Illinois Regiment. I am now confined here with Macrae, Evans, Frank Wheat, and some others. They are to be sent on to Richmond for exchange. *I* am held for I know not what. Some say they have me put down as an 'independent scout,'" said Jimmie. His mother later added a handwritten notation to the letter: "Poor boy, he was not eighteen years old. He was kept in prison, had <u>two trials</u>. They could not convict him of any wrongdoing, and released him and exchanged him."

In a letter posted from U.S. Ford on May 20, 1863, Vivian Towles reported to his sister: "Yesterday I had the great pleasure of writing to Mother the welcome news of Jim's arrival in Dixie safe and sound. I have not seen him but one of our Co. who was in the same room with him in the Old Capitol prison and who came to City Point on the same boat with him, reached our Camp on day before yesterday and says he left him on the cars at Orange C.H. on his way to Culpeper where he expected to join our Regt. I expect to see him in a few days at most and hope he will be able to visit you all before taking his place in ranks."

For the scouts, there was always the possibility of clashes with the enemy. A clever post-war book, *Autobiography of Arab*, is actually the first-person story of one of the South Carolinians, Sgt. E. Prioleau Henderson, told tongue-in-cheek from the perspective of his horse, Arab. In the book, Arab the horse tells of how the area between the lines of the two armies was "neutral ground," and described encounters with Union cavalry, including a detachment of "Scott's Nine Hundred," a Federal unit anachronistically armed with lances instead of sabers.

An August 12, 1862 advertisement in the *New York Times* had sought recruits for the unit, which it described as "most splendidly equipped and mounted, and being the only United States volunteer cavalry regiment, [enjoying] more advantages than any other in the service. Recruits are mustered into the service at once, and paid bounty, clothed, equipped and mounted—so that they are at once in the receipt of their pay."

Made up primarily of urban and rural New Yorkers, they were known as "Scott's Nine Hundred" in honor of Thomas A. Scott, assistant secretary of war. The attempt was made to organize a unique regiment with distinctive uniforms, accoutrements and horses. In addition to the lances carried by some, the regiment used a different type of horse in order to distinguish one company from another. One company, for example, was given sorrels, another grays, and another used bays.

Henderson (through his horse, Arab) reported a skirmish between Hampton's troops and Scott's Nine Hundred that culminated in a Confederate charge, the result of which he noted: "You ought to have seen those lancers run." Each lance had a miniature Union flag attached, and the road for miles was strewn with lances and small flags. "They were splendidly mounted and their horses sure made good time, for they had some pretty fast horses pursuing them (myself for instance)… only a small detachment got back to Alexandria. That was the last I ever heard of the famous 'Scott's Nine Hundred,'" said Arab the horse.

This engagement may have been the one reported in the *New York Times* in late June 1863. "A DESPERATE CAVALRY FIGHT: A Squadron of Scott's 900 Cavalry Surrounded and Cut Up," read the headline. The article went on to report:

> A squadron of Scott's Nine Hundred cavalry, under Maj. Remington, on their way to Centreville, this morning, encountered near Fairfax the Sixth Virginia cavalry [sic], and dashed at them with the sabre. The Major made two charges, and drove the

> enemy for three miles into a wood, and there encountered a superior force, that checked him with the fire of carbines. The fight from the beginning to the end was fierce. Its termination, from the overwhelming disparity of numbers, was disastrous. Maj. REMINGTON, after having had his horse shot twice, cut his way out and made his escape with eighteen men. Five have come in since. Eighty are reported as either killed, wounded or missing.

While no lances were mentioned, the gist of the skirmish seems indicative of a vigorously disputed cavalry engagement in the territory between the two armies, and the Confederate scouts may have taken part in the affair.

Other adventures involving the scouts (and their horses) occurred in this area that one scout described as full of "dense and dark thickets," where every turn promised a hiding place or perhaps an ambush for the enemy. Such engagements were not without risk. On one occasion, Sergeant Mickler led the Iron Scouts in a skirmish into a Union picket line. "Our brave Sergt. Calhoun Sparks was shot in the right breast, clear through and through," before falling from his horse and surrendering. Mickler rescued the sergeant and returned to friendly lines with no one killed. In addition to Sparks being severely wounded, two men had horses killed, and several Yankee cavalrymen were killed and a number taken prisoner in the fight. Sparks was hospitalized at Richmond's Chimborazo Hospital #3 in March 1863, spent time at home on furlough, and later returned to join his fellow scouts.

For Sparks, the story would not end well. Shortly after returning from his furlough in South Carolina, the intrepid Sparks rejoined his fellow scouts, spending the night of his return with Sergeant Mickler at Mr. Cooper's (on the old Towles property). Although his wound was still not entirely healed, Sparks said he had been longing "to be back with the Boys in old Prince William." Sparks, Mickler, and another scout sallied forth to determine the movements of the Federal army, passing through the "Union settlement," and stopping at the house of a Northern settler, the Widow Bodine. A niece of the widow's surreptitiously told the Confederates that there were three Yankee officers in the house and that the widow had hidden them in the cellar. Leaving Sparks to hold the horses, Mickler and his other companion rushed down to the cellar. Mickler was wounded, and the Federals, firing through the cellar window, shot and killed Sparks. "Poor Sergt. Sparks was killed last Wednesday in Mrs. Theodore Bodine's by Yankeys concealed in the house," wrote Robert in a letter home. "The body laid out in the snow uncared for three days. I passed within thirty yards of it on

Thursday night, but did not know it was there." As Prioleau Henderson observed, "Thus died another gallant cavalryman, and one among the bravest, as well as the most moral and courteous." His body was buried at a nearby church, and eventually, Sparks' brother carried his remains back to South Carolina. "There he is quietly sleeping, awaiting the Great roll call. Sleep peacefully, brave Sparks; your death was noble, as your life was beautiful," wrote Henderson.

On another time, a small band of scouts led by Sergeant Mickler were attempting to gain information about Union troop dispositions:

> The country from Bristow to Warrenton Junction is what is termed in Virginia 'a very open country—that is, there is only an occasional body of woods. Sergt. Mickler [told] several of the scouts before we started, 'Mind, I am going on a running, not a fighting trip this afternoon…I only want men on fast horses.'
>
> The Sergeant's party consisted of five men, all well mounted. We proceeded quietly along after leaving Bristow Station in the direction of the junction, stopping occasionally at the different houses on the route to find out if the enemy had left any clue of their destination. From what we could learn from the citizens, they were only reconnoitering. We did not see a 'blue coat'—only the road freshly cut up by their horses' feet.

The scouts were "off their guard" through misleading information received from a gentleman the scouts later termed a Union citizen. As a result, they walked into a trap. The Federals had concealed themselves, and when the scouts approached the houses, the men riding abreast and laughing heartily at some amusing story, they suddenly were accosted by Yankee cavalry. "Halt! Halt! Surrender! Surrender!" came the cries. Heading on a straight line for the pines, the scouts were saved only by the speed of their horses and the skill of their riders. One scout noted that his horse had saved him from "a term in Old Capitol Prison."

Robert Towles himself soon had a close call. His South Carolinian friends reported the capture of three or four scouts, "Bob Towles for one." Again, Mickler assembled his men for a rescue attempt, laying in ambuscade for the Union troops near Broad Run. Dissuaded from firing by darkness and the close proximity of their captured comrades, Mickler regrettably took no action.

"The next morning…we saw a man advancing across the field from the direction of Mr. Allan Howison's house. He had no hat on his head and seemed to be in a big hurry," said a South Carolinian. "When he came up it proved to be Bob Towles." Robert had escaped from his captors just before they had reached the Union encampment at Dumfries. While proceeding single file in the dark, guarded by two men, one on each side with cocked pistols, he "made up his mind to escape…so he quietly dropped from his horse, remaining perfectly still until the entire regiment passed him."

Clearly, Robert Towles was nothing if not imperturbably daring. His experiences with the South Carolinian "Iron Scouts" helped him develop his scouting abilities and had enhanced his value as someone who could provide valuable intelligence. Such talents were much needed by the Confederates, but also put men like Robert Towles clearly in harm's way, as events would prove.

CHAPTER EIGHT

One would have supposed they had Gen. Lee
The road to Old Capitol Prison

"He said if I did not come out he would burn the barn down."

Diary entry
August, 1863

Gen. Oliver Otis Howard, Library of Congress

Gen. Carl Schurz, Library of Congress

Long Bridge across the Potomac, Library of Congress

confined

Robert Towles

During the summer of 1863, intelligence regarding Union intentions was needed more than ever, as Robert E. Lee pondered how best to counter any Federal move south after Gettysburg.

As the Union presence in Northern Virginia increased, the threat to scouts increased accordingly, as they attempted to avoid Union patrols at the frontier of the war zone. A diary kept by Robert Towles during this time provides a sense of just how dangerous such duty ultimately could become. As he had proven time and again, Robert was possessed of what a young U.S. Cavalry officer, George S. Patton, Jr., would much later list among the essential attributes of a cavalryman—tenacity of purpose and the possession of "a Gambler's Courage." Not long after his brush with capture, Robert was once again aggressively scouting behind enemy lines. This time, however, he would not be as lucky as he had been earlier.

On August 5, Robert was headed back to Confederate lines near Catlett's Station, when he encountered a compact line of Union pickets. For three nights, he attempted to make his way through the active enemy pickets and patrols, but was unsuccessful each time. "A kind lady friend remonstrated with me, begged me not to go, but still I persisted. She was afraid the pickets would halt me, and I would not halt, and they would shoot me," said a determined Robert in his diary.

With sentries standing only fifty yards apart, Robert crawled on his hands and knees through high grass to a fence corner near the road. On the other side of the fence, Union soldiers walked not more than six feet from the young cavalryman. The close proximity of the Union troops required that he exercise great caution in attempting to cross, and having slept little during the past three nights, Robert found himself nodding off in the fence corner while waiting for the opportunity to move undetected through the picket lines.

"Finally, finding it was almost day, I determined to cross the road in spite of consequences," wrote Robert. With his grey uniform providing some measure of camouflage, Robert was able to take several large strides across the road, put his hands on two fence stakes, and hop over "as light as a kitten" without being seen or heard by the watchful Union troops. Unbeknownst to Robert, however, the extended Union lines now consisted of a double line of pickets, the second approximately three hundred yards beyond the first.

With dawn fast approaching, Robert walked on rapidly, not expecting any more danger, when he was accosted with an order to halt. One of the Army of Potomac's "largest size Dutchmen" (likely from the predominantly German-American Eleventh Corps) intoned, "Who comps deer?" "Friend," said Robert, whereupon the sentry asked him to advance. Drawing his pistol, Robert advanced on the man he termed his *intimate* friend and inquired as to where to find his company. When he got close enough to grab the guard's rifle by the bayonet, Robert pointed his pistol at the hapless soldier and improbably ordered the man to surrender.

Instead of obeying Robert's order, the sentry jerked his gun to the side, striking Robert in the side of the head with its bayonet, and fired, narrowly missing the daring young Rebel. Apparently unnerved by so brazen an opponent, however, the Union soldier promptly dropped his rifle and fled. Still holding the other end of the rifle, Robert dropped it and ran to escape other approaching sentries. The grey color of his uniform again made it difficult for the Union troops to see him in the morning haze.

Retreating about a mile back into Union lines, Robert sought a place to hide, and he headed for familiar territory—his family's farm. Mr. Cooper's ("the old Towles mansion") was a safe haven for the young scout. Because day was breaking, Robert decided to hide in Mr. Cooper's barn, expecting to stay only a short while until he could analyze the situation and determine the location of nearby Union cavalry. That night, he hoped to make it safely to the woods, where he would hide during the day. Exhaustion set in, however, and Robert soon unintentionally fell asleep in the loft.

Awakened by the sound of the barn door opening, Robert called out, expecting Mr. Cooper. Instead, "Mr. Dutchman No. 2," gun in hand, loudly inquired concerning Robert's identity. Satisfied as to the inhabitant's hostile intent by Robert's response of a "snapped" pistol, the Union soldier promptly ran out, slamming shut the barn door. Running quickly to the front of the barn, Robert found nearly twenty Union soldiers surrounding the building, ready for him with rifles raised. An examination of the rear entrance revealed an equal number of troops blocking his escape through that quarter.

Climbing back into the loft, Robert hid one of his pistols under the wheat, along with about a dozen leaves out of his pocketbook. By this time, a Union captain in charge of the surrounding detail had come forward to order Robert to surrender. The men under his command seemed less than enthusiastic about attempting a forcible removal of the Rebel, however. The trooper who had first come to the barn door opined that anyone who would be so bold as to put their head inside the door would "have his brains blown out" by the feisty Confederate.

In an attempt at banter, Robert called out to the captain, asking how many men he had. When told that there were plenty of troops to take him captive, Robert crowed that he could "whip that many easily." In reality, Robert knew that he had no chance whatsoever to escape his predicament. When the Union captain threatened to burn down the barn, Robert apparently concluded that it was time to surrender. Throwing his remaining pistol down before the assembled Union soldiers, Robert was made to step back before any would venture forward to retrieve it. The resulting celebration seemed out of proportion to Robert. "Then such crowing was heard, one would have supposed they had Gen. Lee," he noted ruefully.

Apparently, Robert had achieved notoriety during his time as scout behind enemy lines. When he was taken to the local colonel's headquarters on the nearby farm of a Dr. King, the officers and men "made a tremendous fuss" over the captive. Remarks such as, "We've got you at last, have we?" and "You are the boy we have been after for a long time," were examples of the somewhat animated commentary that greeted Robert.

Not all of the authorities were impressed with the young scout, however. Once Robert (accompanied by Farmer Cooper) was taken to Weaversville, he was ordered to be strip-searched by the brigadier in command, who, perhaps as a result, Robert described as "a cross, ill-natured fellow."

From Weaversville, the captive was sent along to Gen. Carl Schurz, commander of the Third Division of the Eleventh Corps. During his latest scout, Robert had eavesdropped on the general when he had paid a visit to Dr. King's (a pre-war neighbor of the Towles family). When told by Robert that they had "met" before when Robert had spied on the general during his stay at the doctor's home, Schurz good-naturedly laughed. He admitted that the doctor's daughter had told him about a daring Rebel scout who had slipped up from the woods to get a good look at the general.

Robert was invited to dine with Schurz and his staff before being sent further up the chain of command to see Maj. Gen. Oliver Otis Howard, the commander of the Eleventh Corps of the Army of the Potomac. Howard had concentrated his corps in the vicinity of the Orange & Alexandria. "My headquarters are at Catlett's house, west side of the railroad, about a mile from Catlett's station," he noted in a late summer report. The Eleventh Corps was spread throughout the area, with the third division on the south bank of Cedar Run between Weaversville and Warrenton Junction, the second division near Catlett's Station, and the first division on the west side of the railroad. One regiment was stationed at Brentsville, one at Bristoe Station, one at Cedar Run, and one at Greenwich.

On the way to see General Howard, Robert found that other Union officers were not as cordial as General Schurz had been. Before he reached Howard's headquarters at Catlett's Station, Robert was interrogated by a colonel he described as "one of the meanest yankeys that ever was." The colonel was pleased to have captured the notorious scout and promised that Robert would "stretch some hemp" if the colonel had his way. "All that I regret sir…is that you were taken with your uniform on. I think we will hang you anyhow." Robert only laughed at the threat, which made the officer furious.

General Howard interviewed his apparently now-infamous "guest" and asked a great many questions about Robert and his family. The general, a teetotalling Congregationalist known as the Christian Soldier, had lost an arm at the battle of Fair Oaks, which Robert noted "may have cooled him down somewhat." By this time, Howard's career had experienced several ups and downs. At Chancellorsville, his troops had been routed by Stonewall Jackson's flank attack. On the first day of Gettysburg, however, Howard had been largely credited with stabilizing the deteriorating Union lines along Cemetery Ridge. Soon to be transferred west, he would serve honorably there. After the war, he would fight Indians, serve as head of the Freedmen Bureau, and help found a school in Washington, DC—Howard University, where his portrait hangs.

Howard may have found some sympathy for the Episcopal cleric's son who had landed in his tent. During the interview, the general was given a pocketbook found on Robert at the time of his capture. Robert prized highly the pocketbook/wallet, which he had taken during the August 1862 raid on General Pope's supply train at Catlett's Station. He asked General Howard that he be allowed to keep his trophy, saying that he attached great sentimental value to it. Noting that Robert appeared to be a truthful young man, General Howard allowed him to keep the memento, after examining it thoroughly. The bombastic Pope had not been a particular favorite among the officers in the Army of the Potomac, and Howard may have been exacting a bit of payback by letting the scout keep the wallet.

Asked if he knew Mr. Catlett, Robert admitted that he did, and General Howard allowed him to spend the evening with the stationmaster and his family. Accompanied by friends, Robert slept soundly for the first time in four nights.

The next morning, he was taken by train to Warrenton Junction and then on foot to Germantown, where he was again interrogated and placed in what he called "a hot and dirty guardhouse." There he found many fellow soldiers, friends, and acquaintances, and even a Presbyterian cleric, Reverend Pugh from Warrenton. The captives included many citizens of Prince William and its neighboring counties, collected in a Union dragnet for secessionist sympathizers. The detained "old gray headed citizens" were allowed visitors, among them Miss Bettie Howison, Robert's pre-war neighbor. "Through Miss Bettie I was enabled to send my watch, and love and a great many messages to my friends at Teneriff and other places," wrote Robert.

Time passed slowly as the captives awaited their fate. Some were released on parole of honor. "They sometimes offer an oath of parole or something of that kind which can be swallowed without harm, but I don't think many will take the oath," said older brother Vivian in a letter home. The neighboring Howisons were apparently among those reported taken around the time of Robert's capture. Vivian noted that "Mr. Howison and Allen have not yet returned. Emma/noble girl/ as they were carrying her father away called out to him 'Don't you take that oath Father; Whatever you do don't take that oath' and the last words he said were 'all right, my daughter.' We have heard that they are determined to make him take it, some yankees having said that all that detained him was 'the refusal to take the oath.' So things go with the unfortunate citizens," said Vivian.

In any case, the Howisons and more than forty of the citizen prisoners were released on parole of honor the next day. A parole of honor was a sworn promise, both oral and in writing, made to pledge fidelity to the government of the United States and to not take arms against it. While typically extracted from officers and enlisted men (as part of the exchange process early in the war or at the end of the conflict), citizens were also asked to take an oath or sign a parole of honor when circumstances dictated.

After the release of the citizens, more than a hundred other men remained captive in a space of roughly forty square feet. Confederate prisoners from several different units were formed into details to collect tree branches for bedding. Robert found a number of his new companions to be very agreeable, and managed to find some humor in playing dominos with a Frenchman who would not or could not speak a word of English.

Finally, on August 10, the remaining prisoners were given rations and prepared to start the next morning for Washington City and captivity in the Old Capitol Prison. The men were formed in line and marched through the hot sun and dust to Warrenton Junction, where they were put on a train. Along the route to Washington were a number of landmarks familiar to the young scout. Robert was able to glimpse several houses which he recognized, including those of a number of antebellum neighbors of his family. Other spots he recognized included Catlett's Station and General Howard's headquarters, Cedar Run Bridge—which Robert had unsuccessfully worked to destroy during the September 1862 Catlett's Station cavalry raid—and even a hill on the edge of a local woods, where he had often rested and where he once lost a hat. "I am fast leaving my native haunts, and Oh! Well, it would be impossible to describe my feelings, as I sit and grit my teeth, to think of my condition."

Noting that "blue backs" appeared in profusion all over the fields of Northern Virginia, Robert wished mightily for a pistol, either to personally reduce the number of invaders or to affect an escape from the train that he believed was "dashing on to an earthly Hades." Late in the trip, he noted that the train was passing the Episcopal Theological Seminary in Alexandria, where his father had been ordained into the ministry. Finally, the locomotive crossed the Long Bridge across the Potomac, and the prisoners arrived in the Union capital.

Upon disembarking, Robert and his companions were allowed to rest under some trees near the Depot, and a number of "friends of the South" flocked to them, despite the guards. "Basket after basket of provisions, and bucket after bucket of water were brought to us, and anything else that the men needed, was cheerfully given," stated Robert. After this respite, the men were marched through the City to what would become their new abode—Old Capitol Prison.

In the first week of his captivity, the free-wheeling Robert was already feeling the pressure of confinement. "This is the fourth day of my imprisonment in the old Capitol, and Oh! how sick I am getting. How do I long to see some familiar face. One sweet one, yet I would not wish to see them under existing circumstances." A contemporary letter to the family from Robert's brother, Vivian, seemed to indicate that at least one friend was able to connect with the captive, however. Viv's best friend, Lee Macrae, had also been at Old Capitol for a time, and being familiar with the prison, Lee's sister Bettie was apparently able to send Robert baskets of fruit and food, as well as clothes.

Recovering from a sudden fever, he noted that his friends had tried to get a prison surgeon to see him, but they were told that Robert would have to come to the surgeon if he wanted treatment. "I will try and not trouble him," wrote the young scout. "I am still improving, but it is very hard for one to improve in this place," he noted in his diary.

Several times there were indications that the prisoners would be exchanged or sent to another, more amenable location, such as Point Lookout, a camp in Maryland. "Any where is preferable to this place," wrote Robert. Unfortunately for Robert, when the roll was called, Robert's name was not on the list for transfer. "I am still here, yet I know not why," complained Robert.

Confined with new roommates—three South Carolinians allegedly held as hostages for three black soldiers captured at Ft. Sumter—Robert bided his time while hoping for some connection to the outside world. Not long after his capture, he received a letter and ten dollars from family friend Rev. E.A. Dalrymple, who unfortunately for Robert, was denied permission to visit the young man.

In a late August letter to sister Ella, Vivian reported that news of Robert's capture had come to the regiment through another scout, Dick Shepherd. Shepherd reported that Mr. Cooper, who had been taken with Robert, had been released, along with many other citizens of Prince William, Fauquier and Stafford Counties. Robert, however, had been taken to Washington City and Old Capitol Prison.

Vivian urged Ella not to worry about Robert's capture. "His being taken in Prince William will secure his confinement in the Old Capitol which is undoubtedly the best prison they have as to cleanliness, food, comfort and health. His confinement there may cause him to escape some worse fate…and I am certain that you stand a better chance of seeing him in a few months in good health than if he had remained at large," comforted Vivian. Subsequent events would demonstrate how prophetic Vivian's words were.

Time would also tell whether the Old Capitol would live up to its advance billing as a comfortable and healthy environment for Confederate prisoners. And Vivian's assurance that their sister would see Robert soon would prove to be true, though not through the means Robert's older brother expected.

CHAPTER NINE

An Earthly Hades
Imprisoned in "the Bastille of the North"

"Summer is gone, today is the last day, and I am still here...
O for wings like a dove."

Diary entry
August 31, 1863

Old Capitol Prison, Library of Congress

prison

William P. Wood, Commandant of Old Capitol Prison

The Register of Prisoners at the Old Capitol Prison shows that "Robert Towle" [sic] was captured at Harris Ford on August 3, and identified him, incorrectly, as a Sergeant in the 4th Virginia Infantry [sic]. A subsequent entry indicates that, almost immediately upon his arrival, Robert was transferred to the "State list" by order of General Martindale, the military governor of Washington City. Much to his concern, Robert became increasingly convinced that the authorities were refusing to treat him as a prisoner of war, despite his having been captured in uniform. Indeed, a guard confided to Robert that there was a very serious charge made against him—that of being a spy.

On September 6, 1863, the young cavalryman had been held in the Old Capitol Prison for nearly one month, and he celebrated his twentieth birthday in less-than-ideal circumstances. "I shall undoubtedly miss my cake, however it cannot be helped. There is no use in grieving over spilt milk. I should be thankful if I do not have to spend another in the same embarrassing situation," wrote Robert in his diary.

Although Robert noted that he was fortunate enough to get into one of the most pleasant rooms in the building, in the third story fronting the street, Old Capitol Prison was not the type of establishment where one wanted to spend very many birthdays. Its history was unique, and the atmosphere challenging.

Situated at the corner of A and First streets in the City of Washington, Old Capitol's history would give little clue as to its ultimate use as a "bastille" for prisoners during the Civil War. In August 1814, when British troops entered Washington, they burned the Capitol and other public buildings. Faced with a dilemma concerning where Congress could conduct the public's business, the government acquired the three-story structure, which had been serving as a tavern and boarding house. Within its walls and in the space which would come to be known as "the notorious Room 16" of the prison, the U.S. Senate and House of Representatives met to conduct public business until the Capitol could be rebuilt. Two presidents had been inaugurated at the Old Capitol, and many distinguished statesmen began their careers in this somewhat unlikely venue.

Doubtless many Confederate prisoners would have found it ironic that the Hon. John C. Calhoun, South Carolinian, vice president of the United States under Andrew Jackson and champion of nullification and states' rights, died in the very same building.

Upon the completion of the restored Capitol, the structure became known as the "Old Capitol," and in the years before the outbreak of the Civil War, it served alternately as a boarding house and school. In 1861, faced with the need to secure incoming prisoners of war and a growing number of state or political prisoners, the government reacquired the property and converted the Old Capitol to a prison.

After the subdivision of its spacious rooms, Old Capitol's capacity was approximately five hundred persons, although during the course of the war many more prisoners were housed there and at its adjacent annex, Carroll Prison. After the war, a *Washington Star* newspaper article would claim that "altogether nearly 20,000 persons [had been] confined in these buildings," including more than 15,000 Rebel prisoners of war.

Relatively few changes were made to complete the building's transition to what one inmate called a "dungeon for the victims of despotism." Bars were placed on the windows, but security was primarily due to the presence of an armed guard of about sixty troops taken from a local infantry regiment and stationed throughout the building and on the adjacent streets.

A description of the facility that greeted Robert Towles in August 1863 paints a bleak picture indeed. The entrance on First Street was under a large arched window, which "admitted light to the former Senate Chamber, but which, through its broken and filthy panes, permitted the winter's wind and drifting snow to fall on the unhappy inmates," noted an observer. According to another prisoner, the accumulated filth in the prison was "better imagined than described."

In summer, the heat and stench from the adjacent open "sinks," or latrines, were nearly unbearable. The sinks were wide trenches, fronted by a long wooden rail and, unlike field latrines, were not regularly covered and re-dug. The presence of these sinks, used for months by several hundred men, "did not contribute, it may be safely said, to the beauty of the scenery or add sweetness to the tainted air," said an inmate. During the prison's heyday, a small herd of hungry pigs waited daily for the slush that comprised the offal, which seemed to "ooze" from the prison yard.

The subdivided rooms, "filled with filth of every imaginable kind" and less than thirty-feet square, were numbered and fitted with a triple tier of bunks but little furniture and usually housed from eighteen to twenty-five prisoners. Continued and regular calls of sentries on the landings and outside the rooms, combined with the "clanking of arms" and the changing of the guard every two hours made sleep difficult. More than one "guest" testified to the presence of a fierce cadre of bed bugs, which required nightly efforts to resist the onslaught of the bloodthirsty "grey backs."

Despite Vivian's previously expressed sentiments to his father that Old Capitol was the "best" Union prison for brother Robert, it was not living up to its reputation. Reality trumped familial wishful thinking, and Old Capitol clearly was not the acme of Union prisons when it came to "cleanliness, food, comfort and health."

Into what Robert had earlier called an "Earthly Hades" were placed a wide variety of persons: Confederate prisoners awaiting exchange or transfer, alleged spies, bushwhackers, blockade runners, alleged "disloyal" citizens, and even border-state legislators arrested under martial law and in the absence of *habeas corpus*. "Contrabands," or escaped slaves, were also held in protective custody at Old Capitol until an outbreak of smallpox in early 1863 forced their relocation to Arlington House, Robert E. Lee's estate, where there remained a Freedmen Village for nearly thirty years.

A few of the recorded enumerated charges against prisoners include notations of "open and unrelenting secessionist," "suspicion of infidelity to the government," and "having had correspondence and commercial intercourse with rebel states." Some of the more colorful inmates included a patient of a Kentucky lunatic asylum—sent to Old Capitol as a "prisoner of state." Another delusional prisoner known as "General Thunderbolt," who fancied himself as the rightful commander of the Federal army, was sent to Old Capitol after seeking an interview with President Lincoln, presumably to ascertain the status of his "command."

Non-military Southern sympathizers were also a common sight within the prison. Robert described twenty citizens brought in from Culpepper County, Virginia. "Our particular friends, the Yankeys," he said, "have a peculiar way of arresting everybody and everything they see. I heard a man say this morning that he had a dog at home that he was very much afraid they would get. The dog had but one eye yet he was afraid they…would get him." It was alleged that some of these Northern Virginia farmers had been taken in order to commandeer any of their valuables, such as livestock, that the army coveted. Most were soon freed upon taking a loyalty oath.

By the time Robert arrived, Old Capitol had also welcomed a number of celebrity prisoners, including the famous Confederate women spies, Rose O'Neill Greenhow and Belle Boyd. All in all, the mix of prisoners at Old Capitol was impressive in its diversity.

Many Confederate prisoners of war were held briefly at the Old Capitol and were then sent to other prison camps or south for exchange. Prisoners (including Robert) transferred to the "State" list, however, were those suspected of being spies. State prisoners were rarely exchanged and could be held indefinitely while their fates were determined.

Partisan rangers of Col. John S. Mosby—the Grey Ghost of the Confederacy—sometimes made their way to Old Capitol, where they were segregated and given special attention. Mosby's men were a rough bunch, who amused themselves at times by throwing bricks through the windows into the surrounding streets.

The "keeper" of Old Capitol and Carroll Prisons was a Mexican War veteran named William P. Wood, who eventually would be named the first head of the U.S. Secret Service when it became part of the Treasury Department.

After the jurisdictional transfer of the Old Capitol from the Department of State to the War Department, Wood was placed in charge of the prison by Secretary of War Edwin M. Stanton. Young Maj. William E. Doster, who became the Washington provost marshal when the Army of the Potomac took the field, said that Wood "was deeper in the War Office than any man at Washington, and it was commonly said that Stanton was at the head of the War Office and Wood at the head of Stanton."

Wood met and interrogated each incoming prisoner.

Although described as "undersized," he was reputed to possess great physical strength, which he used to good effect, sometime shaking prisoners forcefully when he became agitated during interrogations. Wood was involved in the most mundane of daily routines at the prison, including mail distribution and the call to services on the Sabbath. Wood himself protested that he was merely there "to carry out the orders of the Government," and served "but as the custodian of the prisoner," responsible only for receiving and holding inmates until they were released. He professed to know little or nothing regarding the charges against individual prisoners, and despite his occasional outbursts of temper, many prisoners came to view Wood as a sympathetic, if strict, overseer. All information obtained through individual examinations by Superintendent Wood undoubtedly went directly to the War Department and weighed heavily in the final disposition of espionage and disloyalty cases, however.

By enforcing strict segregation of prisoners between rooms, and by utilizing spies and detectives placed in the prison population, Wood maintained a rigid discipline that discouraged escapes and dissention. During the course of the war, only sixteen men would escape from the Prison. On more than one occasion, Superintendent Wood was heard to exclaim that nothing occurred in the Old Capitol Prison about which he did not know.

While he awaited the disposition of his case, Robert went about a daily routine that was, by all description, exceedingly dull. The amusements of the prison were few and simple. Most of the prisoners played cards all day long with the favorite game being "bluff," or poker, and the stakes consisting of one-cent pieces. Dominoes, checkers, and an occasional song and dance by the prisoners enlivened an otherwise boring routine.

Papers were allowed, so news from the outside world did make its way into Old Capitol. On September 22, Robert noted the confirmation of the rumored defeat of the "Yankey Army of the Cumberland" at Chickamauga in the West. As might be expected, this news created a great deal of excitement among the Rebel prisoners.

For a great many of the inmates, the daily routine consisted of daydreaming. Robert confessed that this was his principal enjoyment. "I do have some delicious dreams of friends I have left behind me…I do a great deal of dreaming while I am awake." For a cavalryman accustomed to "living among the pines," prison life must have been tedious, however.

A common pastime appears to have been observing daily life outside on the streets of Washington City. Through the great arched window above the entrance to the prison, the Capitol Dome could be seen, ironically now topped by a statue of Lady Liberty. "I have rubbed the hair off each side of my head, looking through these iron bars," said Robert in a September diary entry. "It seems to me an age [since capture], and none know how many weary months may pass, and still find me looking through the bars."

Looking through the bars was not without its dangers, however. Jesse W. Wharton of Prince George County, Maryland, was shot by a sentry for standing at the window to his room. Wharton, thinking that the rules allowed looking out the windows as long as the bars were not touched, paid no attention to a warning from a member of the 91st Pennsylvania regiment, who shot and killed the unfortunate prisoner.

Notwithstanding occurrences such as this, however, Robert and others took great pleasure in surreptitiously greeting the "pretty Ladies" of Washington as they passed the window. Waving a little Confederate flag, which may have been among those smuggled into the prison by accused Confederate spy Belle Boyd, Robert noticed that some of the ladies would smile, while others would shake their head emphatically. Many "kiss their hands, and slyly wave their handkerchiefs to us," wrote Robert.

Such innocent behavior was not without its risks, however. According to one commentator, "scarcely a day passes without the sentry…arresting on the sidewalk or from carriages, ladies or gentlemen who dare to recognize…by look or salutation, a relative or friend." The June 7, 1862 issue of *Vanity Fair* reported the arrest of three ladies, "two of whom were the wife and daughter of a prominent officer of the Senate." While passing the Old Capitol Prison, one of the ladies was reported to have "raised her handkerchief to her face, and passed it several times with rapidity over her mouth." This movement was observed by a guard, who stopped the carriage and arrested the occupants for violating a public order "prohibitory of any waving of handkerchiefs or making any other sign…or signal to the prisoners." The lady stated that she had been eating oranges and was merely wiping her mouth. Her presumed fastidiousness nevertheless earned her a short stay at Old Capitol.

Not all passers-by were ladies. Robert noted that "the only familiar face I have seen—at liberty—since I have been here is that of my old sorrel horse…familiarly named Bones, who walks majestically past my window every day carrying the worthless carcass of a big yankey sergeant. I think if Bones knew how little his rider became him, he would throw him and break his neck."

Exercise was limited to the half hour granted each day for a walk in the prison yard, weather and space permitting. Since the half hour was also the time allotted for meals, many prisoners dispensed with exercise to indulge in the adventure of Old Capitol cuisine.

The dining room at Old Capitol was described as a "dirty, dismal room." Food was set out on a table "of what material constructed it was impossible to determine on account of the accumulation of dirt," wrote an observer. The long, gloomy-looking room was permeated by an odor that "assailed the nostrils as if coming from an ancient garbage heap." A freed black server typically stood at the head of the long table, dispensing tin cups filled with a liquid "by courtesy called coffee." With a twist of the wrist, the "waiter" would send cups spinning down the table, to be snagged by each man as it slid past.

The daily staples consisted of bread—the one item sometimes described as good—and meat, often described as not fit to eat. As one prisoner noted, the beef "had the appearance, when cooked, of a piece of thick sole-leather," and it was steeped in grease and fried in an iron skillet, no doubt adding little to its appeal. Those who had good teeth might masticate it, with an effort, but swallowing such morsels was no doubt difficult.

"Our fare is most miserable," stated Robert in one of his early diary entries. Another prisoner described the meat as "putrid," and noted that few of his friends could stand to eat their bread when such meat was before them. The food was generally considered by the inmates to consist of condemned army provisions. This perception seems borne out by an observation early in the war from a military governor, who advocated the regular prison issuance of salt pork and hard biscuit—the worst that could be procured. "They are all traitors, or they would not be here, and that is good enough for them!" he noted contemptuously.

For prisoners who had access to money—either brought with them or sent by friends—the alternative to the mess hall was to purchase items from the prison sutler. At Old Capitol, the sutler, William P. Wood's nephew, was purported to inflate prices for goods by as much as 500%, giving rise to the sobriquet of "the swindling shop." For those who could afford such luxuries at their inflated prices, the sutler did provide a regular daily supplement of butter, pies, tomatoes, and melons. Even tobacco and whiskey were sometimes available. In a diary entry, Robert noted that he had been able to sample a sutler's wares. "We bought a watermelon today, paid half [a] dollar, rather indifferent it was, tho."

Occasionally, outsiders were allowed to bring food to the prison. In late August, Robert reported that "the whole prison was treated to watermelons, peaches, tomatos, etc. by some Ladies from Georgetown." Such largess was the exception, rather than the rule, however.

Worship was an available option for the prisoners. Superintendent Wood, a self-proclaimed atheist, was purported to have personally announced competing services for all prisoners so inclined—one for what he termed the Gospel according to Jeff Davis and one for all who wanted to hear the Lord God preached according to Abe Lincoln. When asked what those who chose neither alternative should do, Wood replied, "Oh, then, they should stay in their rooms." For his part—and as the son of an Episcopal rector—Robert must have found some solace in Sabbath day services that he described as being conducted by chaplains of "Morgan's command".

Increasingly, Robert became frustrated by his lack of contact with the outside world. He feared that what friends were in the area were "too strong Union to help a poor Rebble" by visiting. His only outside contact was through an occasional letter, with money enclosed, from a family friend—"Old Dal" Dalrymple, who had instructed his brother Viv at the Episcopal High School.

Although he was under suspicion of being a spy, Robert continued to hope to be exchanged as a prisoner of war. Until 1864, most Confederate prisoners of war were sent to Point Lookout prison or other locations for transfer and exchange under the existing cartel for exchange of prisoners. For Robert and other prisoners suspected of being independent scouts (synonymous with being a spy), exchange was usually a forlorn hope, however. Unlike their fellow Rebel soldiers, such men were generally segregated to be held for trial by military tribunal, and their fate could be incarceration with hard labor or even execution.

Another Confederate scout, Col. Harry Gilmor, in his autobiography, *Four Years in the Saddle,* recounted how, when captured, his name was inscribed on the books as a "spy," and the entry forwarded with him to Ft. McHenry. There, "I was detained for five months, in direct violation of the cartel between the two governments, which, if regarded, would have released me in ten days." The commander at Ft. McHenry opposed Gilmor's exchange, saying that there were "serious charges against me"—a somewhat uncanny mirror of comments made to Robert Towles. "As frivolous as this was, it was deemed sufficient to confine an officer in a cell, keep his family under painful anxiety, and dishonor the cartel solemnly established," said Gilmor. Eventually, Gilmor was released, most likely because he was an officer. For a non-commissioned officer such as Robert Towles, such a solution was not so readily available.

Robert probably did not help his own cause when he was interviewed by the Officer of the Day, who inquired as to Robert's occupation and unit: "'Do you belong to Mosby's guerillas?' 'No sir,' said I. 'What guerillas do you belong to?' 'First Regular Bushwhackers,' said I, and amid the cheers of my companions, Mr. Officer of the Day withdrew."

Finally on September 16, Robert was informed that he was to be transferred to the Old Capitol annex, Carroll Prison, where the most notorious spies were housed. Built by Daniel Carroll in the early 1800s, the five houses of Carroll Row (also known as "Duff Green's Row") served a number of uses. The city's first Inaugural Ball, held for James Madison in 1809, was in a Carroll Row hotel. When additional space was needed to supplement the rooms at Old Capitol, the row houses, which had been serving as a boarding house, were converted into the Carroll Prison. The spot is now occupied by the Library of Congress.

Ruefully, Robert noted that there now seemed little hope for an exchange and observed that the inmates of the Carroll "Hotel" were allowed fewer privileges than at Old Capitol. Expressing fears for his safety at his new prison, on October 1, Robert noted in his diary that he had "a slight presentiment, that it will not be long before I leave here; for what place I cannot yet say."

In early October, a letter to Gen. S.A. Meredith, Union commissioner for exchange of prisoners, arrived from the Rev. John Towles, Robert's father. Having heard nothing from their son, the Towleses hoped to elicit a brief letter regarding his health and status through the good offices of General Meredith.

"I beg you will be pleased to consider it consistent with the faithful discharge of your duties to…receive from him and convey to Commissioner Ould to be mailed to me" a letter from Robert. "I earnestly beg that you will consider a father's unhappiness under the circumstances, and especially the anxious fears of a poor sick mother as to whether her son is well or still alive."

The letter was returned through Confederate Commissioner Ould with a terse notation from the officials at Old Capitol. Robert Towles had escaped.

Chapter Ten

Watch those Yankees, boys!
The death of an older brother

"An affectionate Son, a noble heart, a brave and gallant soldier
has left us a willing sacrifice if need be to his country's Cause."

R.H. Colvin letter
October 23, 1863

Lt. Lucien Davis, 4th Virginia Cavalry, Courtesy of the
Manassas Museum System, Manassas, Virginia

yankees

Capt. P.D. Williams, 4th Virginia Cavalry,
Courtesy of the Manassas Museum System,
Manassas, Virginia

Benjamin Merchant, 4th Virginia Cavalry, Courtesy
of the Manassas Museum System, Manassas, Virginia

While Robert Towles struggled with captivity and contemplated escape, the Army of Northern Virginia and his comrades in the 4th Virginia Cavalry continued to face off against the Union Army of the Potomac along the line of the Rapidan River. With the Confederate victory at Chickamauga out West and the perceived caution after Gettysburg by Union General Meade in the East, the result in Virginia was somewhat a standoff. "All quiet on the Potomac; nothing to disturb autumnal slumbers," wired Union Secretary of War Edwin Stanton to President Lincoln.

Despite the setback in Pennsylvania, Gen. Robert E. Lee continued to seek an advantage against Meade. "If General Meade does not move, I wish to attack him," he told Confederate President Jefferson Davis in late August. Such an opportunity was restricted, however, by the disparity in numbers Lee faced after detachment of a corps of his army to the West earlier in the fall.

Instead, Lee sought to jockey his position, much as he had in 1862 against John Pope, looking for opportunities to strike a blow against the Federal forces. The Confederate cavalry guarded the river crossings and protected the Confederate army. The 4th Virginia Cavalry, including Vivian Towles, was part of the cavalry screen, and the period of relative inactivity allowed for correspondence to family.

In August, Vivian had written his younger sister, Ella, commenting on letters he had received from her and again reflecting on the destruction that two years of war had wreaked on Northern Virginia. "I hope and pray that you all may never be driven again from a sheltering roof by such a flood of destruction as here rules the plain," he wrote. "In a section of the Country smaller than Prince Wm. six battles have been fought and the marching and counter marching of mighty hosts of armed men felling forests, entrenching hills obstructing in places and destroying obstructions in other places has laid waste all that was convenient and prosperous which actual battle did not reach."

Others found scenes of similar destruction. One of General Hampton's cavalry passing through Culpeper decried the desolation left by the Yankees, "these notorious scamps who were committing every species of depredations, from negro stealing down to robbing the roost of the last old hen…Farms wantonly laid to waste, houses pillaged, not a living domestic animal nor a grain for bread left for these unfortunate people." Such experiences no doubt spurred the Confederate troops on to defend their homes and their communities.

At times, the pageantry of war also inspired the men and their loved ones at home. Vivian's letter in the late summer of 1863 tells of a particularly memorable experience—the review of the 4th Virginia Cavalry by General Lee, himself.

Aug. 23rd

Dear Sister,

Yesterday, after I wrote the within letter our regiment was reviewed by Gn. Lee in accordance with previous announcement in the level plain around our camp. At five o'clock we were drawn up in order for review and soon Fitz [Lee] splendidly mounted and dressed came to the front with his uncle and staff and we then went through the usual evolutions upon such occasions in splendid style. Col. Wickham said he hoped we would make no blunders and with the exception of some company officers saluting Genl. Lee when he was inspecting no blunder was made. A number of ladies were near the flag of the Gen. and the 2nd regt. band gave us inspiring music and we passed in review by platoons first at a walk next in a trot and finally in a grand charge twice around and then were fronted into line at a gallop, halted and then the companies were inspected front and rear and the review was over. It passed off so unusually well that the spirits of the men were raised very high. Fitz is reported to have said to his uncle as he rode on the field that we would show him something fine.

A later letter expressed his continuing concern for brother Robert, who he expected was still in prison, but presumably eligible for parole. Vivian also had some hope that he might be able to leave the regiment to see his family, although such a visit would likely have been without authorization.

Vivian also had news of a matter involving one of the Towleses' former neighbors. Mr. Michael Roseberry had been arrested for treason against the Confederacy and was being held in Richmond for trial. Vivian—and his father Rev. John Towles—had been called as witnesses in the trial. "Through design or otherwise, the case has been made a very important one," wrote Vivian. "Mr. R. was arrested by some of Hampton's scouts, they say, at the request of some neighbors and on charges made by them. Most of us are summoned by the Government but will be witnesses for Mr. Roseberry, not knowing any treasonable act of which he was guilty but knowing much in his favor. I hope those who know him to be a traitor will prove it."

The Roseberrys were one of about thirty families that had moved from a Quaker settlement in New Jersey to Prince William County in the decade prior to the war. The "Yankee Settlement" or the "Jersey Settlement near Brentsville," as it was known, was a section of the county with adjoining farms and families that were known to have Unionist sympathies. Whether these sympathies had resulted in active support for the Union remains unclear, and at least some of the families contributed their own to the Southern war effort. Two of the New Jersey-born Deats family sons, for example, fought with the 4th Virginia Cavalry. Nevertheless, the Jersey Settlement families had generally been opposed to secession and were suspected by many of their neighbors as being loyal to the Union even after Virginia became part of the Confederacy. Perhaps Mr. Roseberry was one such patriot.

Coincidentally, shortly after the Battle of Bristoe Station in the fall of 1863, the famed Union Iron Brigade was sent through Thoroughfare Gap and passed by the Brentsville area. On November 2, the Brigade commander, Lysander Cutler, was "outraged" to learn that some of his troops had stolen hogs and chickens from the farm of "Mrs. Mitchell [sic] Roseberry." Cutler noted that Roseberry "was a good Union man and was currently being held in Richmond awaiting trial for voicing Union sentiments" and demanded that the guilty parties be identified for punishment. When a private in the brigade acknowledged stealing the livestock, he also implicated General Cutler's negro servant, leading to the discovery that Cutler had himself (unknowingly?) partaken of the stolen goods for his own supper. Needless to say, the investigation was halted, no one was punished, and Mrs. Roseberry received no compensation for the stolen poultry. It is telling that the commander of the Iron Brigade believed the Roseberrys to be strongly Unionist, however, so perhaps the Confederate charges against him had some merit.

In any case, exigencies at the front prevented Vivian from attending the trial, and Mr. Roseberry apparently was eventually freed. No record survives of the results of his trial in Richmond, but that may be a result of lost documentation or an imperfect process for dealing with alleged sedition on the Confederate home front. Later in the war, in recognition of the difficulties encountered in the prosecution of treasonable offenses against the Confederacy, a bill "to define and punish conspiracy against the Confederate States" was introduced in the Confederate Congress and approved by President Jefferson Davis. The act listed a series of offenses which were declared to be high crimes, punishable by a fine not exceeding $5,000 and imprisonment—with or without hard labor—for a period not exceeding five years. It may be that Mr. Roseberry merely outlasted the Confederacy. In any case, he apparently escaped punishment.

After the war, Roseberry appeared before the Southern Claims Commission to prove he was loyal to the Union in seeking compensation for property destroyed by Federal troops during the conflict. The purpose of the Southern Claims Commission was to allow Union sympathizers who had lived in the Southern states during the Civil War to apply for reimbursements for property losses due to Federal confiscations during the war. "Southern loyalists," i.e., those who were Union sympathizers, made more than 20,000 claims, of which less than half were approved for payment. The claimants typically used the testimony of their neighbors as evidence of their loyalty to the Union and of their property losses.

Extensive records exist for the post-war claim of Michael Roseberry, and testimony from a neighbor seems to indicate that the suspicions of Hampton's scouts and the Confederate authorities were indeed justified:

> I resided in Brentsville during the war and was acquainted with Mr. Roseberry. I knew him long before the war. I have heard him talk about secession—talk against it. I was against secession myself. I was a Union man. There were not many Union men in that section. I knew them pretty much all. I know Roseberry was one of them. I know he went very often and tried to give the best information he could…he went to Bristoe, and I think he went to Union Mills once. *I know of his being imprisoned* [emphasis added]. I think a squad of South Carolinians took him prisoner to Richmond. Mosby made a report that he was going to hang him just before the war closed. All I know is that he was a loyal Union man.

Mr. Roseberry's claims—for hogs and other items—were paid by the government, as one would expect for someone called the "old Yankee" by his neighbors.

Another letter from Vivian during this time expressed relief that various family members were recovering from illness, particularly John Towles. "[I hope that] our Dear Father will now have a chance to recover from the effects of the severe trial he has undergone," wrote Vivian, presumably referring to Robert's capture and the strain of being exiled from the family home. "I wonder at his being able to bear up under so much anxiety and fatigue."

Vivian's letter dated September 26 gave some indication of the disposition of the Confederate cavalry patrolling the river crossings:

We are having cool weather here now. Some of the nights are really cold, preventing sleep, etc. The night of our first frost I waked up with my ears and nose, which were exposed, stinging with cold and almost my first thought was that I would do good in Lancaster.

Our Brigade left Fredericksburg on the occasion of the Enemy's advance into Culpeper and except two days when we were pursuing the late yankee raid out of Madison County we have been camped here near Clark Mountain and Raccoon Ford ever since. Our Brig. is reduced to the 1st, 2nd, 3rd and 4th Va. regts. The new Brigade of Lomax is in our Division and composed of the 5th Va. and Md. Battalion from our Brig. the 15th from W.H.F. Lee's and the 6th from Jones'. W.H.F. Lee's is also in our division [Fitz Lee's] and we are all camped near together. I went this morning to see our cousins in the 9th Va. but they were out of Camp on some duty and I did not see them.

Vivian went on to tell his sister about riding to visit pre-war friends in the area. "But I found the yard, garden and premises generally literally torn to pieces by redoubts and breastworks commanding Morton's Ford on the Rapidan. Gen. Johnson had his Hd.Qrs. in the house and the family were gone. I could not tell where. Such is war," wrote Viv.

Soon, however, Vivian and his comrades would be once again actively engaged with the enemy. Maneuvering by the opposing forces along the Rapidan River fords resulted in a series of skirmishes between the Confederate cavalry and their Union counterparts in early October. In his report regarding what would be called the Bristoe Campaign, October 9–22, 1863, Confederate cavalry chief Maj. Gen. Jeb Stuart articulated the plans involving Fitz Lee's Division, which included the 4th Virginia Cavalry:

[Fitz] Lee's Division, supported by two brigades of infantry, the whole under Major General Lee's command, was left to observe the enemy opposite the lower fords of the Rapidan, and guard against a movement which it was foreseen would probably be made by the enemy in that direction, with a view to discover the position of our troops and the commanding general's designs. This anticipation was speedily realized. Disconcerted by the movement of our forces in the direction of Madison Court House, and anxious to ascertain its character and extent, the Federal commander dispatched Buford's division of cavalry, with a battery of artillery, to make a reconnaissance in force toward Orange Court House…Major General Lee had promptly made his dispositions to give the enemy a warm reception.

In his own report, Gen. Fitzhugh Lee described an attack he instigated against encroaching Federal cavalry that had crossed the river at Germanna Ford and was moving up river towards Morton's Ford.

Early on the morning of the 11th, I attacked them…while I crossed the river above them at Raccoon Ford with Wickham's brigade…and moved down upon their flank and rear. Its effect was to cause the enemy to rapidly recross the Rapidan at Morton's. They were then driven to Stevensburg, from there to Brandy Station, from there to the Rappahannock River, being dislodged from every position in which they made a stand by simultaneous attacks in front, rear, and flank, with considerable loss to them.

During the battle, as Wickham's brigade crossed Raccoon Ford, they ran into heavy fire from enemy sharpshooters. John T. Williams of the 4th Virginia wrote, "We found the enemy there in strong force, and soon after crossing we were attacked by a large body of cavalry." The Yankees were under the command of Gen. John Buford, one of the heroes of Gettysburg, who had recognized the importance of the high ground on the first day of that battle. Now Buford's men were attempting to prevent the Confederates from making headway at the ford.

Despite Buford's resistance, Hampton's division pushed the Yankee cavalry back towards Stevensburg, and Fitz Lee's Division attempted to flank the Federals. As Union troops formed their battle line, the 4th Virginia dismounted and took cover in the woods. The Federals advanced, and the 4th charged on foot. "The enemy's sharpshooters were strongly posted on our front," wrote one Confederate. "The ground between us was very much broken, and partly in the woods and brushes."

The ensuing struggle "compelled [Buford] to yield," but the fight cost the Confederates dearly. Several "gallant spirits"—including two captains of the 4th Virginia Cavalry, William Brockenbrough Newton of Company G and Phillip

D. Williams of Company A—were killed in an attack by the regiment. Captain Newton had drawn his sword and spurred his horse to lead the charge. Captain Williams was with the lead squadron by Newton's side. The Federals held their fire and then fired a barrage. It shattered the ranks of the 4th, and the men recoiled in confusion. Among the dead was Vivian Towles.

The grief-stricken men of the 4th charged again to recover their fallen comrades. The enemy line broke, and the Union troops were pushed back across the Rappahannock. "We laid a bloody hand upon the enemy in the after conflict of that evening, and the recollection of our beloved Newton lent an energy to every blade that gleamed that unhappy day," wrote one participant.

For a skirmish, the engagement had resulted in a disproportionate number of casualties among the cavalry. The historian for the Black Horse Cavalry, for example, noted that the battle among the farms of Stevensburg cost the Black Horse more dearly than any other single day of the war, eleven wounded and two captured. To many, however, the death of the two captains was a singular and enduring loss.

Lt. G.W. Beale of the 9th Virginia wrote that Captain Newton "was one of the noblest offerings Hanover County laid on the altar in the army of Lee." Lauded as "an officer of extraordinary promise," the captain had died of a wound to the brain. His troops wept openly as they encamped at Brandy Station that night.

At a meeting of Company C, 4th Virginia Cavalry, held at their camp later that month, the following resolution was adopted regarding the fallen Newton:

> Whereas, it has seemed best, in the dispensation of the All-wise and just Providence, to take from us our beloved Captain, William B. Newton, who fell shot through the brain while leading most gallantly the 4th Virginia Cavalry in the charge at Raccoon Ford, on the 11th October. The officers and men of his company do resolve—
>
> 1. That, in his death, our Confederacy has lost one of its most earnest, faithful and devoted defenders; wise in counsel, gallant in the field, with the highest order of intellectual abilities and social qualities of the most winning character, he was universally respected and admired as the model of a soldier, a patriot and a man; and so early a death has cut short a career which promised to be of distinguished honor to himself and great usefulness to his country.

2. To us, the officers and men of his company his loss is irreparable. We mourn him as our trusted leader, our beloved companion, and our best friend.
3. To his afflicted family we tender the assurance of our deepest sympathy and condolence in their sore bereavement.

The other captain lost was also heavily mourned. P.D. Williams's brother, John Taylor Williams, wrote:

> Our brigade of cavalry commenced the advance by way of Raccoon Ford, Culpeper County on Sunday morning the 11th of October. We found the enemy there in strong force, and soon after crossing the river, we were attached by a large body of cavalry. We found them some time when our regiment [the 4th] was ordered to charge a body of sharpshooters. The regiment was commanded by Captain Newton, of the Hanover Troop, and our squadron by P.D. Williams, whose squadron was in front [and, of course, had to bear the brunt of the fight]. Captain Newton was killed instantly, and [my brother] fell mortally wounded. He received a ball in his left arm just below the shoulder which shattered the bone and entered the breast. His horse was killed and fell upon him…After the Yankees were put to flight…he was taken to Mr. Stringfellow's in the neighborhood, and died a short time afterwards in my arms while I was in the act of giving him some brandy which had been sent in by the chief surgeon. Thus passes away in the prime of life (he had barely reached his twenty-fifth birthday) one who in the words of a fellow soldier 'was as brave a soldier as ever drew a saber or fired a gun.'

For the Towles family, the skirmish had an even more devastating result. Their oldest son had fallen, and the family would never be the same. Vivian's death was recorded in poignant detail by a regimental correspondent, self-styled as "C", who reported for publication:

> It is my painful duty to announce the death of another of Virginia's noblest sons. Private John Vivian Towles, member of company A, 4th regiment Virginia cavalry, and son of the Rev. John Towles, of Prince William county, was killed instantly on the 11th instant, near Stephensburg, Culpeper co., Va., whilst gallantly

serving in a cause to which he was devotedly attached. Early in life, one of the most promising of his age, endowed by nature with the brightest qualities, greatly improved by academical and collegiate study he has been snatched from life, and from his friends at a time when all eyes were turned upon him as a love and hope. The strains of eulogy are not needed to call forth the grief due his memory. He was esteemed in his Company as an ornament to it and to the army, and "like a lofty tree that shakes down its green glories to battle the winter's storm, he laid aside the trappings of place and pride," and walked the humblest path in our army. He gained the admiration of those around him, and has bequeathed us a legacy we feel proud to inherit. As a beloved son, a true friend, and a gallant soldier, his loss is deeply mourned.

The commanding officer of Company A, Lt. Lucien A. Davis, wrote Reverend Towles from the regimental camp on October 22. "It becomes my painful duty to announce to you the death of your son, John Vivian, a member of my company. He was killed instantly on the 11th inst[ant] near Stephensburg, while gallantly engaged in defence of the cause to which he was so singularly devoted." Describing the particulars of the mortal wound and requesting clarification on the disposition of his effects, Lieutenant Davis also took time to eulogize Vivian's character—and what his loss meant to the unit. "By his death my company has lost a bright criterion for bravery—coolness and self-possession in time of danger, and his death is deeply mourned," wrote Davis.

Another comrade of Vivian's later wrote to Reverend Towles and his wife from the 4th Virginia's camp near Brandy Station, conveying "melancholy tidings" and providing the circumstances under which their son had lost his precious life. "Our cavalry were engaged with the enemy on road from Raccoon Ford to Stephensburg, many of our cavalry were dismounted and among them was Viv… under a raking fire of rifle balls grape and Shell when a grape shot struck him on the right side of the head inducing death in about half an hour. He never spoke after the wound. His last words before being shot were 'Watch those yankees, boys.' A brave and gallant soldier has left us a willing sacrifice if need be to his country's Cause," wrote R.H. Colvin ("a bosom friend to poor Viv"). Colvin went on to say that Vivian's friends in the company made him the best coffin that circumstances would allow and buried the oldest Towles boy and several others near where he fell, "under some beautiful oak trees." The sorrowful writer assured the Towleses that Viv's belongings, including his horse and his memorandum book, would be returned to the family.

Among the mementos eventually returned to the family was a Bible, given to Vivian in September 1857 by his mother, Sophronia. The Bible has a gash on its cover from another battle, where, in Viv's breast pocket, it deflected a sabre strike "from the hand of a Federal officer," while the cavalryman was fighting during an earlier 1863 skirmish as a dismounted sharpshooter. At Raccoon Ford, Vivian Towles was not as lucky.

It was left to Reverend Towles to convey the loss to Vivian's siblings. A letter of October 20 was addressed to younger brother Jimmie, apparently in response to the young man's own letter to his parents dated October 15, vowing revenge for Vivian's death. In Robert's absence, Jimmie had arranged to look after Vivian's body and had marked the spot where he was buried. "Some day it may be in the power of your mother & father to go up the Country & it will be a melancholy pleasure to us to visit the spot & water it with our tears," wrote John Towles. "But why, my son, speak of <u>avenging his death</u>? Leave vengeance with Heaven, for 'vengeance is mine, saith the Lord.'"

Reverend Towles went on to caution Jimmie against a perceived intent to go on "a secret and perilous adventure" that would be "rash in the extreme." "Is it not <u>unkind</u> to your parents? You ought not to peril your life for their sakes; and not to let them hear from you is to leave them prey to fears and apprehensions for your safety. Would it not be better for you, at present, to gather up every little memento of your brother that would be prized by your mother, sister, or myself and come down to see us all, if it be only for a few days, and, hereafter, when you go into battle with all your courage and determination?"

More pointedly—and not knowing definitively whether Robert still was in prison or, indeed, lived—Reverend Towles implored his youngest son to caution. "You may be the only one of our soldier boys now left alive to us. How necessary then to counsel prudence with you, who, I fear, are by <u>nature rash</u>. Your poor brother, who possessed far more prudence, may have been rash for <u>once</u> in the noble effort to try to extricate Captain Newton and Captain Williams." This reference seems to indicate anecdotal evidence of Vivian's role in the charge. Whether he died in a rash act of bravery or merely as part of his squadron's charge, however, it seems clear that Viv died courageously fighting by the side of his comrades.

Reverend Towles also took the time to draft a letter to his middle son, Robert, whose fate in prison and beyond was not yet known. "Two sad changes have taken place in the family since your capture. Your mother, who, as you know was in bad health before, was taken extremely ill the very day she got the news of your imprisonment. Thank Heaven her health is now better than it has been for many months. This has enabled her to bear the last sad shock, the news of Vivian's death. Yes, Dear Robert, your poor brother Viv was killed in battle near Stephensburg, Culpeper Co., along with both Captains of his squadron, Williams and Newton, on Sunday, the 11th instant. Taylor Williams writes me word he was decently interred & the grave well marked."

Having not heard from Robert, Reverend Towles went on to express his fears for his son's health and urgently pressed the particulars of how Robert might communicate with his family:

> Your mother and I have had many anxious fears for your health. We had hoped it would occur to you to try to write to us by flag-of-truce boat. Having waited long and received no letter, we now mourn and are sad, lest you may not be alive. Do write immediately on the receipt of this, & let us know how you are. Let your letter be brief: one line to say how you are, will answer our purpose. Remember if your letter contains one improper word, it will not be sent. The gentlemanly commissioners on both sides, to whose kindness we hope to be indebted in this matter, must see there is no word improper to be sent, or improper to be delivered. Place your letter in an open envelope, ready to be mailed in Richmond. Direct to me, Montague's P.O. Essex County, Va. Put your own name & company HQ? on the back; & say on the back, 'By way of flag-of-truce boat, through U.S. Commissioner Gen. Meredith, to Confederate Commissioner Ould.' Enclose your open letter in a separate & sealed envelope to 'Gen. S.A. Meredith, Commissioner for the exchange of prisoners, Washington, D.C.' Send it to the City P.O. prepaying the drop-letter postage.

What John Towles would soon discover from other sources was that his son had escaped his captivity, although Robert's safety was by no means yet secure. While he waited for additional news, Reverend Towles and the family would have time to grieve the loss of their eldest son—a thoughtful, educated, and potential head of the family, whose life was cut short in battle.

Vivian's letter of October 4, 1863—never sent, but found on his body after his death the following week—expressed what he called "a certain melancholy," which he noted his horse seemed to share, and was almost a presentiment of events soon to come. "I seldom get 'homesick' too long for a house to cover me, generous fare, a soft warm bed and the good things of this world generally, but I often, when idle, muse for hours, not about air castles, but about those dearest objects of affection who draw my thoughts to Greenvale House. It is when toiling along through a desolated Country, in rain and mud, hungry and tired, horse and rider, that my thoughts turn to bright fires in warm well furnished rooms, with smoking viands for a ravenous appetite," he said. "It is when the march is over and I have to feel in the swamp, maybe, where dark night finds us, for a place with no briars, no water, no stumps, in which to spread my miserable oil cloth and blanket and seek refuge from gnawing hunger in joint stiffening sleep, that I think of the soft down, the fire, clean linen and slumber secure from rain and storm."

Regrettably, such was not to be.

CHAPTER ELEVEN

Escape and furlough
Reporting back for duty

"At home in the woods. I am now in the height of my enjoyment."

Diary entry
October 3, 1863

Belle Boyd, the "Cleopatra of the Secession,"
Library of Congress

News article about escape from Old Capitol,
"Washington Evening Star" archives

ESCAPE FROM CARROLL PRISON.—A young
man named J. G. Thompson, son of a restaurant keeper in this city, confined in Carroll
prison, charged with being a rebel mail carrier,
succeeded in effecting his escape on Thursday
night. Thompson was confined in the upper
part of the prison, and succeeded in getting
upon the roof of the building, on the corner of
Pennsylvania avenue and First street east,
used as a boarding house, and escaped by going
down the lightning rod to the ground.

freedom

Map of Washington with fortifications

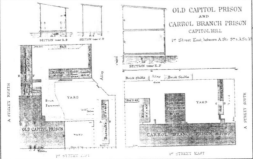

Floorplan for Old Capitol/Carroll Prisons

While his brother Vivian was fighting and dying, Robert Towles was making his escape from prison. Taking advantage of a dark night, Robert had slipped out the window of his South Attic room and onto the roof of the Carroll Prison's row houses, which had been added as an annex to the Old Capitol Prison. From there he made his way over the surrounding fences and into Washington City. "I found myself on Pennsylvania Avenue in Confederate Uniform," noted the young Virginia cavalryman with some chagrin.

He was not alone. With him went a young friend named Thomas Thompson. A watchmaker by trade and son of a Georgetown jeweler, Thompson had been arrested as a Confederate courier during the previous summer and charged as a Confederate "mail carrier"—a serious crime in the security-conscious Northern capital. On what had been ostensibly business trips to and from Richmond, young Thompson had agreed to convey letters from Confederate sympathizers in Washington City to friends and relatives in Virginia. For counter-espionage officials, few transgressions were more worthy of a stay in Old Capitol and Carroll Prisons.

An excerpt from contemporary Union orders relating to prisoners of war and state noted that "hereafter all persons found within our lines who commit acts for the benefit of the enemies of our country will be tried as spies or traitors and if convicted will suffer death." The order includes "carriers of secret mails," as well as "persons found concealed within our lines belonging to the service of the enemy." It seems that young Thompson and Robert Towles were exactly the type of target contemplated by the directive.

"Secret mail" was often more than just routine correspondence carried between loved ones. While letters from comrades to their families would comprise some of such mail, the definition of the contraband also included not readily available open-source material, especially Northern newspapers, and sometimes intelligence reports and other documents intended for Confederate officers and officials. An ever-changing "Secret Line" was made possible by volunteers—men and women who slipped in and out of taverns, farms and waterfront docks along routes that connected Baltimore and Washington to the Confederacy. This secret Rebel mail service provided valuable information to the Southern cause and involved participants as diverse as Washington high society's Rose O'Neil Greenhow (incarcerated for a time in Old Capitol) and watchmaker Thomas Thompson.

The vicissitudes of Civil War Washington and its prison system resulted in Tom Thompson making the acquaintance of Robert Towles. Both had been transferred to Carroll Prison as spies, and when Robert shared his plans to escape, there was apparently little hesitation on the young watchmaker's part. According to Robert, Thompson had already been adjudged a spy and had been condemned to execution in the not distant future. For Tom Thompson, there was little to lose and much to gain by attempting to escape with Robert.

Plans for the escape had apparently been in the offing ever since Robert was transferred to Carroll from the adjacent Old Capitol. Carroll Prison was a grim place, even more so than Old Capitol, and many of the more notorious prisoners were transferred to Carroll to keep a closer watch on them. Prisoners were kept in small rooms, sometimes with a guard or detective to watch over them. Frequent interviews were conducted to ascertain the facts of each person's case. A great many Southern independent scouts were held under the accusation of espionage, even if they were captured in uniform. While a small number of such prisoners were actually executed (the *Washington Star* reported that there had been five executions within the walls of Carroll during the war), those eventually convicted by a military tribunal of spying could at least be expected to endure a lengthy incarceration at hard labor.

Nevertheless, several of Robert's roommates, including a Mr. Kelley from Fauquier County, debated the wisdom of attempting to leave the confines of the Carroll "hotel." "They all…opposed it bitterly," wrote Robert, "thinking that I knew nothing about the situation of things in [other] parts of the building. Here they were mistaken." Robert's eye for detail and his experience as a scout had led him to examine the layout of the prison and formulate a plan for escape.

Robert and his co-conspirators may also have had some help from the inside. One of the most famous inmates in the fall of 1863 was the Southern spy, Belle Boyd. Belle had become a celebrity of sorts during Lt. Gen. Thomas J. "Stonewall" Jackson's Valley Campaign of 1862. Before the battle of Front Royal, the 18-year-old had reputedly ridden across Union lines to warn Stonewall of the Federal troop dispositions. An outgoing, vivacious young woman—if no great beauty—Belle made no secret of her sympathies and did her best to assist the cause whenever possible. Her aptitude for self-promotion likely added to her notoriety, and she had become somewhat of a *cause célèbre* in the South.

Union authorities took note of her and arranged for her arrest and incarceration in Old Capitol Prison during the summer of 1862. After being exchanged in late August of that year, Belle had defied parole restrictions to return to her ailing mother in Martinsburg, behind Union lines, which led to her being taken into custody again in the late summer of 1863. During her second stint as a prisoner, she was sent to Carroll, not long after Robert Towles had been captured and transferred to the prison.

Over the next several months, Belle's fragile health and public sympathy for her plight—even though she was a self-proclaimed Confederate spy—made it politic to release her with the condition that she be banished beyond Union lines for the duration of the War. Her release was scheduled for December, but in the meantime, she took an active interest in the activities of the other inmates.

In her diary, Belle noted that "one evening, whilst I was looking out my room door, a significant cough attracted my attention, and…I perceived a note, tightly rolled up, thrown towards me. I picked it up quickly…and found that it was from Mr. K. of Virginia, begging me to aid himself and two friends to escape." This may well have been Robert's roommate, Mr. Kelley, who must have come around to the idea of Robert's plan to escape. According to Belle, unobserved, she handed the mysterious Mr. K. forty dollars and contrived to assist him in getting to the upstairs garret occupied by his two friends.

The night of the attempt, Belle sent a note to Superintendent Wood, asking for an audience to discuss a matter of feigned importance. According to Belle, she proceeded to detain Mr. Wood with idle conversation until a commotion began in a corner of the building. Shouts of "Murder! Murder!" rang through the complex, and during the confusion, the prisoners managed to make their way over the three fences surrounding the prison building, eluding frantic sentries as they went.

In his diary, Robert described a somewhat different—but no less dramatic—sequence of events. Robert told how his small band of escapees made their way to the window of the South Attic, where they descended from the attic by using a light pole, which had been fixed "by taking a hook from my iron bedstead and driving it into the end of the pole." This jury-rigged ladder allowed the men to slide down to the next level of the Carroll row houses, which happened to be living quarters for the family of Superintendent Wood.

Armed only with a pocket knife and "one long cavalry boot" (which he presumably would wield as a club), Robert led the way down the stairs of the tenement, which he had previously observed to be laid out in the same manner as the other buildings in the complex. With sleepers within the Wood family quarters snoring audibly, Robert and his companions "passed on as quietly as three kittens" to the ground floor, where they unbolted the back door, avoiding the sentinel at the front door, and crossed the small back yard to confront the first of three plank fences enclosing the compound.

Robert had intended to fulfill a wager by pausing to eat a peach from a tree overhanging the first fence, but was forced to flee more expeditiously when one of his fellow escapees tripped on a rick of wood stacked against the fence, creating a commotion. Once over the fences, Robert and his young friend Tom Thompson set off to find sanctuary for the night with Tom's father, a British expatriate who lived in Washington. Robert noted that the third member of their party (Mr. Kelley?) started in another direction.

The War Department records for Old Capitol and Carroll Prisons show three escapees during the month of October 1863, and individual entries in the Prison Register for Towles and Thompson confirm that two of the three persons who escaped from Carroll Prison on October 2 were the two friends. Only thirteen other escapes were recorded from the facility during the course of the war.

Interestingly enough, the report of the escape in the *Washington Star* the next day mentioned only that "*J.G.* [sic] Thompson, rebel mail carrier," had escaped. Under the headline of "Escape from Old Capitol", the newspaper told how Thompson, confined in the upper part of the prison, "succeeded in getting upon the roof of the building, on the corner of Pennsylvania avenue and First street east…and escaped by going down a lightning rod to the ground." No mention of Robert Towles or Kelley was made. Perhaps the military authorities felt the public would be less concerned if a mere civilian spy had escaped, rather than one or more Confederate soldiers. As a side note, a post-war story in the *Star* reprised the report of the escape and noted that Thompson "was never retaken, but some time after the capture of Richmond, he made his appearance here [in Washington]." Tom Thompson had come home.

Leaving Washington City and crossing the Potomac to safe territory proved to be much harder than either of the young men expected. By the fall of 1863, Washington was the most fortified city on the planet, with a ring of more than forty forts and countless patrols and checkpoints. The plains around the city were crowded with camps, sheds, and trains, and the streets were filled with soldiers. In order to safely make their way past this gauntlet, Robert and Tom found it necessary to take an indirect route back to Dixie.

"I took the precaution to cut the stripes off my pants…and taking my jacket off, rolled it up—wrong side out—took it under my arm and started down the Avenue accompanied by my friend Tom," wrote Robert in his diary. Later, the two secured civilian coats and pants, which Robert placed over his jacket to complete his disguise.

Having spent one night in the stable loft at the home of Tom Thompson's family, they made their way out of the city by way of Georgetown and Rockville's Tenellytown Pike, spending a night in a convenient haystack along the way.

In Rockville, they found a large Union meeting and barbecue going on in town. The *Washington Star* reported on October 4 that the Union Convention and

Mass Meeting at Rockville attracted between one- and two-thousand people from as far away as Baltimore and produced a "very animated spectacle throughout the afternoon and evening." The event featured bountiful refreshments and patriotic speeches by local dignitaries. Editorial comment noted that the abundant display of Old Glory must have been "gall and wormwood" to the people of Rockville—citizens of the slave-holding border state of Maryland.

The crowd was probably mixed. Maryland contributed troops to both sides during the War, yet, despite having a star on the Confederate flag as a border state, its sons did not flock in great numbers to the Southern cause, even when the Army of Northern Virginia had crossed into Maryland during the 1862 Antietam Campaign. If there were sympathetic locals, they were not likely to be in great numbers at this event, however. The meeting's theme, prominently displayed throughout the Rockville Fair Grounds, was "The Union, it must and shall be preserved." All in all, it was not a healthy environment for two escaped Southerners.

Robert noted that he did not feel in the least comfortable due to nearly two companies of Union cavalry present. Deciding to be bold, however, Robert noted that "we walked straight through the crowd cheering for President Abe, as bold as any other Union Man." This brazen deception allowed them to pass through to a road leading away from Washington. "We are now in the woods among friends," reported Robert.

Loose in the country, Robert soon found that their prospects for reaching Southern lines would depend almost entirely on his skills as a scout and outdoorsman. While bold enough, Tom Thompson was not accomplished in practical matters. Robert called him "the most perfectly green young man," when it came to the great outdoors. "He knows nothing of traveling off the roads, will get lost in the fields, knows very little about doing anything, yet is willing to undertake anything."

By contacting what appeared to be an extensive underground network of Southern sympathizers, the fugitives found food and shelter over the course of the next few days, as they attempted to find a safe river crossing. Along the way, Robert and Tom slept in haystacks and in barns of friendly farmers—judiciously referred to only by their initials in the diary accounts. It was not until October 24 that the duo managed to elude detectives and hire a boatman to take them to the far shore of the Potomac, near Leesburg, Virginia and the site of the Battle of Balls Bluff. At this juncture, Robert and his companion parted ways, with Tom heading for Richmond and Robert making his way into his familiar haunts of Prince William County.

Caution was still the order of the day. Union patrols remained vigilant throughout Prince William County, which had been occupied since the early days of the war. As in the past, union pickets were particularly heavy along the railroads, and Robert reported almost a continuous line of encampments from Catlett's Station to Bristoe Station. Constantly on the lookout for what seemed to be a continual stream of Union soldiers, Robert had some difficulty in working his way further southward. "Oh, that night or General Stuart would come!" he anguished during one tension-filled episode. Once across the tracks, Robert managed to retrace his steps to the place of his capture—"the barn at Vaucluse" (his former home, subsequently occupied by the Coopers). There, he found his pistol, hidden before he was taken, beneath sheaves of wheat in a local barn. "The rats had almost eaten the holster up, but the pistol has not rusted in the least bit. I took it down on Cedar Run today and although it had been loaded nearly three months, not a barrel snapped."

Over the next ten days, Robert worked his way back through the area where he had done considerable scouting and where friends of his family still lived. Many of the local homes were posted with sentries, and Robert used all of his guile to elude them in order to pay visits to people he knew.

Crawling up in the shrubbery of the home of a family friend, Dr. Macrae, Robert found three guards on the porch, one whistling "When This Cruel War is Over." At another house, Robert came close enough to overhear a trooper of the 8th Illinois Cavalry boast that "no Rebs [were] within many miles" of the place. Despite the sentries, Robert was able to make contact with a number of acquaintances and friends as he made his way south.

On November 4, just three months to the day when he had been captured and taken to Old Capitol in "that far famed city of Washington," Robert found himself once more at Teneriffe.

> But oh! What a change—no, not in my friends…the same glow of spirits, the same hearty welcome as of old, but I could hardly realize that it was the same place…the fencing gone, the cornfield packed as hard and stripped as clean as any road, with ditches cut and heaps of stone collected together somewhat in the shape of chimneys, huts, etc. Yet, it is really gratifying to see how well it is all taken. The girls laugh and talk about it as if it were all a good joke.

Yankee pickets had only recently been moved from around the mill, and the girls told Robert that Union General Birney had used their parlor as his headquarters, but was no longer there. Robert's timing was excellent.

In between stopping at other familiar places such as the Grove (a prominent home in the area) and visiting former neighbors like the Colvins, Manuels, and Peytons, Robert hid in the pines, where he spent a day "much more agreeably than I had the slightest idea of. Four of my young Lady friends have spent the day with me." Challenging duty, that!

As he moved through his former haunts, Robert took note that the area bore little resemblance to the prosperous farming community he had known before the War. Hardship was apparent everywhere. No doubt Prince William County appeared to Robert as it did to Robert E. Lee, Jr. (the commanding general's son). The young Lee described the desolation in a letter to his mother as troops passed by on their way to the Battle of Brandy Station that October: "All that country on the other side of Warrenton—along the railroad and east of it is a perfect desert, not a piece of fencing or any signs of civilization except one or two families." The hard hand of war had come to Prince William.

Although he enjoyed seeing those friends who remained in the area, Robert determined to make his way back to his regiment at the earliest possible time. In this he was nearly dissuaded by a female friend who thought it too risky an attempt. "I think I must be cruel enough not to heed her advice tonight," thought a determined Robert on November 7.

During a desperate attempt to cross the railroad, Robert encountered a "Mr. Yankey Cavalry man" riding up the road ahead. Running ahead and flanking the Union soldier, Robert came upon the man who had been thrown from his horse and rendered senseless. "He was the most splendidly equipped yankey I think I ever saw. He has all a cavalryman could call for…I took his horse, equipments… and let him go." Presumably, the Union soldier was grateful for his life, if not for the loss of his weapons and his belongings.

Thus equipped, Robert headed for the area where Maj. Gen. Stuart's command was purported to be camped. On Friday, November 13, the prodigal cavalry scout noted in his diary that he was "with General Stuart at last." His comrades from Company A of the 4th Virginia Cavalry were very much surprised to see him.

Having been told that his mother was deathly ill, Robert requested a furlough to visit her. "No furloughs are granted now, but General Stuart has made a special application to General Lee for a furlough for me, and I am waiting its return." The approval was not long in coming. Signed by General Lee's chief of staff, Walter Taylor, and containing Stuart's personal endorsement—"recently escaped from the enemy"—the furlough paper authorized a fifteen-day absence for Robert C. Towles and sent him homeward bound.

A three-day ride found Robert in Lancaster County, Virginia, twelve miles from Greenvale Manor, the home where his parents, sister, and brothers had fled when they left Prince William County at the beginning of the war. Riding up to the gate of the house, Robert asked if he could be accommodated for the night. With surprise and great joy, he was welcomed by his family.

"Home once more. Oh what a joy, what a blessing after being separated so long from Father, Mother, Sister and brothers, to be once more suddenly clasped in their arms. But oh! What change time has made, all have changed so much, I hardly would have known them; and two are no more—two the brightest, two happiest, have gone, gone to their eternal rest." The loss of younger sister Rosalie to illness during the summer and older brother Vivian's death in action affected the young soldier greatly.

Despite his grief, Robert noted that he would not wish them back to the darkness of the world. "They are free, forever free, from Sin and sorrow...from War and strife." Expressing his belief that the home circle, though broken on earth, would be united again in Heaven, Robert prepared to leave a sad, but grateful family. His furlough was ending. The war, General Stuart, his comrades, and duty beckoned.

A Bushwacker's life
Back in the field...and scouting

"Thus you see My Dear Sister
I have pictured to you a bush whackers life."

Robert Towles
Jan. 5, 1864

A Civil War snowball fight

bush whacking, ambushes, and winter

The Grey Ghost of the Confederacy. Col. John S. Mosby and some of his Rangers.
University of Maryland Department of History

After reporting back to his regiment, Robert Towles suspended keeping a diary "because of the nature of the duty to which I've been assigned." Once again, Robert was to be detached as a scout behind enemy lines. Intelligence from the area remained important, and Robert was still one of the best-qualified individuals to provide it. The Union response to Confederate scouting had intensified in recent months, however.

In 1864, Maj. Gen. Henry W. Halleck, Union chief of staff, at the direction of the secretary of war, ordered that, "in retaliation for the murderous acts of guerrilla bands, composed of and assisted by the inhabitants along the Manassas Gap Railroad…you [shall] proceed to destroy every house within five miles of the road which is not required for our own purposes, or which is not occupied by persons known to be friendly." This directive was particularly aimed at partisans under John Singleton Mosby, but it shows how seriously the Federals took the scout, partisan, and "bushwacker" threat.

Opinions differed somewhat as to the nature of the enemy the Federals faced. The provost-marshal-general of Defenses South of the Potomac, in forwarding a list of what he called "guerrillas" for confinement in Old Capitol, called them "men of bad character [who] ought not to be exchanged, but confined in some prison remote from Virginia, where they will not be likely to escape." He went on to say, "They are generally rebels, cut-throats, and thieves, and only await a release to return to their old avocation." The report mentioned Robert's compatriot, Dick Shepard, who "was captured with great difficulty by Lt. Jackson in November," but who had escaped and was back with the guerillas, much to the apparent annoyance of the general.

Earlier in 1863, another Union general, Brigadier William W. Averell, had opined that their adversaries were "mostly young rebels who assemble, mount, and form scouting parties at the shortest notice." Averell proposed to "cause the arrest of all such that can be found…if the major-general commanding approve." If only it were so easy.

As a Union corps commander noted, "They are men who have been selected for the particular duty upon which they were engaged by reason of their peculiar qualifications for it and their knowledge of the country. One of them would give more trouble to us than half a dozen ordinary soldiers."

This assessment had certainly proven true in the case of "the Grey Ghost of the Confederacy," John Singleton Mosby. Mosby knew a great deal about bushwacking. Between 1863 and 1865, a 125-square-mile triangle of northern Virginia encompassing parts of Fauquier and Loudoun counties was so firmly under the control of Col. John S. Mosby's 43rd Virginia Cavalry that it became known simply as "Mosby's Confederacy." Mosby's guerrilla fighters were known as the "Partisan Rangers" or "Mosby's Rangers."

Supported by a fiercely loyal, civilian population, Mosby and his ubiquitous partisans blew up trains and bridges and harassed Union supply lines so effectively that significant numbers of troops had to be diverted to guard against them. Although Union penalties for sympathizers could be severe, civilians did all they could to help the Rangers melt invisibly into the landscape, providing food, lodging, and guidance through the web of country roads and paths. "Every farmhouse in this section was a refuge for guerrillas and every farmer was an ally of Mosby, and every farmer's son was with him or in the Confederate Army," said one Union observer of life in Mosby's Confederacy.

Mosby himself noted, "We were called guerillas and bushwackers. These should not be opprobrious epithets, since the exploits of the 'embattled farmers' at Concord and Lexington have been sung in Emerson's immortal ode. Now, while bushwacking is perfectly legitimate war, and it as fair to shoot from a bush as behind a stockade or an earthwork, no men in the Confederate army less deserve these epithets than mine." While often operating in stealth and using the element of surprise, Mosby's men and other scouts also fought in mounted charges and used close-in weapons such as pistols.

The impact such Rebel forces had on the Union war effort is plain from the frequent commentary on the topic and from actions taken to ameliorate the perceived problem. Time after time, official reports detailed examples of Confederate forays and Union reactions. No matter how vigorous the efforts to suppress behind-the-lines Rebel activity and raids, the partisans and scouts seemed to remain impediments to the pacification of occupied Southern territory.

Capt. Andrew H. McHenry of the 13th Pennsylvania Cavalry reported on a scout from Bristoe Station to Brentsville in March of 1864. "Along this road to near Cedar Run bridge is skirted with small second-growth pines on either side, generally favorable for bushwackers to carry out their mode of warfare."

Union logistical genius Henry Haupt wrote to Chief of Staff Henry Halleck, "The chief danger to our trains and construction forces arises from the cavalry companies of Prince William." Haupt proposed a force of "not less than 200 sharpshooters" to ride on top of rail cars and to assist in unloading trains.

In the spring of 1863, the 8th Illinois Cavalry was instructed as follows: "… pickets report a company of Rebel cavalry in the vicinity of Brentsville. The colonel commanding the brigade directs that, in accordance to the detail for pickets, you send a squadron tomorrow morning, under an energetic officer, to scout in that vicinity, and to endeavor to capture them."

George Stoneman, the brigadier commanding the Union Cavalry Corps in May 1863 had gone even further. "These annoyances will continue until some stringent measures are taken to clear that section of the country of every male inhabitant, either by shooting, hanging, banishment, or incarceration…The country is infested by a set of bushwacking thieves and smugglers who should be eradicated, root and branch."

In March 1863, Stoneman's predecessor, Alfred Pleasonton, has said much the same thing. "It is recommended that the rebel partisans and bushwackers be cleared out from the vicinity of Occoquan and Brentsville by a command from this division. One brigade and a couple of guns should be sufficient." Probably much to the chagrin of Union commanders like Stoneman and Pleasonton, such efforts did not uniformly succeed. Rebel scouting operations continued in the area throughout the war. As late as February 1865, the Official Records reported on an expedition of one hundred men from the 8th Illinois that had resulted in "complete success," capturing fifteen prisoners and a Union horse that had been captured the previous fall. "The camp of the gang is burnt, and a quantity of clothing and blankets was destroyed."

Whether a gang, partisans, bushwackers, or simply cavalry scouts on detached duty, it was clear that such men were making an impact on the Union war effort in Virginia. With the increasing Federal focus on such activities, the duty to which Robert Towles had again been assigned was more dangerous than ever. Robert seemed not to mind, however. With him were what he called his "squad," several trusted comrades who formed a small command to harass and observe the enemy.

Fellow 4th Virginia Company A members John Sinclair—whom Robert called his adjutant general—and family friend Lee Macrae—self-styled "aide-de-camp"—were extremely familiar with the local territory. Robert and his men sallied forth as was practicable, using their familiarity with the area and hiding in what their old Iron Scout companions had called "those old Virginia pines."

On Christmas Day 1863, Robert wrote his mother, describing a typical routine for the scouts:

> This is such a beautiful day that if I were not compeled to spend it in the pines I could not realize there was any war. I came across the R.R. last night with two of my squad Lee McRae & Jno. Sinclair. stoped at Tenariffe [Mill] until one o'clock this morning. had a most excellent time. then rode all over the neighborhood,

woke every body up to tell them Christmas gifts and now have
fallen back into the pines to remain until night—will again allow
us to launch forth.

I am now half wrapped up in my blankets, my two men
sleeping at my back, having been up all last night and my hand is
so stiff I can scarcely hold the pen.

The winter weather made it challenging to obtain much useful information
from the Federals. Because of the cold, the small force of Northern infantry
camped at intervals along the Orange and Alexandria Railroad rarely ventured
outside of their shanties. When it snowed, Robert and his men found it expedient
to take to the pines and remain still to prevent their being tracked in the snow by
any Yankee patrols that did go out. "We are now what might be called snowed up,"
he said at one such juncture.

Such conditions did not mean that the scouts were not comfortable, however.
In an early January letter to his sister, Ella, Robert described the men's situation:

I am now at leasure for the first time since my return to
Prince William, it commenced snowing yesterday morning,
continued all day and part of the night, and now is about eight
inches deep.

I and my Agnt. Gen. Jno. Sinclair are very comfortably fixed
indeed. We have a haystack in the thick pines about three miles
from the R.R. the Stack constitutes one side of our house and the
pines which surrounds the stack the other sides, poles running
from the stack to the fence covered with oilcloths constitute
the rufe, one end is open the other stoped with an oilcloth, we
have an ample supply of bed cloths, two blankets, two shawls,
three quilts, and our overcoats. Our house is large enough for
our saddles and corn besides ourselves, our horses are tied to the
fence near us enjoying plenty of hay and corn. We are convenient
to the houses of several friends and suffer for nothing. In fact we
are as comfortable as we would be in a three story brick Mansion
with coal fires burning in the grates.

Thus you see My Dear Sister I have pictured to you a bush
whackers life.

Some noted that the term "bushwacker" had different meanings, depending on one's perspective. "We were planning to *bushwack* them (as they called it), or rather we were going to *ambush* them (as we called it)," said a Confederate scout. With partisans such as Mosby harassing the Federal troops in nearby counties, it is no wonder that apprehension was high among the Yankees when it came to independent scouts. "Every effort is made to get away from the bushwackers, the bad Johnnie Rebs," said a Federal soldier.

Certainly, in an area where the terrain still afforded concealment in dense thickets of pines, it was possible to remain concealed, in order to observe Union troops (particularly their numbers and disposition), and to "make a dash" to harass any who strayed outside of their lines and encampments. One such ambush was noted in Union reports on February 14, 1864, when twenty-five cavalrymen from the 13th Pennsylvania observed "three rebel soldiers having run from the town [of Brentsville] into a thicket of pines in the direction of Cedar Run." A volley from the hidden men killed two Federals and wounded four others. Subsequent searches failed to turn up the squad of scouts. Perhaps the perpetrators were Robert Towles and his men.

In addition to the woods, Confederate scouts still often afforded themselves of the hospitality of the remaining local populace who were sympathetic to the Rebel cause. As he had earlier in the war while partnering with the Iron Scouts, Robert sought out familiar territory and friends. "I saw Bettie, Emma, and their Ma [Howison], Saturday night, staid with them until twelve o'clock. Saw Lou [Latimer] the morning before and the girls at Tenariffe [Mill] Friday," wrote Robert. "They all send a great deal of love to you all."

Particularly after the success Mosby's partisan rangers had achieved in the area, Union troops were on high alert. "Have all houses in that vicinity searched for arms and ammunition. Arrest all men known to be disloyal and leave no horses which can be used by guerrillas," ordered Union Maj. Gen. Samuel P. Heintzelman.

Despite the extra vigilance, locals still managed to help Rebel soldiers who sought shelter. One such example involved the Towles's family friend, Mr. Cooper. A scout was hiding at the Cooper residence when troopers from the 8th Illinois Cavalry arrived. Mr. Cooper's daughters woke the man, saying, "Get up, Sergeant, a whole regiment of Yankees are advancing up the avenue to the house." Confronted by another body of Union cavalry approaching the rear of the house, the scout had no option but to hide on the premises. The two daughters offered to hide him in their upstairs bedroom, and thus the Rebel scout escaped capture.

There certainly was a risk to local families who sheltered Confederate scouts. Speaking of the Towles's neighbor, Allan Howison, Prioleau Henderson related a story about two scouts who visited the Howison house and were conducted to the basement, which was used for meals and sometimes as a sitting room. The Howison daughters, including Miss Emma—whose beauty some thought was unrivaled in the county—offered some cake and wine to the scouts, when the party was interrupted by two Yankees, who the scouts quickly took captive.

Allan Howison, "looking grave and very solemn," pulled the scouts aside with a serious matter. "Boys, have I not always treated you scouts as hospitably as I was able to do?" Upon receiving their answer in the affirmative, Howison surprised the scouts by making the men promise to kill the prisoners, noting that the local Federal commander had decreed that any house in which a member of his command was captured "should be immediately burnt." Pleading a defenseless family, including daughters, he would rather see the Yankees "disappear" than put his family at risk.

The scouts, having given their word, nevertheless found themselves unable to perform "so cowardly and cruel a deed," and let the Yankees live, after eliciting a promise not to tell of the incident accompanied by "more learned oaths than I ever heard of before or since." Prioleau Henderson could not imagine what tale the men told their superiors, but he felt that the Union soldiers had kept their word, "for Mr. Howison's house was never burned." Nor could he blame the man. "Mr. Howison was a good, moral, hospitable gentleman, but his first duty was to his unprotected family," wrote Henderson.

When not in Prince William scouting, Robert spent the winter months of 1863–1864 back with his regiment in camp. On January 10, he wrote his sister, noting that "I am now on the east side of R.R. crossed Thursday night in the snowstorm." Soon, Robert would be back in camp, awaiting better weather.

Camp life often consisted of a rather dull routine, but occasionally, the soldiers conspired to have a great deal of fun. In a lengthy, almost stream-of-consciousness letter home, Robert Towles described a snowball battle that involved many of his cavalry comrades, in heated competition with infantry camped nearby.

> As I have thrown about a thousand snowballs today, my arm is almost too sore to write, we have had a grand fight today which I will endeavor to describe—vis—…
>
> About nine o'clock this morning we were attacked by three brigades of infantry. We only have one reg[iment] the second, seven companies of the first and four of ours, the fourth, the

fight was opened by one brigade of inft., which is camped on the opposite side of the plank road from us, who charged into the camp of the second reg. The charge was gallantly met and repulsed and before we could get out to the edge of the woods to see what was going on the whole mass came scrambling back over the hill, pressed by the second the inft. sallied along the plank road behind the fence, the second regt. rallied and formed for a charge on the top of the hill about four hundred yards from and to the right of a hill where our company was collected as spectators. The second charged the inft. left flank which was slowly stubbornly giving way, just then your humble servant who was mounted, gave his horse to another man and proposed we should charge the inft. right flank. about twenty said they would follow and down we came like a tornado on the astonished infants. (Sargent Williams and I leading) routing the entire wing. Just then some of the first regiment reinforced the second and seeing us driving the right made one tremendous charge and routed the whole line. it was really a grand sight. We had about fifty mounted men and when the rout commenced they dashed in upon the scattered infantry with their arms full of balls taking numbers of prisoners. We drove them about half a mile to their camp where they received reinforcements and fought desperately for half an hour. I by this time was completely run down and sent back for my horse, mounted him and went through the rest of the fight as cav. I armed myself by reaching down from the side of my horse catch up some snow, make a couple of balls, pick out some inft. mounted officer who would be at the head of his men waving his hat, charge him, run him back through his lines and fall back for more ammunition. just then another brig[ade] of infantry came down the road which compelled us to fall back across it. Reinforced by a fresh brig[ade] the infants came on with doubled vigor and pressed us back to our camp where we fought for an hour and a half desperately during which time a third brig[ade] of inf. came in. they then numbered about five to our one yet we kept them all at bay. Our officers seeing we were fighting against such large odds, met the inft. officers under flag of truce and agreed to pick two hundred men on each side and let them have a fair fight in the open field. The arrangements were agreed to and the whole party passed through camp into a field back of camp and two hundred men were picked on either side. Major Breckenridge of the 2nd Cav. commanded our men and an infantry Col. commanded theirs. All noncombatants were cleared from the area, the contesting forces were drawn up in lines about a hundred yards apart, the word was given and the inft. colonel ordered a charge and the whole line dashed forward with a yell. The Cavalry line which were all dismounted stood perfectly firm, not a word was spoken until the infantry got within about twenty yards of them, the order was given to charge and the two opposing columns rolled together and as the huge gigantic wave rolled against the stubborn rock.

So with the infants for a moment all were observed in a cloud of snow, but only for a moment, the infants were routed the most complete stampede I ever saw, down a steep hill and over a deep wide ditch into which many tumbled headlong and others on top of them out of sight in mud and water. the inft. Lieut. Col., a Capt., a Lieut. many men were taken before they got across the ditch. Here another stand was made by the infantry and the fighting for a few minutes was tremendous—the lines were drawn up on opposite sides of the ditch, each cavalryman had his foot planted on the bank and stood as firm as a rock while the infantry under a tremendous shower slowly gave way until sufficient room was given for the cav. to jump the ditch, when the whole inft. lines broke again, the immense mass of inft. spectators standing in the rear along the edge of the woods seeing their fellows completely routed came down the hill with a yell determined to clear the field, then came our attack and about 150 well-mounted men charged them from all directions, some with haversacks and saddle blankets full up with snowballs and others with long switches cutting each side of their horses heads to prevent them from catching their bridles, charged through the mass spreading terror and confusion wherever they went. and the whole mass scampered off and have not since made their appearance. We followed them about a mile, caught many prisoners among them some of the higher officers.

When not engaging in such frivolity, the young cavalryman pined for home. "I have written several letters home lately but have not heard a word from you all since I left," wrote Robert. "You must sit down and write to me immediately. Tell me how Mother, Father, & Aunt Anna are getting and whether you, Jim and Churchill have stoped Shaking yet or not. I am afraid it will be some time before I will be able to send those mules down as we have orders now to turn over all captured property to the government. Give my love to all."

Spring of 1864 brought renewed campaigning, and in the Army of Northern Virginia, men knew that the coming year would bring desperate and perhaps decisive action. Every able-bodied soldier in the ranks would be needed for the anticipated struggle with the Army of the Potomac and the new Union general-in-chief, Ulysses S. Grant.

Writing his younger sister, Robert noted that there was now little likelihood that he would be allowed to visit the family in Lancaster County:

> You spoke in your letter of the furlough. I have been expecting, vain hope, no more furloughs are granted, I am too late, how I regret it, you say all my Soldier Cousins are at home. I would like to share their pleasures but Gen. Lee and duty say not and I must fight on, hope on that the day may soon come then we may meet in peace, I believe the day is not far distant. The war is almost over, I believe that before Christmas is passed if God sees fit to spare his life through the coming desperate struggle you will be able to greet your Soldier brother back from the war no longer a soldier, Oh sister what joy then will be ours, I can satisfy myself in my long and uncertain absence from you all. so how I look forward to that joyful day when I shall be once more clasped in the arms of the loved ones at home, No more a Soldier, a boy again. Dear Sister pray on, hope on, that that day may come that it may not be far distant.
>
> Then Sister in the midst of our joys how we will miss those loved ones who have gone to their blessed rest. Poor darling Rosa, poor dear Viv, yet they are happy and though we mourn their loss we should not wish them back to this dark and unhappy world. It is God's will, God is just, God is allwise, his will be done.

Soon, Robert's life as a bushwacker would come to an end, and he would be called back to permanent service as part of the regiment. The long-awaited, Overland Campaign of General Grant and the Union Army of the Potomac would require all available Confederate soldiers to defend Richmond.

CHAPTER THIRTEEN

A lonely brother's tears
The death of another brother

"With deepest distress, I write to tell you
that poor brother Jimmie is no more."

Letter to Rev. John Towles

U.S. Grant and staff planning the Overland
Campaign, Library of Congress

John Taylor Williams, 4th Virginia Cavalry,
Courtesy of the Manassas Museum System,
Manassas, Virginia

the
generals

Lt. Gen. Ulysses S. Grant,
Library of Congress

Towles family 'carte de visite' of
Gen. Lee

Marshall Weedon, 4th Virginia Cavalry,
Courtesy of the Manassas Museum System,
Manassas, Virginia

By the late spring of 1864, the new general-in-chief for the Union forces, Ulysses S. Grant, had one goal—to bring the war to a successful close. His predecessors had failed to do so, and war weariness was beginning to appear in Northern cities. President Lincoln had high hopes that he had at last found a commander up to the task. "Unconditional Surrender" (U.S.) Grant was now in charge.

Grant had been extremely successful in the Western Theater of the war, having engineered the fall of Vicksburg on the Mississippi and restoring Union fortunes in Chattanooga after Chickamauga. As a consequence, Lincoln gave Grant command of all the Union armies. With the new job went the three stars of a lieutenant general, a rank not held by any U.S. officer (except honorifically) since George Washington. In March 1864 Grant came to Washington, met Lincoln for the first time, received his promotion, and prepared for the spring campaign.

Grant shared Lincoln's strategic view, namely that capturing key points on a map and occupying Southern territory meant little as long as the Confederate army remained viable and in the field. Instead, his goal would be the destruction of General Lee's Army of Northern Virginia. Historian J. Edward Smith writes, "The clarity of his conception and the simplicity of his execution imparted a new dimension to military strategy. Grant ignored Southern cities, rail junctions, and other strategic points and concentrated on destroying the enemy army." Grant's instructions to his subordinate, the commander of the Union Army of the Potomac, George Gordon Meade, were characteristically simple: "Wherever Lee goes, there you will go also."

Grant refused to direct operations from Washington and decided to make his headquarters with the Army of the Potomac. He had good reason for doing so. The army was an established force that had engaged the Confederates on many occasions, albeit with little success. Except for its single defensive victory at Gettysburg, the Army of the Potomac had a record of stalemate or defeat, and it had never won a clear-cut offensive victory against Lee. The army had traditionally suffered from its close proximity to Washington, which made it strongly susceptible to political pressures in its deployment. The army had also been rife with intrigues and factions within its officer corps.

Simply stated, the Army of the Potomac needed Grant's on-the-scene direction far more than the other Union armies in the field. Grant had never met General Meade before his arrival in Virginia and did not know what to expect, but Meade impressed Grant by offering to step aside immediately if the general-in-chief wished to put someone in his place. Grant declined the offer and Meade remained in command. Even so, Grant exerted such close supervision over the Army of the Potomac that it quickly became known as "Grant's army."

Grant and Meade had two options: move right and try to get around Lee to the west; or move left, slipping through the Wilderness and getting around Lee to the east, forcing the Confederate commander to fight in the open. Eventually, they chose the direct route, through the Wilderness, where the lines of supply would be shorter and less vulnerable to the Confederate cavalry and to Mosby's partisan rangers. "The art of war is simple enough," Grant wrote in his memoirs. "Find out where your enemy is. Get at him as soon as you can. Strike him as hard as you can and as often as you can, and keep moving on."

On May 4, 1864, the Union Army of the Potomac crossed the Rapidan River into the Wilderness, the same tangled thickets where its previous commander, Major Gen. Joseph P. "Fighting Joe" Hooker, had been defeated by Robert E. Lee and Stonewall Jackson the year before at Chancellorsville. Lee's army was positioned some miles to the west, awaiting Grant's move. By crossing at the Rapidan, Grant opted for an "Overland Campaign" that hoped to turn Lee's right flank and compel him to retreat. Instead of retreating, however, the same day Lee responded in his characteristically aggressive manner, and early the next morning, he hurled his veteran troops against two Union corps as they struggled along the narrow lanes of the wilderness.

Grant's first encounter with Robert E. Lee ended on the evening of May 6, 1864. The fight was a brutal, two-day series of engagements that would become known as the Battle of the Wilderness.

Outnumbered nearly two to one (64,000 men against Grant's 119,000), Lee had wanted to force a battle in the Wilderness, where thick woods would dilute the Union numerical advantage and make it difficult for the Federals to use their numerous and well-trained artillery. During the next two days, he savaged the Union army with a sustained intensity Grant had not experienced in his previous campaigns. Those who had experienced it were not slow to offer advice. On the second day of the fighting one Union general told him, "General Grant, this is a crisis that cannot be looked upon too seriously. I know Lee's methods well by past experience; he will throw his whole army between us and the Rapidan, and cut us off completely from our communications." Usually taciturn, Grant permitted himself a rare show of annoyance. "Oh, I am heartily tired of hearing what Lee is going to do. Some of you always seem to think he is suddenly going to turn a double somersault and land in our rear and on both of our flanks at the same time. Go back to your command," he snapped, "and try to think what we are going to do ourselves, instead of what Lee is going to do."

The fighting in the wilderness cost the Union nearly 17,000 casualties; Lee, by contrast suffered no more than about 10,000. In earlier days, the Army of the Potomac would have retreated after such a battle to lick its wounds. Grant, however, decided simply to disengage and continue his effort to get around Lee's flank.

Early on the morning of May 7, Grant issued a directive to the Army of the Potomac, ordering Meade to "Make all preparations during the day for a night march to take position at Spotsylvania Court House." Unlike his predecessors, Grant was not deterred by losses or tactical defeats, and was determined to press the issue, "if it takes all summer." Clearly, this was a different type of Union commander than Lee was used to facing. After suffering for years from a chronic sense of inferiority, the Army of the Potomac found itself led by a man who never thought in terms of defeat and who did not lose his will to fight when confronted by casualties.

With the Fifth Corps of Gen. Gouverneur K. Warren leading the way, the Federals headed for Spotsylvania, ten miles southeast of the Wilderness and a strategically important junction, the control of which would place the Union army between Lee and Richmond. The army began moving during the evening of May 7, hoping to steal a march on the Confederates.

Rebel cavalry—including the 4th Virginia Cavalry—got there first. During the night of the seventh, Fitz Lee had dismounted his cavalry division and, using his men as infantry, had created rudimentary defenses of trees and rails across the Brock Road and stayed the advance of the enemy until joined by the Confederate First Corps under Richard Anderson. The Confederates had won the race to the critical crossroads, and both sides settled in for another engagement—one that was destined to last for the coming twenty days and that would result in some of most ferocious fighting of the war.

On May 9, Grant sent Gen. Philip H. Sheridan with his cavalry on what amounted to a raid, with the aim of destroying Lee's ammunition train, threatening the Confederate capital of Richmond and luring the Confederate cavalry into a decisive engagement. In response, Lee sent his peerless cavalry chief, Jeb Stuart, to intercept the Union cavalry. Sheridan succeeded on passing to Stuart's right and threatened Richmond, but Stuart gave chase, and at the Battle of Yellow Tavern on May 11, Stuart was shot by a dismounted Yankee cavalryman. He died soon after.

In a tribute to Stuart, General Lee observed:

> Among the gallant soldiers who have fallen in this war,
> General Stuart was second to none in valor, in zeal, and in

unflinching devotion to his country…The mysterious hand of an all-wise God has removed him from the scene of his usefulness and fame. His grateful countrymen will mourn his loss and cherish his memory. To his comrades in arms he has left the proud recollection of his deeds and the inspiring influence of his example.

The Confederacy mourned the loss of another of its heroes, but the action on May 9 had an even more tragic aspect for the Towles family. Shortly after dawn on the morning of May 9, when Sheridan had begun moving south, Wickham's brigade, including the 4th Virginia Cavalry, pursued and harassed Sheridan's rearguard. "It was hot and the roads were very dusty. To impede our pursuit, the fences on both sides of the road were set on fire and our march was through dust and smoke…", wrote William Wallace Scott of the Black Horse Cavalry.

Wickham attacked Sheridan at Jerrell's Mill as the Union cavalry was attempting to ford the Ta River. It is likely during this engagement that the Towles family lost another son.

A handwritten list of Company A casualties from the battle at the Museum of the Confederacy's Brockenbrough Library shows James Towles listed on May 9.

> Jas. H. Towles
> Killed in a dismounted charge against infantry near Spottsylvania C.H. on the morning of May 9th 1864. Buried at Kenmore, the residence of Mr. McKenney near the C.H.

The particulars of Jimmie's death are given some substance by an entry in the Confederate States of America Roll of Honour, written by Edgar Weir, a member of Company A of the 4th Virginia Cavalry. Weir was the son of a prominent slaveholding Unionist landowner in Prince William County, William Weir. The father was ambivalent to the Southern cause and believed that slavery should be ended by a gradual emancipation and exportation to Africa—an idea once espoused by Abraham Lincoln, among others. Like some other families, the Weirs were of divided loyalties. Edgar Weir, however, was "the most committed to the secessionist cause," and he was a proud member of the Prince William Company. Edgar was captured and paroled several times during the war, but survived to document exploits of Confederate soldiers for the Roll of Honor. He was the recipient of the United Daughters of the Confederacy Cross of Honour in 1902.

His entry for James Towles indicates that Jimmie was only thirteen when he had attempted to enlist. This is actually incorrect, inasmuch as James's birth date of October 19, 1845 would have made him fifteen at the start of the war. The Roll of Honour entry goes on to say that he was not an enlisted soldier ("being too young for Service") and was with the regiment "just staying around with the boys." The youngest Towles brother does have muster cards in the National Archives, however, and although he was quite young, he also was apparently determined to follow in his older brothers' footsteps. Far from being just a boy tagging along with his brothers, he had already been seasoned through scouting in Prince William and by enduring captivity at Point Lookout and exchange.

On May 9, Edgar Weir reported that James was one of a detail to hold horses for dismounted men, Weir said that Jimmy went to him, borrowed his horse and went into the charge with the mounted cavalrymen and was killed. "This shows," says the Roll of Honour chronicler, "like many other such instances, the spirit that animated the youth of the 'Sixties.'"

It was left to Robert Towles to inform his family of the loss of another soldier boy. In a letter penned shortly after the battle, Robert wrote his parents:

My dear Father

With the deepest distress, I write to tell you that poor brother Jimmie is no more. In a dismounted charge on Monday the 9th of May, he was instantly killed. We were fighting against infantry—The ball entering near the left corner of his left eye, lodging in his head.

My poor brother—he too is gone. I trust his soul is at rest with his Savior. It was a very warm day, & it was with the greatest difficulty I succeeded in bringing his body from the field. Two of my Company—whom I shall never forget, assisting me. Marshall Weedon & Taylor Williams. I got my horse, Marshall mounted and we laid brothers lifeless body across the horse in front of Marshall. All this was done under a heavy artillery fire. It seems a miracle we accomplished it, but we succeeded in bringing his poor body off. We then carried it back to the rear about two miles to a Mr. McKennys near Spotsylvania C.H. Who kindly furnished us with some strong good plank, and hired us a man to dig the grave. I was too distressed to do any thing, but the boys made a nice Coffin, nicer than I could expect, and I lined it with my shawl, made a pillow of his overcoat cape; and with his clothes buttoned around him, his hair nicely combed, the blood washed from his face, he looked very natural excepting the deep ugly wound in the side of his face. We buried him, a lonely brothers tears watered his grave, a lonely brothers prayers followed him.

This blow will fall most heavily on poor Mother. do Father try and console her, I fear she will never be able to bear up under the shock. My poor brother, so lately in full health, so full of life and now he is gone. It is Gods Will, we should try and not murmur, God must do what is right, let us all try and say "Thy Will Oh God be done

Jimmie is buried at Kenmore the residence of Mr. McKenny near Spotsylvania, C.H.

love to Aunt, Mother, Sister & brothers.

Your affectionate Son

Robert C. Towles

Kenmore Woods (historically known as Kenmore) survives today and is a Federal-style house with Colonial Revival additions on the National Register of Historic Places. The main dwelling house, approached by a long, tree-lined drive, was built in 1829. A compact early nineteenth-century house, it is an outstanding example of the architecture of rural plantation homes built at that time in Spotsylvania County. The prominent position of the property, astride two roads leading to the Spotsylvania Court House, during which the house was the command site of Colonel Walker of the First Corps artillery of the Army of Northern Virginia.

Although the owner of the main house during the 1860s was Mrs. H.C. Harrison, 378 acres of Kenmore had been sold to Addison L. McKenney and his wife Sally Ann (Beazley) McKenney. A "vigorous man in commerce," McKenney had overcome partial paralysis that crippled him for life. A Surgeon's Certificate of Exemption, dated February 1, 1865, described Addison as thirty-five years old and "exempt from military duty on account of hemiplegia." McKenney, with R.W. Colbert and George Collin, furnished provender for the Confederate army in 1862–1863. His other business interests included blacksmithing and sawmilling activities with his brother Edgar McKenney in Caroline County, all while living at Kenmore during the war.

During the Battle of Spotsylvania Court House, Confederate artillery had strengthened the area south of the town, expecting the infantry thrust through this route across the Massaponax Road. Kenmore is called "Frazier House" in written communications, but is referred to as the McKenney Place on both Confederate and Union maps. Two Civil War maps show trenches extending across the east end of the Kenmore property. It was, perhaps, to be expected that a great many soldiers who died during the battle would be buried nearby.

For the Towles family, however, only one grave mattered—that of a "mere youth" who followed his older brothers as they served their state and country… and who paid the ultimate price.

Spotsylvania would not be the last battle of the war, nor was it the most costly. But many have argued that it was among the most brutal fighting that took place during the conflict, and its savagery proved once again that, as General Grant's subordinate William Tecumseh Sherman had said, "War is hell."

CHAPTER FOURTEEN

Joyfully, Joyfully
The Battle of Trevilian Station

"He is more perfectly resigned than any one I ever saw…"

Sallie Conner

trevilian

Gen. George Armstrong Custer,
Library of Congress

Phil Sheridan and staff, Library of Congress

Gen. Wade Hampton,
Library of Congress

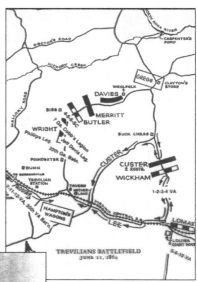

Trevilian battle map

Charge of the cavalry at the Battle of Trevilian Station (print)

As General Grant's overland offensive continued in the early summer of 1864, the cavalry of both the Union and Confederate armies increasingly came into play. In the aftermath of Gen. Jeb Stuart's death, command of the cavalry corps was initially undecided. Some felt that Robert E. Lee's nephew, Fitzhugh Lee, was closer to the mindset established by Stuart when it came to utilization of the Southern cavalry. Wade Hampton, a South Carolinian and aristocrat, was a gifted horseman, who had distinguished himself at Gettysburg and elsewhere, and had proven conspicuously brave. During the war, he had several mounts shot out from under him, and he was highly respected by his men. After some deliberation, Lee placed Hampton in overall command of the Confederate cavalry, with both Hampton and Fitz Lee commanding divisions.

After Spotsylvania and several subsequent lateral maneuvers, the Battle of Cold Harbor had brought an end to a month of bloody fighting in Virginia. The cost had been high on both sides. Since the 1864 campaign had opened, General Grant had lost more than 60,000 men, yet he had been unable to either destroy Lee's army or to take Richmond.

Stymied in his efforts to capture the Confederate capital directly, Grant decided to maneuver to capture Petersburg, Richmond's essential rail conduit. In order to take Petersburg, however, the Army of the Potomac would have to detach from Lee's army and move to the south side of the James River. Knowing that the Confederate cavalry continued to provide valuable reconnaissance to the Army of Northern Virginia, Grant had again decided to draw off Lee's cavalry by sending Gen. Philip Sheridan and two divisions of Union cavalry on a diversionary raid towards Charlottesville. Sheridan's force consisted of 9,300 Union cavalry with twenty pieces of horse artillery. Grant instructed Sheridan to destroy as much of the Virginia Central Railroad track as possible and to link up with another Union army under General David Hunter, who was working his way south through the Shenandoah Valley.

Sheridan's Union troopers left the Army of the Potomac on June 7 and headed west up the North Anna River toward Trevilian Station, a stop on the Virginia Central. Lee sent the cavalry divisions of Hampton and Fitz Lee in pursuit. The Confederate force consisted of approximately 6,500 cavalry. With Fitz Lee's division was Wickham's brigade, comprising the 1st, 2nd, 3rd, and 4th Virginia Cavalry, the latter including Robert Towles, erstwhile scout and the sole remaining Towles son in Confederate service.

Aggressively riding along interior lines, Hampton reached the Trevilian area on June 10, one day ahead of the Union cavalry. Rather than stand on the defensive, Hampton decided to attack the Federals at their camp. His division and Fitz Lee's took separate roads as they approached Sheridan's troops, and early on the morning of June 11, Hampton engaged one portion of the Federal cavalry in stubborn, dismounted fighting. Fitz Lee's division approached from the southeast, as part of what Hampton envisioned as a pincer movement that would trap Sheridan between the two Confederate divisions. Fitz Lee advanced tentatively, allowing a somewhat detached portion of Sheridan's force under Gen. George Armstrong Custer to take advantage of the gap between the two Confederate divisions and to capture Hampton's supply trains, 800 horses, and several horse artillery caissons. Much later, in post-war correspondence with his former subordinates, Hampton would criticize Fitz Lee for slowness in executing an attack that might have resulted in Confederate victory on the May 11. A Hampton biographer claimed that the plan of the battle was "frustrated by the failure of Fitz Lee's Division to advance in the manner ordered."

Whatever the facts of the matter, Custer was able to interpose his troops between the two Confederate divisions. By midday, however, Custer had been boxed in by Hampton's reserves under Gen. Thomas L. Rosser and as Fitz Lee committed his division against Custer's left and rear.

The developing situation resulted in a turn of events. Fitz Lee's troopers recaptured the spoils the Union cavalry had taken earlier, and also took Custer's own headquarters wagon along with his colored cook, Eliza Brown, sometimes referred to as "the Queen of Sheba." Eliza accompanied Custer's troops in the field, riding in what was described as a somewhat decrepit carriage, along with Custer's personal baggage. After her capture, the "Queen" later escaped and returned to the Union camp that night with Custer's valise. Custer's love letters from his wife, Libbie, were lost, however, much to the chagrin of the general and his wife.

Custer certainly had more to worry about than a missing servant and lost correspondence, however. Both Hampton and Lee converged on the "boy general" and forced him to take up a defensive position around Trevilian Station. Custer later noted, "From the nature of the ground and the character of the attacks that were made upon me our lines very nearly resembled a circle." Drawing a comparison to Custer's fate at Little Big Horn a dozen years hence, some have called this action "Custer's First Last Stand." In this instance, however, Custer managed to stave off his attackers, and Fitz Lee eventually fell back to Louisa Court House.

The second day of battle on June 12 was a hard-fought Confederate tactical victory, involving fierce dismounted fighting by both sides. As John Esten Cooke noted, "the Infantry are apt to sneer, and think, if they do not say it often, 'We do the hard fighting, the cavalry the fancy work!' or 'Here comes the cavalry, going to the rear, a fight is on hand."' Notwithstanding other continuous, demanding work such as reconnaissance, dismounted fighting certainly gave lie to such generalizations, and Trevilian Station was only one such example of that fact.

Finally, at 10 p.m. on the twelfth, Sheridan broke off the fight and returned his cavalry to the Army of the Potomac, having failed to unite with Hunter's army or to inflict any permanent damage on the Virginia Central Railroad. Confederate losses in the battle are not precisely known, but probably numbered near one thousand. Among the casualties was Robert Towles.

During the engagement with Custer's troops on the May 11, the 4th Virginia Cavalry had been part of Fitz Lee's clash with the Michigander. It is not clear whether Robert was wounded in the initial engagement or as part of the afternoon's efforts to retake the Confederate supply trains, but Robert and his company were likely involved in heated exchanges with Custer's troops throughout the afternoon, and during that time, Robert fell wounded. The diary of Horatio Nelson of Company A (Robert's company) noted the following:

> June 11, 1864 SATURDAY. On the road towards Gordonsville. Fell in with the Yanks 3 miles from the Ct. House. Had a considerable fight. Our company had 1 man mortally wounded and 3 severely. We lost in Rgt. Heavy. Captured 3 caissons good many mules and Yanks.

Another member of Company A, Thomas P. Ellicott, is buried at Oakland Cemetery near Trevilian, with an inscription on his headstone that he was mortally wounded "while bearing a comrade off the field." Perhaps that comrade was Robert Towles.

In any case, after the battle, Robert was among the wounded taken to the local hospital, where he and other Confederate casualties were treated.

Shortly thereafter, the family received news about Robert from a young woman who was among those tending the wounded. In a letter dated June 13 from Louisa Court House, Sallie Conner wrote Robert's mother Sophronia "with a heavy heart," complying with the young cavalryman's wish that she let his parents know the particulars of the wound he had suffered.

Sallie Conner is listed in the 1860 Federal Census as a young woman of twenty, which would have made her twenty-four by the time of the Battle of Trevilian Station. Like many other local women, she undoubtedly volunteered to tend to the many wounded soldiers from the battle.

"[Robert] was brought immediately here to the Hospital, where he has been well cared for I can assure you," wrote Sallie. "He is certainly very dangerously wounded, shot through the abdomen." While his wound was serious, Sallie thought there was a chance for Robert to recover. In any case, his state of mind was clear.

> He is more perfectly resigned than any one I ever saw, says he has always tried to live right, and is now resigned to the Will of the Lord, that all he cares to live for is to be a comfort to his parents… He seems very much afraid you will not be able to bear the shock of hearing he is so badly wounded. Says you have seen so much trouble since the War commenced. I have never seen anyone, in whom I feel a deeper interest, than I do in him, he is a noble boy.

A postscript for the letter added that Robert's friend, Lee Macrae, was with him, and that Robert "seems rather better" and was suffering very little. Regrettably, Sallie Conner's optimism was misplaced. On the June 16, Robert died.

News of Robert's wounding had spread to relatives in another unit. His cousin John William Chowning of the 9th Virginia Cavalry wrote in a diary entry for June 20 that he had started to Louisa Court House "to see Bob Towles who was very seriously wounded on Saturday." The next day, his diary notes, "Got to the C.H. in the evening and find that poor Bob is no more. I go to see Macrae and talk with him. I stay that night with Dr. Perkins." The next day, John William wrote his "Dear Aunt," Sophronia Towles, to report the sad tidings.

> I was down near the White House when I heard it. Our Brigade was not with the rest of the Cavalry after Sheridan but at Coal Harbor. As soon as the fourth Regt. got with us I went to Co. A and heard that Bob had been very seriously wounded. I immediately applied to Lieut. Ball to let me go to Louisa C.H. thinking I might possibly be of some service, but just before I got there I heard the dreadful news. He died on the 16th. Lee Macrae was with him all the time and gave him all the necessary attention. I have talked with him and also to the Miss Connor who (said he) did not suffer for anything at all. They did everything that ladies could do. I assured them and Lee Macrae that they would ever be remembered with gratitude for their kindness by all of the family.

"Poor Bob has nobly done his duty always and now he has died a triumphant death," wrote John William. "He said, 'Tell my mother and Father that the only thing I wish to live any longer for is to comfort them. I'm not afraid to die.'" Robert's cousin went on to say that the dying cavalryman had asked for a local minister to preach his funeral, even choosing the Bible text and hymn.

The Bible text was the parable of the talents, Matthew 25, verse 23: "His lord said unto him, "Well done, good and faithful servant; thou hast been faithful over a few things, I will make thee ruler over many things: enter thou into the joy of thy lord."

The hymn was "Joyfully, Joyfully," a now-obscure hymn found in a nineteenth century Shape-Note Tunebook. Shape notes are a music notation designed to facilitate congregational and community singing. The notation, introduced in 1801, became a popular teaching device in American singing schools. Shapes were added to the note heads in written music to help singers find pitches within major and minor scales without the use of more complex information found in key signatures on the staff.

The sentiments of the lyrics for "Joyfully, Joyfully" convey the wishes of a good Episcopal son to hasten home to heaven:

> Joyfully, joyfully, onward I move,
> Bound for the land of bright spirits above;
> Angelic choristers sing as I come,
> Joyfully, joyfully haste to thy home.
> Soon with my pilgrimage ended below,
> Home to the land of spirits I go;
> Pilgrim and stranger no more shall I roam,
> Joyfully, Joyfully resting at home.

Perhaps thinking of his siblings who had preceded him in death, Robert no doubt found solace in one particular verse of the hymn. "Friends fondly cherished have passed on before, Waiting they watch me approaching the shore. Singing to cheer me thro' death's chilling gloom, Joyfully, Joyfully, haste to thy home."

In his letter to his aunt, John William Chowning included a message for the Towles brothers' beloved younger sister. "Tell Ella to try to bear this with Christian fortitude, and to remember that Bob died a tryumphant death, and requested that all his friends would meet him in heaven. For that let us try." As for Robert's possessions—including his "account book" (the diary *Kept, While a Prisoner*) and "the book he captured" (the wallet from General Pope's headquarters tent)—John William indicated that all would be sent home to his grieving parents.

Other members of the family mourned, as well. Representative of this is a letter from J.L. (Jimmie) Ewell, another nephew of John and Sophronia Towles. Jimmie Ewell, like John William Chowning, was from Lancaster County, the ancestral home of the Towles family, and was also a member of the 9th Virginia Cavalry. From Cavalry Camp near Rheames Station in July, he wrote "painful lines" from "your devoted yet unworthy nephew."

> I have it from those that were with him that he had every attention that could be desired, more than this I learned he had bore his wound heroically never complaining & expressed no fears of death, even said his greatest care was for his dear mother. Dear Aunt yours for the past few years has been a hard life. An interesting daughter just budding into woman hood snatched away from earthly friends and winged her flight to join the Immortal choir in that bright world of eternal bliss, shurely this was hard to be borne, but God is just and with peaceful submission we should bear his visitations.

The letter conveyed throughout a religious certitude typical of the family, capturing the high regard in which the brothers were held—and their sacrifice in the service of cause and country.

> Three noble boys than whom moreso our country could not boast, One at a time in close succession are they called from us while nobly defending their cherished country, Life could not be lost in a nobler cause, their memory will long be cherished longest by those with whom they were best acquainted, their examples will be held up to others as a moddle, by which to shape their actions. To a careless observer it would appear that God had forsaken you but no My Aunt this is not the case, for "God chasteneth those he loveth". It sometimes looks strange that the vile sinner and worthless character is permitted to remain in the world apparently of no use to himself or benefit to mankind while the noble youth of the land are being snatch away by the ruthless hand of death, but we should remember that our finite minds cannot comprehend the workings of an all wise God "who moves in a mysterious way his wonders to perform", these

afflictions are with out doubt for some good purpose and while I deeply simpathize with you in your severe bereavement, I am fully persuaded all will work together for your eternal welfare, God grant that when he sees fit to call your now troubled spirit from this cold world of vice and immorality you may take your flight to bright mansions beyond the skies there meet to part no more with those who for the present are lost to you and join with them in giving eternal praise to him who doeth all things well.

As George Rable pointed out in his recent book, *God's Almost Chosen Peoples,* the thought of an eternal home embodied a "concrete picture of reunited families" gathered with their Lord. In this context, many who suffered from wounds or disease often articulated that they would *prefer* to die, in order to be once again with loved ones who had passed on. In her acclaimed book, *This Republic of Suffering,* Drew Gilpin Faust also discusses the concept of a "good death" and "triumphant" movement from an earthly vale of tears to a heavenly home. Certainly, the sentiments embodied in Robert's choice of funeral hymns and the content of letters to and from the family, are excellent examples of such a mindset.

A fierce, two-day struggle—the largest, all-cavalry battle of the Civil War—had ended in the retreat of the Union forces. Sheridan had failed to execute Grant's plans, but some put the best face possible on the result. Northern newspaper editor Horace Greeley, for example, in his book—ponderously titled—*The American Conflict: A History of the Great Rebellion in the United States of America, 1860-'65, its Causes, Incidents, and Results: Intended to Exhibit Especially its Moral and Political Phases, with the Drift and Progress of American Opinion Respecting Human Slavery, from 1776 to the Close of the War for the Union,* noted that Sheridan's raid "was less effective than had been calculated, because Gen. Hunter, who was expected to meet him at Gordonsville, had taken a different direction, leaving more foe's on Sheridan's hands than he was able satisfactorily to manage." Hampton's Confederates would certainly have agreed with that wry assessment.

After the battle, many of the wounded and dying were cared for in nearby homes and in the towns of Gordonsville and Louisa. Some of the wounded were sent to the Confederate receiving hospital at the Exchange Hotel in Gordonsville. Others who died in the town were buried in Oakland Cemetery, which a local historian noted "was begun after the battle." The cemetery was the last resting place for eighty-three unknown casualties as well as "for some whose names and companies were known and who had died in hastily established hospitals in the

Methodist Church and the Courthouse." It was there that Robert Towles was laid to rest.

As for the importance and complexity of the battle in which Robert gave his life, writing in 1909, Union cavalry Col. James H. Kidd wrote that "the planning and fighting of the battle, with its artful maneuvers and tactical strategems, have been compared to a game of chess. To my mind, no cavalry engagement of the Civil War had more points of resemblance to the moves of knights and pawns upon the chessboard than did the first day at Trevilian Station."

One of those so-called pawns was, of course, Robert Towles. His death was the last in a series of tragic events that would fundamentally change the Towles family. The young man's death may have been triumphant, but his passing would leave yet another hole in the fabric of a family already torn asunder by other losses.

No amount of consolation could obscure the fact that, in relatively quick succession, and in separate but documented tragic detail, the three Towles brothers had given "the last full measure" for their cause and comrades. What remained was how the family would endure and commemorate its losses.

Chapter Fifteen

The insatiate wretches
Yankee Raiders, a salt works, and "The Bonnie Blue Flag"

"They did anything to make life harder on us."

Reminiscence of a local
from the Northern Neck

Cannonball found at Chowning Ferry Farm

Sophronia Chowning Towles

U.S.S. Jacob Bell, Official Records of the Union and Confederate
Navies in the War of the Rebellion, Series 1, Vol. 5

the manor

View from Greenvale Manor

Union Sailor, Library of Congress

Sophronia Towles, the matriarch of the Towles family, spent her remaining years documenting and maintaining family memories and traditions, and among the most vivid was an incident that was both traumatic and somewhat ubiquitous in the Northern Neck during the Civil War.

> On the last day of June-64, the crew from a Yankey Steamer landed here; and after burning the barn, Cornhouses, Stables, etc. with all their contents, stripped the house of all the bed clothing, wearing apparel, eatibles, in fact everything they could find, excepting in my room. I managed to save most of my clothing, & the greater part of my Husband's & little boys'. Among other things which they took from me, were many treasured articles—more or less valuable—belonging to my dear dead children & which I kept in one trunk. Tho' I told them what & whose they were, the insatiate wretches would not even spare me these, even all their letters & worse than all the loving letter which dear Robert wrote us about poor dead Jimmie's death, with the lock of hair cut from his head after he was killed, and which I wished to preserve until my little boys were old enough to appreciate and read it—for themselves. That letter was all I had in relation to the dear childs death.

Sophronia went on to say that she would "try and copy it from memory for the especial benefit of my little boys should they live," and her reconstruction of that letter appears earlier in this manuscript.

The frustration of such extremely personal mementos being lost would remain with her throughout her life, and one Union ship, in particular, was the subject of Sophronia's ire. No doubt to ensure a vivid remembrance, she burned the memory of that ship into her surviving daughter's memory. "As a refugee," Sophronia wrote, "young Ella Towles suffered the fright and indignities afflicted by the crew of the Yankee gunboat *Jacob Belle* [sic] when she came into Greenvale Creek for supplies or to plunder."

Part of the dreaded Potomac Flotilla, the *U.S.S. Jacob Bell* was a 229-ton, side-wheel gunboat, built in 1842 at New York City for commercial employment. The U.S. Navy purchased her in August 1861, placing her in commission at that time under her civilian name. She served throughout the Civil War on the rivers along the Chesapeake Bay and would eventually be lost at sea in 1865 while being towed to New York.

The *Jacob Bell* was a veteran of incursions into the Northern Neck waters. Since the Potomac Flotilla's creation in 1861, the *Bell* and its sister ships had enforced a Union presence on the area. A typical report from the vessel dated July 15, 1863, listed "contraband goods" taken from the Rappahannock River area:

> SIR: I have the honor to report to you that on the 13th of this month, I landed near Union wharf, Rappahannock River, a force of 50 men, and captured the following contraband goods, etc., viz: Thirteen large flatboats (all engaged in blockade running), 32 barrels alcohol, 18 barrels whisky, 27 barrels (700 pounds) copperas, 14 barrels fine salt, 31 barrels soda, some rope, and machine belting. These goods were scattered over a space of 5 square miles, and I had to destroy all of them for want of transportation. I have also captured a large canoe (appropriated) and flatboat (destroyed), loaded with contraband goods, and have sent Acting Master's Mate R.L. Omensetter in charge of them with price lists to Washington.
> Very respectfully,
> G.C. SCHULTZE,
> *Acting Master, Commanding*

The *Jacob Bell* and other ships in the Potomac Flotilla were known to have used naval gunfire as part of their activities in the area. Between such bombardment and shore parties, few families in the Northern Neck felt safe. Local historian and author Miriam Haynie reports that "throughout the entire war the shoreline was systematically shelled and many houses were burned. A number of Federal naval officers confirmed that when private houses were used to shelter rebels or the home guard, they would be burned to the ground." Chowning Ferry Farm, an ancestral home owned by relatives of the Towleses, was one such house that was shelled. During excavations and construction of a septic system in the early 1980s, cannon balls were found in the front yard from such a bombardment.

The Gresham family's home in Lancaster County was another such target. Fortunately, Mr. Gresham's ill wife had been moved to an outhouse for protection, because a shell exploded in the room where she had been staying. "These piratical cruisers have bombarded so many unoffending private residences and have carried desolation to so many peaceful homes," noted a contemporary Confederate report.

Often, marines also landed from the ships. When that happened, destruction often followed, despite assurances to the contrary earlier in the war from Flotilla and U.S. Navy officers. During such actions, the character of the Northern marines was almost always unfavorably commented upon. One woman declared that the Northern invaders were recruited "from thieves and cut-throats released from jail," and another stated that they were being gathered "from the riffraff, the offscourings of the cities and the 'scum of Europe.'"

A special target of the Union raiders was local salt production. The Northern embargo meant that the South had to produce its own salt, and even though salt mines existed in the South, mining and transportation of the substance was difficult and oftentimes impossible. Large quantities of salt were needed for preserving meat, fish, butter, and other perishable foods, as well as for curing hides. To produce salt for local consumption and perhaps for transport to Confederate forces elsewhere, local salt works were established in discreet locations, usually on creeks or tributaries that had access to salt water.

The destruction of such salt works became a major objective for the Potomac Flotilla and was deemed an essential component of the Union Navy's effective restriction of Confederate industry. Salt works, providing as they did both a foodstuff and an invaluable preservative, were a constant target for the fast-strike Union boat expeditions aimed at drying up the source of intended supplies for southern armies and communities. In the fall and winter of 1862, the Official Records document several preemptive actions against local salt works. A typical entry was as follows:

> *Rappahannock River, October 9, 1862.*
>
> SIR: I most respectfully take the liberty of reporting to you that…this morning I observed a large smoke about 6 miles above where I lay when you were down here. I immediately got underway and proceeded up the river, and found it to be a large, extensive salt works, consisting of five large boilers, and attended to by negroes. They informed me that they had made a great quantity of salt, and that their master takes it to Richmond, and that he was at present off with some, to some place. So I destroyed all the boilers and tore the place down.
>
> I remain, very respectfully, your obedient servant,
> HUGH H. SAVAGE,
> *Acting Master, Commanding.*

Even relatively small salt operations drew the notice of the Flotilla. "Pa told me the Yankees would come around and steal and break up everything they could find. They would even break up our brine pots," wrote a local man. "Most everybody had cast-iron pots that were used to boil salt water in, and when the water evaporated out it would leave salt in the bottom of the pot. That's the way the old people around here got salt. So, the Yankees would go around and break up all these pots. They did anything to make life harder on us."

Other salt operations were on a much larger scale. These involved collecting water from the Rappahannock River in wooden troughs and allowing it to evaporate. Larger salt works sometimes employed vats and tanks as well. One such facility—according to family lore—was started by Rev. John Towles. It, too, attracted the attention of the Potomac Flotilla.

In "The Reminiscences of Rectors at St. Paul's Church, Haymarket, Virginia," the section on Reverend Towles describes how, after fleeing with his family to his native Lancaster County, John Towles found sanctuary at the old Church of St. Mary's White Chapel, where he had been baptized, confirmed, and married. The church needed a rector, and he gave that service during the time he and his family were in Lancaster. The report also tells of how he "greatly helped the people" by establishing a salt works, extracting salt from the Rappahannock River tidewater.

It must have been this salt works that became the target of the expedition by the Potomac Flotilla to the Rappahannock River in late June 1864, and it was the impetus for the raid that Sophronia Towles recalled so bitterly. The salt works in question were apparently established on Chilton's Creek (not Shelton Creek, as indicated in the Official Reports, there being no such named creek in the area). Chilton was a family name, and likely the property in question was owned by the cousins of the Towles.

Towles family tradition, as well as Federal Naval records, document the matter. "The Yankees destroyed his salt-works that had proved such a blessing to so many people," wrote Sophronia in a diary entry. Reports of the action in the Navy's Official Records are more voluminous.

Destruction of salt works in Shelton Creek, Virginia, June 30, 1864.
Report of Commander Parker, U. S. Navy, commanding Potomac Flotilla.
U. S. S. ELLA,
Potomac Flotilla, July 6, 1864.

SIR: I have the honor to inform the Department that on the 30th ultimo an expedition sent to Shelton's Creek, on the Rappahannock

River, Virginia, by Acting Volunteer Lieutenant Hooker, succeeded in destroying a salt works recently established there, with its evaporators and tanks.

A number of buildings connected with the works, with carts, wood, and grain were burned.

I am, sir, very respectfully, your obedient servant,

FOXHALL A. PARKER,

Commander, Commanding Potomac Flotilla.

Hon. GIDEON WELLES,

Secretary of the Navy.

* * *

Report of Acting Volunteer Lieutenant Hooker, U. S. Navy, commanding First Division Potomac Flotilla.

U. S. S. COMMODORE READ,

Rappahannock River, Virginia, July 1, 1864.

SIR: I have the honor to report that from information which I had received I became convinced that within a short time extensive salt works had been established on the Rappahannock, and consequently started yesterday to look for them, having in company the *Bell* and *Freeborn.* During the afternoon I sent Acting Master Arthur, with three armed boats, to examine Shelton's Creek near the Corrotoman, and he there discovered the salt works, built in an excavation which completely hid them from view. There were several large evaporators and tanks, and the negroes there stated that the works would make 75 bushels of salt per day; that they had been in operation about three weeks, and were at work for the Confederate Government.

In connection with the works was a large stable, a granary containing about 200 bushels of corn, a number of wagons and carts, about 100 cords of wood, and several flatboats, used to carry the salt across the river; that there were also a few barrels of salt. The evaporators and tanks were broken up, and all the buildings, grain, carts, wood, etc., burned. The boats also were destroyed. The horses, 12 in number, the negroes said, had been taken away when they saw our boats approaching.

Very respectfully, your obedient servant,
EDWARD HOOKER,
Actg. Vol. Lieut., U. S. Navy, Comdg. First Div. Potomac Flotilla.
Commander F. A. PARKER, *U. S. Navy,*
Commanding Potomac Flotilla.

* * *

Report of Acting Master Arthur, U. S. Navy, commanding *U. S. S. Thomas Freeborn.*

U. S. S. FREEBORN,
Potomac Flotilla, June 30, 1864.

SIR: In obedience to your order I took two armed boats from this vessel, accompanied with one from the U. S. S. *Commodore Read,* and landed at Shelton's Creek, about 30 miles from the mouth of the Rappahannock River, where I found an extensive salt works, six large kettles containing 30 gallons, and a large vat or tank containing about 150 gallons of water. The construction was entirely hidden from the river, a place having been cut in the bank for its erection.

I also found a large quantity of grain, agricultural implements, and tinner's tools. As I had no means of getting them off, I set fire to the buildings and burned them. The salt works I entirely destroyed, with about 100 cords of wood which had been hauled there for the purpose of making salt.

Information I received from the negro that attended the works was that he could make 75 bushels of salt per day, which was conveyed across the river in boats and sent to Richmond.

It had been in operation only three weeks.

Very respectfully, your obedient servant,
W. A. ARTHUR,
Acting Master, Commanding.
Acting Volunteer Lieutenant EDWARD HOOKER,
U. S. S. Commodore Read.

At the time of the expedition to destroy the salt works, the *USS Jacob Bell* and the *USS Freeborn* apparently also offloaded marines near Greenvale, where the Towles family lived. Whether this was because they had connected Reverend Towles to the salt production or merely because Greenvale was a convenient target remains unknown. Ostensibly, the landing party was looking to capture guerrillas in the area.

The log abstracts of the two ships give little insight into the actions allegedly taken on June 30.

Abstract log of the *U. S. S. Thomas Freeborn*, March 22, 1863, to June 17, 1865.

June 30—At 2:45 p.m. sent two armed boats ashore; destroyed salt works, grain, agricultural implements, etc.

July 3—At 9 p.m. came to anchor in Dividing Creek. Sent 10 men and 1 officer on an expedition with the *Read's* and *Fuchsia's* men in charge of Acting Master W. T. Street.

July 4—At 10 p.m. men returned from expedition.

Abstract log of the *U. S. S. Jacob Bell*, March 8, 1863, to May 13, 1865.

June 23—Off Jackson Creek, watching for signals from shore. From 4 to 8 a.m. embarking men from shore. Brought off six prisoners. Got underway at 6:30; proceeded out of the river; went alongside of the *Commodore Read*; delivered one horse and six prisoners.

July 13—At 2:20 p.m. made fast to the guard ship at St. Inigoes; took on board a 30-pounder Parrott gun.

Neither abstract seems to show much. The *Freeborn's* does mention the action against the salt works, but the *Jacob Bell's* has a large gap in its coverage, including for June 30. The actual logbook of the *Jacob Bell* survives in the archives of the Library of Congress and sheds some limited additional light on the activities of the Potomac Flotilla at the end of June 1863.

For the period in question—late June 1864—the entry for in the *Jacob Bell's* log for June 30th says simply:

> Passed Smith's Point, Dividing Creek, up the River with *Freeborn*.
> Came to anchor abreast of wharf.

No mention of marines being offloaded, raiding parties, or any other action of significance appears for dates either before or after the thirtieth. All in all, such an entry is the equivalent of "nothing special happened."

One might infer that the relative lack of information in either the abstract or actual logs reflects turning the proverbial blind eye to actions against Southern civilians. The entries certainly contain much less detail than was required by the U.S. Navy. The department's Bureau of Navigation in a General Order dated January 19, 1863, had stipulated that log books for each vessel be kept "strictly in accordance with the following instructions: 1) State of weather in general terms; 2) All movements of the vessel…with such brief remarks of all occurrences as will render perfectly intelligible the service performed by the vessel; 3) Any exercises; 4) All circumstances of engaging the enemy; and 5) If boats or goods are taken and destroyed, state the reasons why."

In any case, the log of the *USS. Jacob Bell* perhaps is representative of how infrequently (or inconsistently) vessels in the Potomac Flotilla adhered to this order. Likely the officers simply chose not to document what must have become a commonplace occurrence by 1864—the punishment of Southern citizens and sympathizers.

What *is* clear is that such activity *did* happen and perhaps on a regular basis. "The steam transports came into the mouth of the Rappahannock and the crews from both vessels went on shore [in Lancaster County] and robbed the houses on shore, breaking into women's trunks, taking their jewelry and clothes, and taking their beds away with them," wrote another report. Such stories certainly dovetail with what Towles family tradition has documented at Greenvale.

While Home Guard troops sometimes responded to such attacks, oftentimes the local populace was at the mercy of the raiders. In the case of the Towles family, Sophronia chose to resist in her own way. Outraged by the destruction of her family's personal effects and property, and fresh from receiving the news of her son Robert's death, she angrily confronted the Union marines who were destroying her family's property. "She (Sophronia) defied the Yankee marines from the ship *Jacob Belle* [sic], singing 'The Bonnie Blue Flag' in the face of their reprehensible actions," noted a family diary.

Sophronia's choice of songs was likely not without purpose. Its lyrics and history were intertwined with the Southern cause, and "The Bonnie Blue Flag" had a unique Southern heritage in both origin and symbolism. Originally displaying a five-pointed star on a field of blue, which symbolized fellowship, the flag dates back to the early 1800s, when the U.S. government was encouraging American landowners in Southern states to rebel against Spain, which controlled the frontier territories. It was essentially, even then, a symbol of rebellion.

In February of 1861, several Southern states that had seceded from the Union met in Montgomery, Alabama, and formed the Confederate States of America. On the day when Jefferson Davis was elected president of the Confederacy, a large flag with a single white star on a field of blue was raised as both a symbol of fellowship amongst the seceding states, but also as a symbol of rebellion against the Union. Upon the unfurling of the flag, one observer waved it with the exclamation, "The Bonnie Blue Flag." In the audience, a traveling showman, Harry McCarthy, was inspired to write the rousing song of the same name.

Soon, another flag was designed for the Confederacy, but the Bonnie Blue Flag, though never officially adopted, remained popular throughout the war because of the song. It gradually became a recognized banner of independence for the Southern states, and the song was considered by many to be the unofficial national anthem of the Confederacy, more popular than even "Dixie" or the little known official National Hymn of the Confederacy, "God Save the South."

It has been said that during the occupation of New Orleans during the war, Union Gen. Ben Butler made quite a profit by fining every man, woman, or child who sang, whistled, or played the tune on any instrument. He also arrested the local publisher and destroyed copies of the sheet music. The tune for the song was borrowed from the old song, "The Irish Jaunting Car," and is still heard today as the fight song for Georgia Tech University.

We are a band of brothers
And native to the soil
Fighting for our liberty
With treasure blood, and toil
And when our rights were threatened,
The cry rose near and far
Hurrah for the Bonnie Blue Flag
That bears a single star!

Refrain:
Hurrah!
Hurrah!
For Southern rights, hurrah!
Hurrah for the Bonnie Blue Flag
That bears a single star.

"We all loved to sing and a merry time we had around the piano," noted diarist Nannie Brown Doherty in her unpublished manuscript, "Some Recollections of the Civil War." "One of our special favorites was 'The Bonnie Blue Flag.' O, the zest with which we sang, 'Hurrah, Hurrah, for Southern Rights, Hurrah!'"

The song lost some of its popularity when, late in the war, its lyricist, Harry McCarthy, abandoned the South and moved to Philadelphia. The song did remain popular among Confederate veterans after the war, however—a remembrance of fellowship with family, friends, and acquaintances, and a symbol of rebellion. One Northern Neck woman remembers that, years after the war on Memorial Day, Southern school children would practice the song for weeks. "When we were children, we would [not] have even considered putting a rose or flower on a Union grave," she noted. After her experience at Greenvale—and having lost three sons in Confederate service—Sophronia would no doubt have agreed. No amount of defiant singing would bring back her "noble boys," however.

Chapter Sixteen

The Sulphur Spring Academy
Arson at a school for Freedmen

"Thus perished the subject of many hopes and prayers and toils."

Southern Churchman
Sept. 13, 1866

news

SOUTHERN CHURCHMAN.

The Gospel of Christ

Communications.

Letter from Bishop Meade.

To the Editor of the Southern Churchman.

Yours,
WILLIAM MEADE.

The Church Monthly.

The "Southern Churchman," Episcopal Diocesan newsletter

In April 1865, General Lee surrendered the remainder of the Army of Northern Virginia to General Grant at Appomattox Court House. Days later, Richmond had fallen and the Civil War was over. The South braced itself for Reconstruction, and both sides began the process of recovery from a conflict that had resulted in as many as 750,000 deaths.

For those Southerners who had become refugees further south, it was time to try to rebuild their lives. Following the war, thousands of refugees returned to find their former homes in ashes, only blackened brick chimneys still standing to remind them of happier days. Now and then, former refugees discovered their homes ransacked and mutilated, but still livable. Even the trip home, however, was often a tortuous, desperate journey.

John Towles was one such former expatriate who had decided to return home. "Hearing that the enemy had left 'Vaucluse,' and feeling homesick for his old parish, his beloved parishioners and his home, he came back to Prince William…and again took up his ministerial work," reported an Episcopal journal.

The scene that greeted him and his family upon their return must have been shocking. A war diary of an Alabamian on picket duty at Kelly's Ford (not far from Prince William) noted that "the country round about [is] one vast field of destruction and devastation. Where once elegant, happy homes stood, bare chimneys rear their tall forms sentries over this cruel waste, halls that once resounded to the merry laughter of happy childhood, now reecho to the mournful whistling of the autumn winds. Everything we see is a memento of the relentless cruelty of our invaders."

Another citizen passing through the Culpeper area observed, "The whole country is a widespread desolation, as far as man could destroy. Houses that were vacant, barns, stables, fences, enclosures of graveyards, whether stone walls, brick or wood, with much of the timber, were all swept away, and the country which one rejoiced and blossomed as the rose was left a wild waste. Those of our people that remained and had encountered the storm, were stripped of everything but house and land—all their horses, mules, and stock of every description, with even the poultry of the country, were swept away. Thus poor and peeled, they are now struggling for bare subsistence." The writer could easily have been talking about Brentsville and Prince William County.

Brentsville, which before the onset of the Civil War had grown to include forty houses, fifteen taverns and inns, a church, as well as the courthouse, jail, and, lerk's office, was a shadow of its former self. During the war, Federal details had been sent to salvage bricks (for an unnamed general) from the courthouse and clerk's office. One such procurer noted that his men "commenced at the top [of the Courthouse] to get bricks, beginning with the chimneys and working down, while with the clerk's office, they commenced at the bottom and worked up." Valuable county records—"some of great antiquity" and including documents signed by George Washington when he was president—were found strewn on the floor of the courthouse "fully 2 feet deep." A Union officer noted wryly that "when they next begin to govern Prince William County, it is thought that they will have to commence their county records where the war left off, and it is hoped that they will appoint a county clerk who will take better care of his papers in the future."

Another passing Union officer had noted in 1864 that he "came to Brentsville, examined the place, found 5 houses occupied, including the jail. But two men reside in the town; the Courthouse has but a part of the roof remaining on; the houses are generally in ruins." Not much had improved by the time John Towles returned, and his parish had suffered as well.

> He found his town churches dismantled and indeed largely wrecked by the war. They had been used as hospitals and barracks...In 1865 there was nothing left of St. James Church, at Brentsville, except the walls and roof. The building had been stripped of windows, doors and floor, and was used for a stable.
>
> The building was partially restored through Rev. Towles' efforts and he was assisted in the work by the people of Brentsville, "and especially by Mr. Allen Howison, whose family was among the few Episcopal families left in the community." Windows, doors and floor were partially restored, and "the building was occasionally used by Mr. Towles and other ministers of the Piedmont Convocation...."

The damage at St. Paul's in Haymarket had been extensive. After the first Battle of Manassas (Bull Run), Confederate authorities had removed anything from the church that "might interfere with it being used as a hospital." And after the second Battle of Manassas, the Church was once again used as a hospital, this time by the Federals, who "left only the walls standing." Pews and pulpit had been used for firewood. Windows and doors were gone, and it was said that horses were stabled in the sanctuary. As one local noted, the "despot's heel" had been felt at St. Paul's, as it had on the floor of many a church in Virginia.

Few things were off-limits during the occupation. A wartime diary noted that, in the winter of 1863, the Yankees in Warrenton needed wood to burn, and since crosses in the cemetery were convenient, they were used for firewood.

In many cases—including Reverend Towles's church in Haymarket—sanctuaries had been used as stables. This common practice brought widespread condemnation after the war. The Historical Magazine of the Protestant Episcopal Church decried "what appears to have been a settled policy of the Federal forces as they overran seceded states—a policy of destruction far beyond the needs of an invading army." It was, of course, a recognized military necessity to use any available building, even a church, as a field hospital to take care of the wounded during a prolonged campaign. "But why, in a climate as mild as that of Virginia," wrote the magazine, "should it have been deemed a military necessity to destroy the interior of a church building in order to use it as a stable for army mules and horses?" Examples cited were tearing out of pews, the destruction of pulpits and chancels, and even the tearing down of ancient tablets on the wall above altars.

The names of soldiers from different regiments were often scratched into plastered walls that survived. Once such example cited "remembrances" left by members of the 8th Illinois Cavalry (Robert Towles's old adversaries), the 51st New York Volunteers, the 48th PA, and 86th Mass, and others. Such "shameful desecration" was often the rule, rather than the exception. The churches that John Towles had served so faithfully in antebellum Prince William County were perfect examples of this type of desecration.

Notwithstanding the damage—and the lack of resources to do much about it—John Towles did his best to minister to the local congregation. The intrepid clergyman preached in schoolhouses and in private homes, mirroring what was a common practice during the occupation, when confiscations and destruction of churches had resulted in a deprivation of public worship. "We worshipped as the primitive Christians did, in our own houses," wrote one parishioner.

The Episcopal diocesan newspaper, the *Southern Churchman,* dealt primarily with matters pertaining to the Protestant Episcopal Church in Virginia. Each issue, however, contained articles and some news of general interest to the church at large. One such article sheds some light on matters that would soon lead to Reverend Towles taking his family north to live. Writing from Catlett's Station in Fauquier County on September 13, 1866, in a column titled "Prince William County," John Towles explained how he sought to reestablish his churches after the war.

> My two churches, as you know, St. James in Brentsville,
> and St. Paul's in Haymarket, were destroyed by the war, nothing
> remaining but the walls and roofs. Knowing that nothing could

be done towards rebuilding them, for the sum of $2,000 each would be required, I undertook to repair a small building, near my house, known as 'The Sulphur Spring Academy,' which also had felt the desolating hand of war, nothing being left of it except the wooden frame and the roof. I thought if I could only fit up this little building, it would answer as a place of worship in inclement weather, for we had no place of preaching other than the grove or woods, and [it] would also serve as a schoolhouse, where I could educate my two little boys (all that are left to me of five sons by the war), and the children of my neighbors, there being no school or school-house within a circuit of four miles around me.

Having been unable to get more than a portion of the anticipated cost by subscription or otherwise, Reverend Towles received some money from Bishop Johns of the Virginia Episcopal Diocese and a donation of $100 each from "two benevolent ladies in Maryland."

I resolved to go through with the undertaking, and succeeded by doing, on leisure days, all the carpenter's work with my own hands, unskilled and untrained as they were to such a task, and by straightening myself in my circumstances, which were already narrow enough, the work was finished. Comfortable sittings provided for the congregation as a house of worship, and every convenience of desks, etc. afforded to the scholars as a place of worship.

With church services already established in the building, plans were made for school to begin the following September.

"But, sad to relate, on the night of Thursday last, the 2rd instant, the building was laid in ashes by the hand of an incendiary," wrote Reverend Towles. "Thus perished the subject of many hopes and prayers and toils."

What Reverend Towles noted as "the saddest part of this affair" was that he believed the motive behind the arson was that the school was to have included children of freed blacks.

I had given notice of preaching by myself to the freedmen on Sunday in the month, and the opening of a Sunday-school for them, under my own care, where an effort was to be made to teach all, young and old, to read their Bibles. Soon I received advice from one young man, and a kind of angry warning, rather than advice, from another, not to preach to the freedmen in the building and not to open a Sunday school for them.

With the support of the majority of the church's Board of trustees and "knowing that I was engaged in God's work," Reverend Towles paid no additional attention to the dissenters, other than to calmly argue the point with them and to "bring them to look at the matter in its true light." Some may have been struck by the irony of an Episcopal rector, who had lost three sons fighting for the Confederacy, and who had provided his own best efforts to support the cause, struggling so mightily to establish spiritual resources for newly free blacks. John Towles certainly felt no such moral conflict.

With a good conscience, and feeling that I was actuated by the purest motives, I put my trust in God, and went forward. I had held one service in the building for the freedmen; had organized the Sunday school; secured teachers and distributed a number of donated primers, spellers, and Bible readers. The Sunday school was to have met in the building for the first time on Sunday the 26th—hence the burning.

Despite the tragedy, Reverend Towles continued the Sunday school for freedmen on his own premises. "These, too, may be endangered," he wrote, "if no effort be made by the authorities to ferret out the incendiary and bring him to punishment at the hands of the law; but I feel that I have put my hand to God's work and must leave consequences to Him."

From the Episcopal Church's perspective, the issue of educating and preaching to blacks was controversial before and during the war, and became even more so after the conflict and the freeing of the slaves. While the Northern and Southern segments of the church had reunited with little controversy (and apparently little rancor) after the war, certain topics—such as slavery and race relations—continued to divide the church. Evidence of such a divide can be found among columns in the *Southern Churchman* and in publications such as the *Richmond Times* that routinely debated the issue after the war, with polemic positions taken on both sides of the issue. No doubt such divisions reflected a wider societal schism that would play out over the course of Reconstruction and into the twentieth century and the Civil Rights movement.

"The future of the Negro is not encouraging," wrote one columnist. "What with their laziness, their carnality, and their superstitions, we fear unless the Church makes *superhuman* exertions, their race is well nigh run in this country." The author continued with lurid accounts of "idol-dances" and the substitution of African pagan traditions for Christianity, and posited that Bishop Johns and the church had better "do something" to address the situation.

A slightly less alarmist article reprinted from the *Richmond Times* in October 1866 discussed "Religious instruction of the Negroes" and reported a ground-breaking address by the Bishop concerning the issue.

> It is proper that I should remind you of the fact that, by the action of the Federal Government, several millions of slaves have been suddenly set free, and are left among us, a potent power for good or evil, in connection with the destinies of this country; and further, that the character of their influence must be determined by their own character, which, under God, depends on their moral and religious education, for which a large measure of responsibility must rest upon us.

Ultimately, by resolution of the Diocesan Council in Richmond, Virginia, a committee of three clergy and three laymen was charged with overseeing the effort to encourage such instruction. Further, a resolution was passed that supported the creation of separate congregations for colored members of the church, sanctioning the creation of such congregations' vestries, wardens, and ministers. All such efforts were intended to encourage the advancement of the freedmen's intellectual, moral, and religious improvement. In hindsight, it remains unclear whether evolving contemporary perspectives viewed religious instruction for freedmen as simply an attempt to "civilize" the race or whether pundits were advocating for strict social control. Most likely, they were simply struggling with a radically changing social landscape. A brave new world now confronted clerics and laypersons alike. At least the church recognized the magnitude of the challenge and the opportunities it presented. "Thus, the important work is inaugurated," noted the *Southern Churchman*. Unfortunately for Reverend Towles, the blessings of the church had failed to sway certain elements of the local Prince William populace.

Reverend Towles noted that his preaching to both whites and blacks was entirely gratuitous. "I neither wish nor expect to receive any pecuniary aid for preaching the Gospel to the community in which I live, impoverished, like myself, by the war." He went on to ask, however, for aid from his friends in the Church to rebuild the Sulphur Springs Academy and to put up a small house on the lot for a family that might provide protection for the building.

A December 1866 entry in the *Southern Churchman's* "Church Intelligence" acknowledged receipt of contributions from various donors towards the rebuilding of the Sulphur Spring Academy as a "Freedmen's Sabbath School." The list included Episcopal Bishop Johns and "Old Dal," the Rev. E.A. Dalrymple, who had taught Vivian Towles at the Episcopal High School and who had sent money to Robert Towles in Old Capitol Prison.

In April of the following year, the newspaper included a brief note in a list of miscellaneous church business: "The Rev. Mr. Towles of Prince William, has been called to a parish in Prince Georges County, Md., and will probably accept." On advice from his Bishops Meade and Pinckney, John Towles had decided to take his young family away from his pre-war home and settle in an area that was not devastated by the conflict nor imbued by hatreds of race and sectionalism. Perhaps he had also come to fear for the safety of his family after the threats and arson connected to the Sulphur Spring Academy.

Not long after, Reverend Towles and his family moved to Accokeek, Maryland, where he took the position of rector for Christ Church, St. John's Parish. He would serve as its rector for the next eighteen years until his death in 1885.

Back in Prince William, a new rector took up the task to rebuild St. Paul's. Records show that "the first minister to serve the church after the war" was the Rev. William A. Alrich, who apparently took over the parish when John Towles moved to Maryland in early 1867. Alrich was originally from Delaware, but had served in the Confederate army. He found the Haymarket church in "ruinous" condition. "The village had been burned, with the exception of four houses, and the whole stretch of surrounding country had been devastated. Not a family, high or low, but had suffered and lost." The new rector at once began to try to raise funds. That year, it was reported that the congregation raised $600 to rebuild the gutted church, added new pews, repaired walls and floors, and replaced other missing items. The first service in the renovated church was held on September 1, 1867.

Although there are no surviving records of communication or collaboration between Reverend Towles and the new rector in Prince William, the former apparently retained an interest in his old parish, even after he accepted the call to Maryland. In June 1867, an article in the *Churchman* had acknowledged additional contributions to the Sulphur Springs Academy fund, including small amounts from Prince William neighbors such as Miss Stella King. A disclaimer noted, "As this is not an Episcopal school, it is not necessary for us to publish the proceedings of the Board of Trustees. We need only say, that the Board has given Mr. Towles their receipt for all the money he has collected and pledge themselves to use the schoolhouse for the purposes for which it was built."

The school may have been reconstituted after Reverend Towles and his family departed. The book *Yesterday's Schools* notes that the first school in the southern part of the Brentsville District was located at "Sulphur Springs/Towles Gate/Vancluse [sic]" and was "probably located in a rented building" until the Brentsville District School Board built a permanent schoolhouse in 1877. By then, Reverend Towles had moved to Accokeek, Maryland. The new school was named the Vancluse (or VanCluse) School, "although the origin of that name is unknown." Could this have been a modification of the name of the original Towles homestead? It seems likely, inasmuch as the school history indicates that Towles' Gate was simply a way to refer to the school by its location in the community, and an annotation to the entry speculates that Reverend Towles may have lived nearby and given his name to Towles' Gate. In 1890, the name of the schoolhouse was changed from Vancluse to Hazelwood, the name of the nearby antebellum farm at the site of the old Truro House, which had been destroyed during the war. Perhaps because the Towles family was long gone by that time—and the institutional memory of the area so disrupted by the war and its aftermath—that in the long term, the new name had come to mean more to the community than the Towles connection.

Leaving Prince William and Virginia behind must have been wrenching for the Towleses, but Accokeek also was an opportunity for a fresh start, far from the desolation of their home county after the war.

The sons of Rev. John and Sophronia Towles
Memorial and Remembrance

"Your letter has dispelled that fond hope of mine that my friend like myself had passed through this struggle unscathed..."

James P. Mosher

Ella Towles Poole

E.A. Poole

family

Churchill Towles and family

Grave marker for Vivian, Robert,
and James Towles, Oakland
Cemetery, Louisa, Virginia

Vermont Marble Company
Obelisk

Robert E. Lee (E.A. Poole Portrait)

In addition to the challenges of attempting to restart his ministry in Prince William County and to rebuild the family fortunes in the aftermath of the war, John Towles and his wife Sophronia sought to raise their remaining children while honoring their fallen sons.

Perhaps the most arduous and impressive example of the latter was to locate and bring together the mortal remains of their soldier boys, no mean feat in a landscape torn asunder by four years of war. Robert had fallen at Trevilian, near Louisa Court House; his brothers each died some twenty-five equidistant miles away at Raccoon Ford and Spotsylvania. This encompassed a large swath of territory, however, especially given the destruction and chaos engendered by the war and what must have been great difficulty in securing transportation.

Nevertheless, armed with detailed descriptions by comrades of where Vivian and Jimmie had been laid to rest, Reverend Towles, perhaps with the help of family members from Lancaster County, located their graves, disinterred the remains, and transported them to Louisa, where Robert had been buried in the newly established Oakland Cemetery.

The perseverance necessary for such a task had to have been substantial, and the effort must have been compounded by the emotional toll such a journey would have entailed. The result, however, was to reunite the three boys in a peaceful setting that remains poignant today. Just inside of the wrought iron gate at Oakland Cemetery, near oak trees that canopy the graves of other Confederate soldiers—many unidentified—rest "The Sons of Rev. John and S.E. Towles." A seven-foot-tall obelisk carries that identification on one side, with each of the three remaining sides devoted to one of the boys. No more need be said; the marker is a simple tribute to family members who had departed this earth to enjoy their heavenly rest.

With this cathartic task completed, Reverend Towles could focus on his new flock in Accokeek. Sophronia and the remaining Towles children would continue to grieve for and remember the brothers. And of course, others also remembered.

In the spring of 1866, while Reverend Towles was still attempting to restore his churches and home in Prince William County, correspondence appeared from an unlikely source—a Michigan acquaintance of Vivian named James Mosher. Responding to an earlier inquiry, John Towles had informed the young man that Vivian had not survived the war. Mosher's response was telling for its earnest sympathy, as well as for its sense of lost opportunities for cross-sectional reconciliation and rekindled friendship.

Coppenopolis, Col.
Apr. 2d - 66
Rev. Jno. Towles

My dear Friend

Some time has elapsed since receiving the reply to my letter to your son "Viv". I have many times endeavoured to answer the same, but as often have I deferred doing so; not that my affection for him now that he is gone is any the less than while in life. but from a deference to yourself and wife in intruding upon a sorrow as sacred as that of yours.

I am well aware that no words of mine, sincere and heartfelt as they are, can alleviate the sufferings of you & yours over this great bereavement. Still my dear Sir! I ask you in all sincerity to accept the sympathies of one who valued the friendship of him who is gone beyond that of all his other companions.

Like him I have been a "soldier" and shared the privations attendant upon a Soldiers life; it's true our courses were opposite. it was ever the boast of myself and comrades however that knew him, meet "Viv Towles" where we would, we met a friend be the circumstances what they were.

Your letter has dispelled that fond hope of mine that my friend like myself had passed through this struggle unscathed. and need I add that it has opened up a train of reflections in my case. how so many of my friends in both armies have by the wayside fallen and I left to mourn their loss? a wise providence has willed it so for ends we in our short-sighted wisdom cannot comprehend. pardon me! but I cannot help but exclaim would God had been as kind to you and yours!

My acquaintance with your late son "Viv" dates back to his entry of the "University of Mich". his bros Robt and James I have frequently heard him speak of but knew them not except through him. in fact I feel that I am personally acquainted with all the members of your family, so often have you been mentioned in my presence and in writing now I can hardly conceive that it is to a stranger. it was often the wish of the subject of this letter and myself that I should visit him during "vacation" in his "Va home" and I doubt not but it would have been carried out had not contention arisen between the different sections of our country.

I am fearful my dear Sir that I am taxing your time and patience in this already lengthy letter. Still allow me to hope and wish, that the future of you and yours may be frought with all contentment and joy; although you are deprived of the "Strong arms and brave hearts of your noble boys to cheer in old age"— may your declining years be as peaceful and free from care that the most hopeful Christian spirit could wish.

In conclusion allow me to express the wish that I shall not be forgotten by you.

The Friend of your son "Viv",
James P. Mosher

The tone of the letter suggests that a special bond had developed between the young men during a relatively brief interlude in a somewhat unique setting. What brought together a young Virginian with a local Michigan boy in a way that established a friendship deep enough to be remembered after more than a decade of war and social upheaval? The university setting may offer some clues.

Michigan at this time was on the far edge of civilization. It was not even organized as a territory until the year 1805, and its population in 1850 would not have been more than a few hundred thousand. A drawing of the campus in Ann Arbor, circa 1855, and a bird's-eye rendering of the campus circa 1865 show a modest collection of a half dozen or so buildings amidst a wooded community. The university—in its infancy—was nevertheless a dynamic institution for its time and was under progressive leadership. "The pre-Civil War University of Michigan regarded the student as a citizen. The faculty encouraged student participation in all sorts of Ann Arbor civic enterprises," noted one journal.

Even given that level of progressive vision, one wonders why the eldest son of an Episcopal rector would travel to far-away Michigan for studies. The *History of the University of Michigan* may provide some clues. Under the aggressive leadership of its first president, Henry Philip Tappan, the university began what one source called "a remarkable growth and expansion." President, or as he was often called, Chancellor Tappan was "a man of wide culture, of established reputation as a scholar, and an author on philosophical and educational subjects." Tappan instituted a scientific curriculum that eliminated Latin and Greek and that attracted students who disliked classical studies and who were vocationally oriented. Perhaps Rev. John Towles found agreement with the assessment of the university's Board of Regents, when they applauded Dr. Tappan for "his views of a proper University education…liberal, progressive, and adapted to the present age."

Tappan, himself a Presbyterian cleric, took pride in the moral conduct of the students. He instituted daily chapel, Sunday church attendance, Sunday afternoon lectures, weekly student prayer meetings, and meetings of the Society for Missionary Inquiry. The professors at the university who came from Eastern institutions were reported to have noted that Michigan students were more religious than those in Eastern colleges—something that must have appealed to Reverend Towles and to Vivian.

From roughly 1853 to the outbreak of the war, the school undertook a transformative curriculum based on university studies typified in the Gymnasia of Prussia. This high ideal of university study included scholarships, faculty lectures, and departmental specialization. This policy "developed a new independence in the student's mind, a swifter transition between boyhood and manhood." Enrollment kept pace with academic progress, and students flocked in at a brisk pace. From a student body of fifty in 1850, the undergraduates a decade later numbered 519, a good percentage of whom were from outside of the state of Michigan. The course study for those years shows an area that may have caught the attention of Reverend Towles and young Vivian Towles.

An agricultural course was outlined in 1852–1853 in the expectation that the state legislature would provide the means for its establishment. When those means failed to materialize, the Agricultural College was organized through other avenues. University records show that the Rev. Charles Fox, a clergyman of the Episcopal Church, "gave gratuitously a course of lectures in the University on agriculture in the spring of 1853." While this educational experiment had apparently run its course by the time Vivian came to Michigan, perhaps his (and his family's) interest in the school had been piqued by the subject matter of the nascent agricultural curriculum and its Episcopal connections.

Other religious inducements may also have come into play. Contemporary school reports show active Episcopal student organizations at the University of Michigan, and a surviving copy of the 1844 Virginia Theological Seminary catalogue exists in the school files, perhaps a tantalizing clue to connections between clergy or Episcopalian peers that might have encouraged youths like Vivian Towles to venture so far from home.

In 1854, Reverend Fox was appointed by the Regents as Professor of Agriculture, but died soon after receiving the appointment. With his death, the university's agricultural department was closed. The legislature later established the Michigan Agricultural College in Lansing, much to the chagrin of Chancellor Tappan.

Vivian Towles would have been eighteen years old in 1857, but it seems possible that the Episcopal connection may have lured him to Ann Arbor to pursue skills that would have been useful on the family farm in Prince William County. With the agricultural department at the university abandoned and with no hope that it would be revived, perhaps Vivian returned to his home in Virginia to seek other opportunities.

The surviving records are inconclusive. Non-graduate records do indicate that James Pierson Mosher attended the University of Michigan from 1854–1855 as a First Year student and that he took partial courses in 1856 and 1857 and again for a time in 1859 prior to the war. No corresponding records exist for Vivian Towles; however, this may be because he spent only a partial year at the university. What is clear from James Mosher's postwar letter, however, is that his and Vivian's experiences in Ann Arbor overlapped.

A final clue as to the connection is found in a contemporary communicant list from St. Andrews, the local Episcopal Church—"Mr. Towles" appears on the list; whether this was Vivian or his father is unclear, but the notation can hardly be a coincidence and confirms Mosher's assertion that his acquaintance with Vivian dated back to his entry of the University of Michigan. That a decade later—and after a great war on opposing sides—the Michigander would write his friend's parents is a testament to the lasting impression that acquaintance made.

After the war, Mosher maintained his connection with the university. An existing post card from Mosher in the university archives from 1900, indicates that he was active in the Panhellenic life on campus. "Should there still be a Chapter of the Delta Phi, kindly inform one of the members to drop me a [letter], as I was one of its founders and still have an interest in the welfare of those who have succeeded us older ones." Delta Phi has been billed as America's oldest continuous fraternity and one of the first three social college fraternities in North America.

The obituary file for Mosher provides a sense of the commitment to cause and country that young men on both sides of the Mason-Dixon Line demonstrated. "Enlisted before terms expired" reads the card. Other alumni records for James Mosher show that he was twenty-eight years old when mustered into the army, which would have made him slightly older but of an age with Vivian. He died in Oakland, California, in 1905.

Mosher had indeed served his country, initially as first sergeant in Company K of the 26th Michigan Infantry and then as second lieutenant. The 26th Michigan served throughout the war in various areas and in different capacities. Mustered in at Jackson, Michigan, in December 1862, the regiment was sent to help put down Northern draft riots in New York City the following year. In April 1863, it was dispatched to Suffolk, Virginia, to assist in its defense against Confederate Gen. James Longstreet, who had been detached from Lee's army to forage. Its winter camp in late 1863 was ironically at Stevensburg, where Vivian had been killed in action that fall. On May 9, the regiment advanced to within two miles of the Confederate lines at Spotsylvania Court House, where on that day, young Jimmie Towles was killed. What some might call "karma" had certainly kept Mosher not far from the Towles brothers during the war…and yet far enough so that they hadn't engaged one another.

Remembrances of the Towles brothers came in other ways as well. In the chapel of the Episcopal High School in Alexandria, a marble tablet commemorated the high school students who "gave their lives in the service of the Army and Navy of the Confederate States." John Vivian Towles was among the sixty-one entries on the tablet.

Having moved north, the Towles family sought to establish new roots, while occasionally being reminded of the Virginia home they had left behind. John Towles continued to watch his old parish with interest and no doubt remained in contact with remaining friends and neighbors in the area. Although few contemporary property records survive, he may even have continued to own some real estate in Prince William, even after his family's move to Accokeek.

In a September 1871 *Port Tobacco Times and Charles County Advertiser* posting entitled "Treasure Found," it was reported that "the rentor of the farm belonging to Rev. Mr. Towles in Prince William County, VA, while cleaning out a well on that farm a short time since, found a jar filled with gold coin." The paper went on to say that Mr. Towles, "who is rector at this time of a Parish adjoining ours, says he has no knowledge of the gold whatsoever." This posting would seem to indicate that Reverend Towles retained some property interest in Prince William County, although no real estate records survive to confirm that assumption.

Life undoubtedly went on, but remembrance remained at the core of Towles family traditions.

For her part, Sophronia Towles did her utmost to commemorate her "brave Confederate soldiers," recopying some destroyed letters from memory and making several handwritten copies of Robert's diary (*Kept, while a Prisoner*) for each surviving sibling. The original diary survives, as do three copies in Sophronia's handwriting. It should be noted that her copies—perhaps in deference to the younger children's sensibilities (or with the editing one might expect from a mother)—conveniently left out a few of the more exuberant escapades of young Robert, for example his flirtations with young women while scouting in Prince William.

The remaining children of John and Sophronia Towles would grow up to be successful adults.

When he was eighteen years old, Churchill Towles moved to Texas, where he married and began a line of the family that continues today. In her diary, Sophronia described her fourth son as being "a youth of great energy." And, in his own way and in a different time, he mirrored his older brothers' military service. During the Spanish-American War, he served honorably as a major in the First Texan Volunteers, and in 1898, he was listed as commander of Ft. Bliss in El Paso, Texas.

In keeping with the family tradition of using loved ones' names for children in succeeding generations, Churchill's children included a Rosalie, a John, a LeRoy, a Vivian, and a Robert. Although Churchill and his family thrived in Texas, they were not without their share of tragedy. In a letter dated June 16, 1892 to his mother Sophronia, Churchill conveyed sad tidings regarding the namesake of his late elder brother, Robert.

My Dear Mother,

Our little "Robbie" Robert Chowning [Towles] was taken sick with cholera infantum last Tuesday night, was out of danger Thursday night and convalescent the next morning, but Friday night was taken with congestion of the brain and from that time his mother & I never left him for more than a minute or two at a time…the poor little fellow was too weak to stand the fever the cholera had taken away his strength and he became exhausted before the fever could run its course, and on Tuesday night at 11:15 the little angel fell asleep and at 6 pm yesterday, we laid him to rest. He was a bright little ray of sunshine to us all & too good for this world…at the very last, he called out, and his uncle Robert must have come and carried him away on his back to heaven, for around his little lips was left the signature that his little call had been heard and answered. We have said it in the past, God's will be done. Your affectionate son, Churchill.

Clearly, sorrow was not limited to one generation of the Towles family. Ever the keeper of the collective family memory, Sophronia marked the envelope with the simple notation: "To be saved."

The youngest son, Leroy, became a respected physician in Maryland. His death in 1900 at a relatively young age of forty-four was noted in the local paper:

9 March 1900
Washington Post
Washington DC

Dr. LeRoy Chowning Towles died at his home, near Accokeek, Prince George's County, Wednesday, after a year's illness, aged forty-four years. He was one of the most prominent physicians in Southern Maryland. He was a son of the late Rev. John Towles, pastor of Christ's Protestant Episcopal Church, at Accokeek. He was educated at Washington and Lee University and the University of Maryland. He married Miss Emma Jones, who, with three sons and one daughter, survives him, besides one brother, Col. Churchill Towles, of Houston, TX, and one sister, Mrs. Eugene Poole, of Bellevue, PA. Three brothers gave their lives to the Confederacy.

The brothers' youngest sister, Ella, to whom so many surviving letters were addressed, went on to marry a Pennsylvania portrait artist, Eugene Alonzo Poole, a contemporary and acquaintance of Thomas Eakins and Winslow Homer. Coincidentally, as a young man, Ella's husband-to-be had painted Robert E. Lee from life. In a preface to the book, *The Lees of Virginia* (the cover of which uses the portrait), the author describes the occasion:

On 7 December 1865, Eugene Alonzo Poole, age twenty-eight and a Baltimore artist, arrived in Lexington, Virginia. He remained for a fortnight, painting a portrait and sculpting a bust of General Robert E. Lee. Poole's family was probably known to Lee, since he was well acquainted with the Baltimore community. The association apparently was close enough to coax the General from his well-known aversion to sitting for artists and photographers. At any rate, Lee was cooperative and, after young Poole had finished his task, the modest General permitted himself a word of cautious praise for the portrait by allowing as how the artist himself was pleased with it.

The Poole family was so gratified to have one of the rare paintings done from life of Robert E. Lee that the canvas has remained with the artist's descendants to this day.

Poole also was known to have crafted plaster busts of other Confederate generals. One of these—a likeness of Gen. Joseph E. Johnston—survives in a private collection.

Perhaps Ella's greatest role in the family was as a fervent and continuing proponent of remembrance. She was instrumental in the erection of a Confederate monument in Lancaster County—one of the first such monuments in the South. In 1912, Ella organized the Lancaster County Chapter of the United Daughters of the Confederacy, with sixteen charter members, and continued as the chapter's president until her death. Perhaps thinking of her lost brothers, she adhered to the UDC's motto of "Love makes memory eternal." Indeed, a surviving plaque in her honor at the Lancaster County Court House incorporates that saying.

She also took the time to visit Prince William County, "taking much pleasure in visiting the scenes of her girlhood and of her father's long ministry." For a number of years, she provided a John Towles Memorial Medal for good scholarship in the Grace Chapel Sunday School there.

Shortly before her husband's death in 1912, Ella and E.A. Poole had moved to her ancestral home in the Northern Neck, taking up residence at Bertrand, another family home near the Rappahannock. Ella had always wanted a landscape of Greenvale, where she spent the years during the war with her family, but her husband the artist said it was "too flat, had no distance, and the house was too conventional." Instead, sitting on the point, E.A. Poole painted a scene looking across Greenvale Creek, along the shoreline of a neighboring family house, "Belmont," on the Rappahannock. "The sky was exquisite, that first day, with an approaching storm," notes the inscription on a reproduction of the painting. At last, Ella had her painting, even if it was more "Belmont" than "Greenvale."

A late-life photo of Ella shows a prim and proper woman with wire-rimmed glasses and bobbed white hair. A trace of a smile accents a distant sadness in her eyes—perhaps a reflection of the family tragedies that influenced her youth. Family members say that Ella lived life with a passion, and she fiercely embraced her self-appointed role in the remembrance of her heritage.

When she died in 1934, Ella Towles Poole was buried in St. Mary's White Chapel cemetery—next to the church where her parents were married and where her father was interim rector during the war. Her headstone is engraved with Stonewall Jackson's last words: "Let us cross over the river and rest in the shade of a tree," followed by the inscription, "A true Southerner."

As for the Towles children who died during the war, one cannot help but imagine "what if" they had lived. But for their untimely deaths, what roles and contributions might have Vivian, Robert, James, and Rosalie made to their post-war family and their communities? One can only speculate, but it seems nearly certain that they would have provided additional continuity and direction to a family that had deep roots in its communities. Vivian and Robert likely would have been yeoman farmers and, indeed, that was listed as their "profession" in the pre-war Federal Census. Perhaps Jimmie, too, would have followed in that vocation. Rosalie—who her mother noted died "when nearly or quite grown"—likely would soon have married and begun her own family. With her training at the Belle Haven Institute for "educated Young Ladies," she may have become a teacher, the "highest position" to which Belle Haven recognized such students could aspire. Educated, literate, and devoted to duty, each child would have contributed in many ways to the family fortunes as the dawn of a new century approached.

It also seems certain that the nuclear family would have been more likely to remain intact and in Northern Virginia, rather than being dispersed throughout the country. By her own admission, one of Sophronia's greatest regrets in later life was the distance that separated her from her remaining family.

Perhaps the most intriguing and poignant surviving piece of evidence concerning the hope and heartbreak of having sons in harm's way survives in a November 1862 issue of the *Southern Churchman*. It's a small entry, really—and may not even have been from Sophronia (since the listing is anonymous). But there, among many other contributions—most identified by name and location—is a donation "Received for the Confederate States Bible Society." The listing notes a modest amount of five Confederate dollars, and says simply, "A Mother, with three sons in the army yet unhurt, a thank-offering." Could it have been Sophronia? The Towles family certainly would have had access to the *Churchman,* and Reverend Towles periodically contributed articles to it. What makes the notation most ironic, of course, is that it was placed before Raccoon Ford, before Spotsylvania, and before Trevilian Station. Three young brothers were still fighting for their cause, and their family was still awaiting their safe return from war's cruel grasp.

One hundred and fifty years after the conflict that cost other parents their "bright ones," one can still hear the lament in the poem that Sophronia penned to help remember her lost children.

Their little feet are seen no more,
Where once in joy they trod,
Those children we have fondly loved—
For they are gone to God.

An even more plaintive poem kept by Sophronia, "My Child", is more direct…and ultimately hopeful.

I cannot make him dead!
His fair, sunshiny head
Is ever bounding round my study chair;
Yet when my eyes, now dim
With tears, I turn to him
The vision vanishes—he is not there!

Yes, we all live to God!
Father, thy chastening rod
So help us, thine afflicted ones, to bear,
That, in the spirit-land,
Meeting at Thy right hand,
"Twill be our heaven to find that—thou art there!

Like Sophronia Towles, many other mothers—North and South—endured heartrending losses during the Civil War. Some who received death notices were so unrestrained in the expression of their grief that fears were entertained for their sanity. "Oh, God! God, they have not slain my boy?" screamed one woman when told of the death of her son. A subsequent swoon "indicated the strong symptoms of an unbalanced mind," according to observers.

"This lock of hair, clotted with blood, is all that I have left, and [my son] will never be far from me," wrote another mother, who perhaps like Sophronia, spent the rest of her life *remembering*.

Might we all hope never to experience such loss! But regardless of our own stories, we can sympathize with those who *did* endure tragedy, even though they are removed from us by time and distance. We can admire and appreciate their fidelity to family and celebrate how, through devotion, they demonstrated how a family's love can, indeed, make memory eternal.

EPILOGUE

I would not live always

In 1885, John Towles died, leaving a legacy of service to his church and communities. An address of the Bishop to the Diocesan Convention of Maryland reported on the occasion:

> On the very next day, April 16th, the Rev. John Towles was called away from earth…He came to work in Maryland in 1867, being received from the Diocese of Virginia, and taking charge of the parish of which he was the Rector at the time of his death, St. John's Parish, Prince George's and Charles Counties. In 1875 he became Rector also of St. Peter's, Montgomery County. In the following year he relinquished the charge of St. John's Parish, and for two years gave his entire work to St. Peter's, Montgomery County; but in 1878 he returned to his first charge, and continued its faithful minster until the close of his life.

After his death, the Rt. Rev. William Paret, bishop of Maryland, eulogized Towles in his annual report as, "Quiet, modest and unassuming, he leaves to the Diocese the memory of eighteen years of faithful service for the Master." "After a life in God's Service," reads his tombstone in Accokeek.

The Southern Churchman wrote:

> On Sunday, April 19th, this old church presented a sad and impressive scene in the burial of its venerable and respected rector, the Rev. John Towles, who had been rector for many years, and whose unexpected death was deeply mourned. The funeral was held at the hour of morning service, and the church was crowded. The Rev. Dr. W.L. Hyland, assisted by the Rev. Messrs. J. Harry Chesley and W.M. Dame, conducted the services, and at the close the three clergymen sang the favorite hymn of the departed rector, Dr. Muhlenberg's "I would not Live Always."

The choice of the Lutheran Dr. W.A. Muhlenberg's hymn might seem unusual for an Episcopal cleric, however the hymn was well-known among interdenominational clerics. Perhaps most important for Reverend Towles's family, it summarized perfectly the oft-stated hope and expectation that something better (including reuniting with lost loved ones) awaited all Earthly "travelers."

> I would not live always; I ask not to stay
> Where storm after storm rises dark o'er the way,
> The few lurid mornings that dawn on us here
> Suffice for life's woes, are enough for its cheer.
>
> I would not live always; no, welcome the tomb:
> Since Jesus hath lain there, I dread not its gloom.
> There sweet be my rest till He bids me arise
> To hail Him in triumph descending the skies.
>
> Ah, who would live always, away from his God,
> Away from yon heaven, that blissful abode,
> Where rivers of pleasure flow o'er the bright plains
> And noontide of glory eternally reigns;
>
> Where saints of all ages in harmony meet
> Their Savior and brethren transported to greet,
> While anthems of rapture unceasingly roll,
> The smile of the Lord is the feast of the soul?

Dr. Muhlenberg penned the hymn in 1824. Its authorship was apparently contested for a time, eliciting an angry response from its author, who pointed out to the *Southern Churchman* that the claimant "would have had to read my mind," in addition to refuting the extensive contemporaneous evidence of Dr. Muhlenberg's work on the hymn.

Other acknowledgements of John Towles's passing poured in:

Diocese of Maryland.
The Rev. Wm. H. Hyland, D.D., acting dean, accompanied by Revs. J.B. Perry, of Washington, and Henry Thomas, of Poolesville, held Convocational services on the 1st and 2nd instants at Accokeek and Pamonkey.

St. John's parish, in which are located the two points above named, a long time was presided over by the Rev. John Towles, a faithful servant of Christ. He became its rector in 1867; in '74 he assumed the rectorship of St. Peter's, Montgomery county, and in '77 he returned to his former parish (St. John's), where he continued till he fell asleep the spring last gone. For fifteen years he was an earnest shepherd, going in and out among his flock. As I stood by his grave in the yard of the beautiful church at Accokeek, where he so often dispensed the word and broke the bread, I could only say here sleeps one, who has fought a good fight, one who has kept the faith, thence forth thou shalt have the crown of life.

THE REV. JOHN TOWLES, for many years connected with the diocese of Virginia, but recently with Maryland, died suddenly at his home and parish in Prince George's county, Md., April 16. It is painful to hear of the death of so admirable a man; but God knoweth best. His family has the sincere sympathy of those who knew and loved him.

TOWLES. At Accokeek rectory, Prince George's county, Md., April 16, 1885, the Rev. John Towles, in the 72nd year of his age.

Thus it has pleased Almighty God to take from us our dearly beloved pastor. "None knew him but to love, none named him but to praise." Sad were the many hearts that attended his funeral on Sunday, April 19th, for they truly felt that they had lost a friend who was ever ready to administer to their wants, both spiritual and temporal. He was truly a useful man, being highly educated, and always willing to give others the benefit of his knowledge. He came to our parish in 1867, and remained until his death, with the exception of two years spent in Poolsville, Md. "He was a good man, and full of the Holy Ghost, and of faith." And is now reaping his reward in heaven. "Well done, thou good and faithful servant." G.R.H.M.

At a meeting of the vestry, April 27th, 1885, the following resolutions were passed unanimously:—

Whereas God in his wise providence has seen fit to visit this parish with sore affliction by suddenly removing from his sphere of usefulness our beloved rector, Rev. John Towles, therefore

Resolved, That we, the vestry and wardens of St. John's parish, Prince George's and Charles counties, in giving expression to our feeling at this sad bereavement, know that we echo the sentiment of not only the parishioners, but those of other denominations. During his sojourn of nearly eighteen years in this community as rector, he had endeared himself to all by his uniform gentleness of character, kindly manners to old and young, rich and poor, knowing no distinction of persons, for he realized that we are the children of God and inheritors of the kingdom of heaven.

Resolved, That to his bereaved family we extend, as the representatives of the parish and on our own behalf, our deepest and most sincere sympathy, and pray the God of all comfort, on whom our beloved pastor so trustfully relied, will give them from his abundance a full measure of heavenly consolation.

Resolved, that the foregoing tribute of our love and esteem be entered in full on the minutes of the vestry and a copy properly authenticated be transmitted to the afflicted family.

Albert M. Clagett

H.W.B. McPherson

J. Henry Murry

John A. Coe

E.J. Jones

J.W.F. Bealle

R.W. Bryan

Vestrymen

E.J. Jones

Albert M. Clagett

R.K. Compton

Church Wardens

R.W. Bryan

Register

For her part, Sophronia never forgot her sons who had been lost to war's cruel hand. In her diary, while she mourned their loss, she seemed to take pride in their valiant deaths (underlining notations for each, "killed in battle.") She also seemed to take solace in the fact that her sons were "all buried side by side" in the Confederate cemetery at Louisa.

Sophronia lived on until 1897 and was buried next to her husband. On her headstone appears the phrase, "He gives his beloved sleep." Both John and Sophronia were interred in the cemetery close to the church, the vestry of Christ Episcopal having asked that they be buried there.

CHAPTER NOTES

PROLOGUE: **Gone to God**
Source Notes and Related Commentary
The evocative poem, "Gone to God" (actually titled "Dear Departed Children"), which forms an integral part of the title for this book, appears to have been penned by Sophronia Chowning Towles, the mother of the three "soldier boys." A copy of the verse in Sophronia's hand, survives in the family archives, and I was unable to find any other source or author. The poem is, of course, even more poignant, since the Towles family also lost a daughter to illness during the war. And, of course, like many families of the time, the Towles family suffered through several instances of infant mortality. This poem does serve to reinforce the underlying family touchstones of faith and belief in a righteous afterlife.

CHAPTER ONE: **A most agreeable and lovable man**
Source Notes and Related Commentary
Early in this project, a very helpful summary of Rev. John Towles' Episcopal career came from an archivist in the Virginia Diocese, Julia Randle. Secondary sources on the Virginia church—and, in particular, the Brentsville area churches of Rev. Towles—included the venerable *Old Churches and Families of Virginia*, by Bishop Meade, Dennis Bratcher's commentary on the High and Low Episcopal churches, and a monograph on history and architecture in the Bishop Payne Library at the Virginia Theological Seminary in Alexandria, titled "Three Episcopal Churches in Prince William County, Virginia," by Wendy C. Thomas. *Prince William: The Story of Its People and Its Places* provided valuable background on the area where the Towles family made their antebellum home. Alice Maude Ewell's *A Virginia Scene or Life in Old Prince William* offered an important collection of observations about the area from someone who grew up there. George Brown's *A History of Prince William County* gave insight into place names and antebellum Prince William, as did the impressively rendered annotated historical map of the county created by Eugene Scheel.

In "A Souvenir Booklet of the Centennial Celebration of St. Paul's Church in Haymarket, Virginia" I found a fascinating summary of Rev. Towles' rectorship prior to the war. For information on the Virginia Theological Seminary, I went to Rev. Goodwin's book on the history of that institution.

Finally, few records from the antebellum period survive, but those that do include the slave manumissions cited and various partial deeds, housed in RELIC (the Ruth E. Lloyd Information Center), an exceptional repository of historical and other information about Prince William County. RELIC is now part of the Bull Run Regional Library. Also, the mid-1800s census records for the county provided invaluable insights into Prince William and its citizens of the time. During my initial research, I looked at microfilm copies from the National Archives; like so many other things, these records are now available online, making historical research so much easier for authors like me! Likewise the Official Records of the War of the Rebellion or often more simply the Official Records or ORs, constitute the most extensive collection of primary sources of the history of the Civil War, and were originally published in 128 volumes. Shortly after I acquired my last volume to complete the set, my wife pointed out that the collection had become available on CD. I suppose they, too, are now online, as well. Sigh.

CHAPTER TWO: A Lincoln Pole and the winds of war
Source Notes and Related Commentary

Lee Wallace, Jr.'s "The Great Cavalry Encampment of 1860" provided valuable insights into the early gatherings of patriotic Southern militia units. Several pre-war units that eventually came to comprise the 4th Virginia Cavalry had their own unit histories, for example Woodford Hackley's "sketch" of Company D (Little Fork Rangers).

Confederate Veteran, a now somewhat obscure and underappreciated source of valuable information on soldiers and units, includes a valuable reprint of the "History of the Prince William Cavalry," by Mrs. M.R. Barlow of Manassas, Virginia. Much of the description of the unit's early formation, appearance and activities were taken from this source.

The early wartime flight of Eppa Hunton, described in an entry "from the Bible of Virginia Weirs" appeared in the *Manassas Journal* in February of 1913.

The reference to "Yankeedom" as a "doomed land" that expressed the conviction that the South was "engaged in one of the noblest causes on earth, namely the defense of our country," came from a letter by Charles K. Pendleton, courtesy of The Virginia Historical Society, which houses an extraordinary quantity of original source manuscripts that I highly recommend. Research at the Society is greatly facilitated by an exceptionally functional online search database of their collections. Next time you are in Richmond, try it; you'll like it!

Details about "the John Brown affair" appear in many sources, but I found the recent book by Tony Horowitz, *Midnight Rising,* to be an exceptional portrait of an individual who had a great impact on sectional tensions leading to war. I recommend it highly.

CHAPTER THREE: The most insignificant must look his best
Source Notes and Related Commentary

An invaluable source about the accoutrements and other observations about the appearance of component companies of the 4th Virginia Cavalry was a study *Uniforms of the Confederacy (No. 58): 4th Virginia Cavalry, 1861,* by Ron Field. The plate includes sketches of various uniforms for the 4th, including individual companies, such as the Prince William Cavalry, portrayed in full dress uniform, circa 1861, as well as the Little Fork Rangers and the Black Horse Troop. Leslie D. Jensen's "A Survey of Confederate Central Government Quartermaster Issue Jackets" includes sketches and photographs of various uniform types, including the so-called Richmond Depot Type 1 jacket, a basic design that many Confederates wore early during the war. A surviving picture of Charles H. Powell, Co. F of the 4th Virginia Cavalry is shown as an example. Ample sketches and engravings of Confederate cavalrymen exist, of course. I particularly like one of The First Virginia (Rebel) Cavalry at a Halt, "sketched from Nature by Mr. A.R. Waud."

Included in the Towles family archives are parts of the uniforms worn by the brothers as members of the 4th Virginia Cavalry. "Buttons worn on uniform and rosette worn on hat of J. Vivian Towles" reads one such notation. Another family treasure includes a fabric "Red Star badge worn by all members of Co. A of the 4th Virginia Cavalry." Perhaps most poignant in the family collection is a circular patch or rosette given to young James Towles (and found on his body when he died) with the notation on the back that it had been a gift to Jimmie "from his brother Robert."

For other references to regimental uniforms, I used Brassey's *History of Uniforms: American Civil War Confederate Army* as well as Haythornthwaite's *Uniforms of the Civil War.* Several photos in the Manassas Museum collection show members of the Prince William Cavalry in uniform, although their "look" is perhaps more indicative of the utilitarian uniforms worn by the cavalry as the war progressed. No doubt the appearance of the newly-minted troops at the start of the grand adventure was much more striking. My thanks to the Museum for compiling such a wonderful collection of images, to which we've now added Robert Towles.

The hand-drawn scouting map contains notations on the reverse from Sophronia Towles, "My son Vivian's work for the army in the War" and "work done for Confederate generals." Historian and friend Bob Krick has called the map a "significant historical document," and the detail and colors are impressive.

A surviving Towles muster card in the National Archives indicates that during these early months of the war, the 4th Virginia Cavalry was "employed nearly the whole time in watching the enemy in Fauquier, Stafford and Prince William Counties," which supports the work that Vivian and others did during the relative calm before the storm.

Sources for the skirmish at Fairfax included transcripts from the Richmond Daily Dispatch. A "hurried" dispatch from Arlington on June 1, 1861 reported total Union casualties of "6" and five Confederate prisoners, including several identified as members of the Prince William Cavalry. Interestingly, someone other than Lt. Tompkins, the commanding Federal officer, penned the report. Tompkins was reported to be "too unwell to report in person." A Confederate account—posted from Fairfax on June 4th, also in the Richmond Daily Dispatch—noted that the Federals allegedly took pains to minimize reports of their casualties. "...when any man fell from his horse, his comrades would get down and pick him up and throw him across the saddles by that means depriving as from finding out how many of the Federal troops were killed." The correspondent also noted that "I must say one thing, that, from the marks of their firing which I have seen, they [the Federals] fired very badly, and if that is their best, we have very little to fear from it." Other valuable sources about this skirmish included, of course, Ken Stiles' regimental history of the 4th Virginia Cavalry, and the hand-written and transcribed "History of the Prince William Cavalry" found in the Eleanor S. Brockenbrough Library in The Museum of the Confederacy, Richmond, Virginia.

Unfortunately, I couldn't find a contemporary picture of "Extra Billy" in full dress regalia (including the unusual headgear he affected from time to time), but I was able to find a more sedate image that is included in the photo montage at the start of the chapter.

CHAPTER FOUR: Pope's wallet
Source Notes and Related Commentary

There are more books in print than you might think about Gen. John Pope, Lincoln's experiment in command during the fall of 1862. Two such are Peter Cozzens' *General John Pope: A Life for the Nation,* and a companion piece, edited by Cozzens with Robert I. Girardi, *The Military Memoirs of General John Pope.* The latter includes a foreword by our late friend, John Y. Simon, who was an expert on all things Grant and the Civil War. In his foreword, John repeats an evaluation of John Pope by Pope's fellow Union officer, Samuel D. Sturgis, who famously intoned, "I don't care for John Pope a pinch of owl's dung."

Information about Pope's "rich father-in-law" and his connections to Salmon P. Chase, Lincoln's Treasury Secretary, came from *Abandoned by Lincoln: A Military Biography of John Pope.* Thanks also to Lisa Leibfacher and the research services of the Ohio Historical Society, through which I found the obituary of V. B. Horton. The details of the raid on Catlett's Station came from a variety of sources, including Beale's *History of the 9th Virginia Cavalry,* Blackford's *War Years with Jeb Stuart, The Confederate Horsemen* by David Knapp, and, of course, the Official Records. John Hennessy's fine article "Stuart's Revenge" in the June 1995 *Civil War Times* was extremely helpful, as was his exceptional treatment of Second Manassas, *Return to Bull Run: The Campaign and Battle of Second Manassas.*

A letter by Gen. Robert E. Lee on the 26th of August, 1862, archived in the Virginia Historical Society, talks about "the recent expedition to the rear of the enemy, with a view of cutting off their [railroad] communication, during a terrible storm at night," that led to the capture of "several hundred prisoners and some valuable papers of Genl. Pope."

One of the many Virginia Civil War Trails markers near Catlett's Station is called the "Stuart's Revenge" marker, as it recounts how Stuart's raid on Catlett's, among other benefits, enabled Jeb to return the favor when it came to the "capture" of his plumed hat by Union cavalry. The story about "a cartel for the exchange of the prisoners," meaning Stuart's hat for Pope's dress coat, has achieved a measure of notoriety, as reflected by the topic of the marker.

The story of the wallet first appeared in an article I wrote for *America's Civil War* magazine a decade or so ago. There is absolutely no truth to the rumor that I carry my credit cards and driver's license (with a few Yankee greenbacks or Confederate scrip) in Robert's purloined wallet.

Chapter Five: Poor darling Rosa
Source Notes and Related Commentary
The Towles family papers provided a great deal of the material related to this chapter, including copies of the poignant obituaries for Rosalie.

Tales of raids into the Northern Neck and descriptions of that important area for the Towles family came from Miriam Haynie's *The Stronghold* and other sources noted below.

In tracking down the Chowning Ferry family graveyard, I owe a great deal of thanks to an obscure publication "In Remembrance: Gravestone Inscriptions and Burials of Lancaster County," compiled by Margaret Lester Hill and Clyde H. Ratcliffe in 2002. Finding this publication motivated my wife and me to set off on a hot July 4th morning to see if we could locate where Rosalie Towles was buried. After determining that there were no apparent graveyards on the Greenvale property, we ventured further down the road to where the Chownings and Towleses had other ancestral holdings. A friendly neighboring farmer pointed us in the direction of property owned by distant relative Randy Chowning (who, at the time lived in Richmond, Virginia). As my wife stayed in the car, I passed by the house and found the overgrown cemetery, with its wrought iron fence, on the edge of a cornfield. A deer had impaled itself on one of the fence's spikes, lending a very surreal atmosphere to the scene. After climbing over the fence (delicately), the first headstone I found—tilted forward—was Rosalie Towles'. Somewhat spooky stuff!

Regarding Rosalie's education, family letters indicate that she attended school at "the Belle Haven Institute." As I researched this, I found that there were apparently several such institutes. One such institution was on the Eastern Shore of Maryland, and another in Columbia, South Carolina. The Young Ladies of Belle Haven Institute in Columbia were reported to have "donated twenty-two dollars to build and equip" a South Carolinian ironclad. Clearly, before, during, and after the War, the young women of the South exhibited their character and patriotism. On the Eastern Shore of Virginia yet another Belle Haven Institute was operated in the 1860s and early 1870s by "university man" Benjamin Haynes and his brother. Haynes had received a classical education in his native Germany, taught in Baltimore before arriving on the Eastern Shore and would eventually serve as a surgeon in the Confederate army. According to local historical sources, this Belle Haven was located on or near the Accomac-Northampton county line. The school likely had two classes, one for the lower grades and one for the upper. The Institute functioned as late as 1882. Upon reflection, however, and given the family overlap and familiarity, the Institute that Rosalie attended was undoubtedly the one in Alexandria.

CHAPTER SIX: Family matters
Source Notes and Related Commentary
The letters that provided original source material for the majority of this chapter came from the collection sent to young Ella Towles from her older brothers. Regrettably, other family letters were no doubt destroyed, as described in chapter 15 ("The insatiate wretches") below.

One such surviving letter was from Jimmie Towles to Ella. Jimmie had joined his older brothers in the war effort and seems to have followed in Robert's footsteps by serving as a detached scout. Among its other collections, the National

Archives produced a muster card for Jimmie indicating that he was captured "at Catlett's Station" on March 30, 1863 and paroled at Old Capitol Prison on May 10th. He is identified as a Private in Co. A of the 4th Regiment of Virginia Cavalry. This is interesting relative to comments about Jimmie's youth and peripheral participation in the regiment discussed in Chapter 13.

Vivian's description of reaction to the death of "Stonewall" Jackson after the Battle of Chancellorsville is an interesting confirmation of the esteem in which contemporaries—north and south—held the legendary general at the time of his death.

The comments about the aftermath of Gettysburg are also intriguing, inasmuch as they show the Confederates, even in defeat, to be highly motivated, optimistic, and eager for a "rematch."

Descriptions of raids into the Northern Neck during the war came from the Official Records and from Moore's *Kilpatrick and His Cavalry*. I also found an excellent article on this topic from the Northern Neck of Virginia Historical Society by Rev. George William Beale, contributed by Lucy Brown Beale.

Larry Chowning's book, *Soldiers at the Doorstep: Civil War Lore,* provided useful color commentary about a challenging time in the Northern Neck.

CHAPTER SEVEN: Back with the boys in old Prince William
Source Notes and Related Commentary

The indispensable source for this chapter turned out to be *Autobiography of Arab,* the slightly tongue-in-cheek narrative by Priolieu Henderson, as told through his horse, Arab. Many thanks to Brentsville's Pam Sackett for alerting me to this unique first-hand account that, to my delight, happened to include several mentions of Robert Towles and other locales and individuals connected to my manuscript.

Manly Wade Wellman is perhaps best known as an author for his definitive biography of Wade Hampton, *Confederate Giant,* but his pseudo-fictional accounts of the Iron Scouts from the 1950s, including *Ride Rebels* and *The Ghost Battalion,* provided wonderful color commentary for the scouts, including the song cited in the narrative. U.R. Brooks' *Butler and His Cavalry in the War of Secession* provided exceptional details about the South Carolinian cavalry and its scouting in Prince William during the war. The story of the murder of Billy Dulin came from this source. Other valuable material was culled from John Esten Cooke's *Wearing of the Gray.* The Moore manuscript "Chained to Virginia While South Carolina Bleeds" also provided valuable insights into the activities and perspective of the South Carolinians assigned to scout in Prince William. Several of the quotes used in my manuscript came from letters transcribed in the Moore piece.

Iron Scout Jack Shoolbred's evocative picture was reprinted from a page in "Scout for the Confederacy" by Retta Dickinson Warriner, of the John D. Kennedy Chapter 308, Camden South Carolina Division. The publication apparently was a special issue of United Daughters of the Confederacy Magazine. Shoolbred's picture also graced the cover of a *Manassas Journal Messenger/Potomac News/ Stafford County Sun* newspaper insert from July 2000, entitled "Reveille! Ride! Rendezvous!" The insert was a companion piece to one of the several reenactment rides and encampments associated with the Friends of Brentsville Courthouse Historic Centre in recent years.

As for the characteristics of a good scout, and in particular the exploits of the "uber-scout" Frank Stringfellow (a fellow member of the 4th Virginia Cavalry, but much more publicized than the Towles brothers), I consulted my first edition of *Stringfellow of the Fourth,* by R. Shepard Brown, as well as David Knapp's *The Confederate Horsemen.*

For the Union perspective, an 1868 book, *History of the Eighth Cavalry Regiment Illinois Volunteers During the Great Rebellion,* by Abner Hard, proved enlightening, both for this chapter and for Chapter 10. The 8th Illinois participated in the engagement that resulted in Vivian Towles' death (see below).

CHAPTER EIGHT: One would have thought they had General Lee
Source Notes and Related Commentary

The Official Records give us an idea of the disposition of Union troops in and around the Orange and Alexandria Railroad (where Robert and other scouts operated). In a July 26, 1863 entry (about the time Robert was captured), Maj. Gen. O.O. Howard indicates that the railroad is to be guarded "as follows: Two companies at Cedar Run Bridge; four companies at Catlett's Station; four companies at Kettle Run Bridge; four companies at Bristoe Station; two companies at Broad Run Bridge; four companies at Manassas Junction. The 168th New York and 173rd Pennsylvania Volunteers are assigned to that duty." For reference, a Civil War company comprised 100 men on paper. The importance of the Orange and Alexandria is explained in Robert Black's *Railroads of the Confederacy* and elsewhere.

Stories about "oath-taking" are common. Numerous examples of Amnesty Oaths from the end of the war survive, and they no doubt were common in areas such as Prince William County that were occupied by Union troops.

Robert certainly seemed destined to encounter several significant figures on the Union side. For information on Gen. Oliver Otis Howard (who founded

Howard University in Washington, DC after the war), Howard's autobiography proved useful. Maj. Gen. Carl Schurz, commander of the 3ʳᵈ Division of the 11ᵗʰ Corps under O.O. Howard, was a significant political general on the Union side. A revolutionary leader at an early age during the German uprisings of the late 1840s, Schurz escaped to America in 1849 and became a political force among the German immigrants in the North. He campaigned for Abraham Lincoln and was rewarded with a military commission, serving with relative distinction at battles such as Bull Run, Chancellorsville and Gettysburg. He lived until 1906 and was active in politics his entire life.

The "Long Bridge" over the Potomac into Washington is today's bridge over the river at 14ᵗʰ Street, a route I took many times when we lived in D.C. In its July 20, 1861 issue, the *Illustrated London News* described the bridge, as follows: "This bridge, which connects Washington with the Virginia shore, is a mile long, and about a quarter of a mile of the centre part is built of masonry, with low parapets, and resembles a country road. The remainder of the bridge is of wood. It is sufficiently wide to take three carriages abreast, and has two draws—one on the Washington and one on the Virginia side. These are nearly always open for the passage of small armed propellers, with which the Potomac swarms. A company of flying artillery is stationed on the bridge every night near the Virginia shore, with the draw raised in front of them. By day the passage across the bridge is unobstructed, and waggons are constantly passing and repassing, although, for form's sake, a company of soldiers is stationed at the extremity of the bridge, and sentinels parade to and fro." Surely a daunting prospect for a young Confederate soldier passing into captivity on the other side.

CHAPTER NINE: An Earthly Hades
Source Notes and Related Commentary
Numerous sources added color to this chapter, notably *Four Years in the Saddle* by Harry Gilmor (where the author described being held as a "spy" in violation of the cartel for exchange of prisoners early in the war). *Death to Traitors: The Story of Gen. Lafayette C. Baker, Lincoln's Forgotten Secret Service Chief* by Jacob Mogelever provided valuable descriptions of the means taken to deal with so-called "enemies of state." Mogelever's book also contains vivid descriptions of William P. Wood, commandant of Old Capitol. The seminal work on Old Capitol Prison must be Williamson's *Prison Life in the Old Capitol,* although others, including Virginia Lomax's *The Old Capitol and its Inmates* (published in 1867) provide valuable

contemporary descriptions of the prison. Other excellent contemporary books on the subject include John A. Marshall's *An American Bastille* (1872), Lawrence Sangston's *Bastilles of the North, by a Member of the Maryland Legislature* (1863) and D.A. Mahoney's *The Prisoner of State* (1863).

A bit of doggerel, apparently in Robert's own hand, survives in family records: "As a rule, man's a fool. When it's hot, he wants it cool; When it's cool he wants it hot, Always wanting what is not." Perhaps more to the point, given Robert's situation, is another line, "Two men looked through the prison bars. One saw mud, the other saw stars."

In the United Daughters of the Confederacy Magazine, Dr. James I. "Bud" Robertson, Jr. wrote an excellent article about Old Capitol and its two celebrated female prisoners (Belle Boyd and Rose O'Neal Greenhow). In *Annals of the War,* Colonel N.T. Colby contributed an extended vignette on Old Capitol, which also provided valuable background. Lonnie Spear's *Portals of Hell: Military Prisons of the Civil War* came out right about the time I began early research on this book, and I found it helpful in establishing perspective about Old Capitol, as it related to other prisons.

Colonel William P. Wood's obituary was cited in a description of the Historic Congressional Cemetery, where he is buried. According to the obituary, his life "was a continuous melodrama, bordering on the tragic," and encompassed several intriguing chapters. Among other duties, Wood was charged by the Treasury Department with capturing counterfeiters. When Lincoln was assassinated, Wood was in Cincinnati searching for such individuals, and Stanton summoned him back to Washington, where Wood helped determine that the assassin had been John Wilkes Booth. During the course of the investigation, and demonstrating interrogation skills no doubt honed at Old Capitol, he secured confessions of several Lincoln conspirators. After the war, he became chief of the secret service division of Treasury, and was noted for his work in the Credit Mobilier case, and for several other significant Treasury cases. He was very close to Secretary of War Stanton, although the relationship was apparently at times stormy. Woods was the last person to see Stanton alive.

The November 28, 1926 edition of the Evening Star contains a story about Wood, and also references an earlier 1903 account of his various exploits, described as part of the commentary associated with his death in that year at the age of 80. Much of the information was taken from Wood's autobiography, completed shortly before his death.

CHAPTER TEN: Watch those Yankees, boys!

Source Notes and Related Commentary

Various topics covered early in this chapter (for example the 'treason' trial of Mr. Roseberry) were fleshed out by references such as William Robinson's *Justice in Grey: A History of the Judicial System of the Confederate States of America*. *Disloyalty in the Confederacy* by Georgia Lee Tatum was another.

Papers from the Southern Claims Commission are now available online through Footnote (now Fold3) and provide intriguing insights into loyalty during the war and reparations afterwards. The original records are stored in the National Archives, and thanks again to my friend Libby Wright (a fellow Civil War enthusiast) who helped track down references in those records that were pertinent to my story.

The Krick files produced an account from an August 1902 issue of the *Atlanta Journal* of a "Cavalry Parade" in Culpeper County on June 8th, 1863—apparently not the review reported on by Vivian in his letter home, but no doubt similar in many respects. Worth a read...

The description of the skirmishes at Morton's Ford, Stevensburg, and near Kelly's Ford that included the fighting where Vivian Towles was killed comes largely from Fitz Lee's report in the Official Records. Other valuable commentary on the action that day came from Mrs. Barlow's piece on the Prince William Cavalry in *Confederate Veteran* mentioned in the notes to Chapter 3. Her article included J. Taylor Williams' description of the action where his brother, P.D. Williams, was killed. Barlow went on to say that "with all due kindly reference to the soldiers of today, we don't think they rank with Capts. P.D. Williams and Newton." Or, for that matter, one might speculate, with J. Vivian Towles!

An important description of the action on October 11th at Raccoon Ford came from the book on Company H of the 4th Virginia Cavalry, the Black Horse Troop—*Black Horse Cavalry: Defend our Beloved Country,* by Lewis Marshall Helm. U.R. Brooks' *Stories of the Confederacy* also provided some insights into the loss, calling it "severe" with respect to the deaths of "some gallant spirits, among them Captain W.B. Newton... a pure and generous spirit and a brave and noble officer."

8th Illinois Cavalry chronicler Hard's description of the battle noted that "the rebels made a charge upon us in an open field, but the noble Illinoisans boldly stood their ground and emptied many a rebel saddle (including)... the Colonel of the Fourth Virginia Cavalry; his men called him to come back, but it was too late."

A copy from the Krick files provided a short note on Benjamin Dyer Merchant, mentioning that "after the death of his captain P.D. Williams at Raccoon Ford, he [Merchant] became 1st Lieutenant" of the unit. Merchant's postwar photo is among those in the Manassas Museum collection and is included here, along with those of P.D. Williams and Lucien Davis (who wrote the grieving Towles family regarding Vivian's death).

And, sometimes the little clues provide the most poignant reminders of how soldiering involves more than simply battles. A microfilm of a payment entry to J. Vivian Towles survives in the National Archives. For service in July and August of 1863, the note authorizes payment of $48.80. Dated October 3rd (roughly a week before Vivian's death), it is ironically countersigned by Capt. P.D. Williams, who would also die in the skirmish.

CHAPTER ELEVEN: Escape and furlough
Source Notes and Related Commentary

The wartime setting of Washington City is vividly described in *Mr. Lincoln's Washington* and in Margaret Leach's *Reveille in Washington*. The latter provided the description of William P. Wood's eclectic approach to church services. *Washington in Lincoln's Time*, by Noah Brooks, includes a description of how fortified Washington was at the time of Robert's escape from Old Capitol. "Within the District of Columbia there were about forty forts making a complete circle around the capital, their guns being trained to sweep every road or possible rout leading into the city. Rifle pits were cut from point to point, making a continuous line of defense… a frowning line of fortifications that enclosed Washington as with a wall." All in all, it must have been a challenge to find a way out and back south.

The story of "Confederate Cleopatra" Belle Boyd is perhaps best told in her own words through her published diary *Belle Boyd in Camp and Prison* (although this work undoubtedly includes some significant self-aggrandizement on Belle's part). Other biographies, such as Sigaud's and Leonora Wood's repeat the tale of Belle distracting the authorities so "Mr. K." and his friends could escape. Interestingly, Hartnett Kane's book *The Smiling Rebel* identifies the initial as standing for "Kernan," not Kelley, but no specific source information is given for that identification. Part of me will always believe that it stood for Robert Towles' diary acquaintance Mr. Kelley. Finding the small contemporary article on the escape in the *Washington Star's* microfilm archives was fortuitous, and, as indicated in the narrative, interesting in its mention of only Tom Thompson, and not Robert Towles or the third party to the escape.

I did attempt to find some record of Tom Thompson's father in Richmond. A surviving contemporary Richmond Business Directory does contain a listing for a John Thompson, "dealer in hats, caps, furs, umbrellas," and assorted other items. Not exactly a jeweler or watchmaker, as Robert surmised, but perhaps the family in question.

Descriptions of the role "Rebel Mail Carriers" played in the war came from sources such as Helen Jones Campbell's *Confederate Courier* and *Absalom Grimes, Confederate Mail Runner.*

A *Washington Star* article from August of 1865, after the war, gives a sense of the role Old Capitol and Carroll Prisons played during the war. The article estimates that nearly 20,000 persons were confined in the buildings, with Old Capitol being used as a "military prison" and Carroll identified as a prison for state or political prisoners. On the day Abraham Lincoln was assassinated, there were more than 800 Confederate officers in confinement. At the time of the article, five executions had taken place, including one for being a "spy." Perhaps Robert's fears were not so misplaced.

Of course, many tales of escapes from Civil War prisons exist, for example Robert Denney's *Civil War Prisons and Escapes.* The fact remains that few escaped from Old Capitol, however, a fact that I confirmed by looking at National Archives microfilm in the company of Bob Krick, lo these many years past as I began this project.

CHAPTER TWELVE: A Bushwhacker's life
Source Notes and Related Commentary
Various accounts of Union attempts to suppress Confederate scouts or "bushwackers" can be found in the Official Records. Additional information on the 11th New York Cavalry—"Scott's 900"—came from Thomas West Smith's book, *The Story of a Cavalry Regiment, "Scott's 900,"* published in 1897.

Snowball fights among soldiers in winter camp must have been a common diversion, and the one Robert describes certainly seems to have included quite a few of his fellow soldiers. At least one other large-scale "engagement" has been recorded—The Great Snowball Fight involving the 4th Texas Infantry after the battle of Fredericksburg. Reported to have taken place on or about January 6, 1863, the fight involved about 400 Texans, who organized a raid on the nearby 11th Georgia. Both units were part of Gen. John Bell Hood's Division in James Longstreet's Corps of the Army of Northern Virginia. According to Val Giles of the 4th Texas, the Texans "filled their haversacks with snowball cartridges... to take the unsuspecting 'goobers' [i.e., Georgians] in the rear… The surprised and routed old Eleventh appealed to their fellow 'goobers' for help," and soon the Texans were retreating, "followed by 1000 Georgians." Others from the Texas Brigade joined in, as did some North Carolinians. Plenty of "ammunition" was available, since the snow was two feet deep. Accounts agree that the ensuing battle lasted most of the day. According to the Brigade historian, the snowball fight made such a racket that even the Federals across the Rappahannock were alarmed.

Another significant account of a large-scale snowball fight occurred at Dalton, Georgia in March of 1864. For the Mississippians and Louisianians involved, the snow must have been somewhat of an anomaly, but the event involved numerous soldiers, captured battle flags and prisoners. Jeff Giambrone describes the action in his excellent online post.

Regarding the legendary "Grey Ghost of the Confederacy," partisan (bushwacker?) leader John Mosby, there are many books available as references. Jeff Wert's biography certainly stands at the head of that list, but others, such as Munson's *Reminiscences of a Mosby Guerrilla* and James Ramage's *Gray Ghost: The Life of Col. John Singleton Mosby* also are noteworthy.

CHAPTER THIRTEEN: A lonely brother's tears
Source Notes and Related Commentary
Sources for the Battles of the Wilderness and Spotsylvania Courthouse are numerous, and included Gordon Rhea's excellent series of books, most particularly *The Battles for Spotsylvania Court House and the Road to Yellow Tavern, May 7-12, 1864*. William D. Matter's classic, *If It Takes All Summer: The Battle of Spotsylvania*, also was helpful in framing Grant's Overland Campaign in the spring of 1864.

The Virginia Historical Society archives contain some excellent contemporary letters that describe the fighting, including one that speaks about "the whip like crack of the rifle…followed instantly by the shrill and spiteful hiss of the bullet."

A handwritten list of casualties for May 9th can be found in the archives of the Eleanor S. Brockenbrough Library at the Museum of the Confederacy in Richmond, Virginia. Likewise, the library contains the Confederate States of America "Roll of Honour" with Edgar Weir's description of young Jimmie Towles' death. Edgar Vaux Weir, a member of Co. A of the 4th Virginia Cavalry, survived the war and lived for many years thereafter, recounting tales of various battles and events. His service record (in the Compiled Service Records of Confederate Soldiers microfilm at the National Archives in Washington, DC) describes a young man of "average height, 5 feet 8 ¾ inches, with his boots on, sandy complexion with brown hair and hazel eyes." He was captured in August of 1862 at Catlett's Station by the Harris Light Guard, paroled, and returned to active duty in early 1863. Weir served the duration of the war and was known to have agitated to raise a mounted company of conscription-age men and deserters in Prince William and Fairfax Counties—an offer that General Lee declined. Weir's (and others') comments in contemporary letters suggest that there were, indeed, many able-bodied Confederates in the area around Prince William… probably fertile ground for recruitment and support for "bushwackers" like Robert Towles (see previous chapter).

The description of "the McKenney Place," otherwise known as Kenmore Woods or the Frazier House, is found in the U.S. Department of the interior National Parks Service records for the structure's National Register of Historic Places application. Plate XCVI in the Official Atlas of the Civil War (the companion book to the Official Records set) contains a valuable map of the Spotsylvania battlefield.

Finally, the envelope in the family archives that contained surviving uniform mementos taken from the pockets of Jimmie after his death, includes a notation in his sister Ella Towles Poole's handwriting that notes her brother was a "Special Scout for Gen'l Stuart" and that he "entered the Confederate Army at the age of 16." Young, indeed, for such horrific duty.

CHAPTER FOURTEEN: Joyfully, Joyfully
Source Notes and Related Commentary

The surviving letter from Sallie Conner tells of how she tended to the mortally wounded Robert Towles. Of interest to me as I crafted the story of Robert's death was another *Southern Churchman* entry, "How a Christian Soldier may Die," in August of 1862, that, among other things, recounts the importance of hymns ("A good hymn is a blessed treasure") and gives several poignant examples of dying soldiers using the message of hymns to reinforce the journey to God, upon which they were embarking through death. Robert's experience is certainly consistent with this perspective.

Numerous other articles and works contribute to our understanding of what has been termed the "largest all-cavalry battle of the war." An early article by Edward Longacre in *Civil War Times Illustrated*—a favorite magazine of my youth, comes to mind. Longacre's article was entitled "The Long Run for Trevilian," and featured the print of the charge of the Confederate cavalry (although a great deal of the battle was fought dismounted).

The definitive book on Trevilian Station must now be Eric Wittenberg's outstanding volume, *Glory Enough for All.*" As mentioned in my Acknowledgements, Eric graciously took time some years ago to walk the battlefield with me, and was instrumental in placing Robert Towles' photograph on the driving tour marker at Oakland Cemetery (Stop 9). His monograph on "Custer's First Last Stand" (and other information on the battle) can be found online at www.civilwar.org/battlefields/trevilianstation.

A somewhat legendary local historian, Col. Walbrook Davis Swank, compiled eyewitness memoirs of the battle, and corresponded with me early in my writing. A picture in his book *Battle of Trevilian Station* shows members of the Mineral Chapter of the United Daughters of the Confederacy, including his wife, at the dedication of the UDC monument in Oakland Cemetery in 1982. Col. Swank spearheaded the preservation of the Trevilian Station Battlefield, and he wrote or edited 17 books on the Civil War—beginning with his first book at the age of 70. In 2005, at age 95, he spoke at the rededication of the Louisa County Confederate Monument. Col. Swank died in 2008 at the age of 97.

I was able to add flavor to the chapter by incorporating diary entries from Horatio Nelson of the 4th Virginia Cavalry (Co. A), edited by Harold "John" Howard, in his piece "If I am killed on this trip, I want my horse kept for my brother." Other original source material included Towles cousin John William Chowning's transcribed diary, currently on file at the Library of Virginia, in Richmond. *Confederate Veteran* includes an obituary for John William, who lived until 1922 and who inherited the Chowning Ferry property in the Northern Neck, described in Chapter 5.

One aspect of this chapter that was particularly gratifying was the research into the old shape-note hymn, "Joyfully, Joyfully" that Robert Towles requested for his funeral. Tracking down the words and music of the hymn led to a truly satisfying bit of closure about a piece of music that no longer appears in hymnbooks, but that meant a great deal to contemporaries of Robert (and, obviously, to him). Once the music was in hand, all that remained was to hear it. Many thanks to Maggie Rockey, our church organist at Christ Lutheran in Marshall, Michigan for playing the tune for me.

The idea behind shape notes is that the parts of a vocal work can be learned more quickly and easily if the music is printed in shapes that match up with the so-called solfege syllables with which the notes of the musical scale are sung. The seven syllables commonly used for this practice in English-speaking countries are the "Do-Re-Mi" tones popularized in Rodgers and Hammerstein's score for

The Sound of Music. For instance, in the shape-note tradition used in the <u>Sacred Harp</u> and elsewhere, the notes of a C major scale are notated and sung as follows:

| fa | sol | la | fa | sol | la | mi | fa |

Shape notes proved popular in America, and quickly a wide variety of hymnbooks were prepared making use of them. The shapes were eventually superseded in the northeastern U.S. by a so-called "better music" movement. But in the South, the shapes became well entrenched, and multiplied into a variety of traditions, including Episcopal.

In the 1800s, shape notes and music using such terminology were part of emerging Anglican (Episcopal) hymns, the Church having remained somewhat divided on hymnody—the "high church" faction supported a long-standing prohibition to hymns, while the more evangelical faction was far more open to hymn singing. Rev. Towles was an adherent of the latter group, and his family had come to appreciate hymns as a legitimate expression of worship.

Playing the hymn on a modern organ reveals a lively and upbeat tune that reinforces the religious optimism of the Towles family.

CHAPTER FIFTEEN: The insatiate wretches
Source Notes and Related Commentary

The service (if not depredations) of the Potomac Flotilla are chronicled throughout the Official Records of the Union and Confederate Navies, Series I. Other sources included the U.S. Naval Institute Reference Library in Annapolis and the Department of the Navy Naval Historical Center in Washington, DC. Naval History Magazine provided a great article on the Flotilla by William J. Bray, Jr. Operations against saltworks are described in the Official Records, as well as in the Civil War Naval Chronology 1861–1865, compiled by the Naval History Division of the Navy Department in 1971. Valuable local color came from an article by William Hathaway Chapman, Jr., "Yankees, Blue Pigs, and a Castle: The Northern Neck and the Civil War." Interestingly, I was able to actually look at the original log book for the *Jacob Bell*, which is housed in the Library of Congress archives. Holding the log book in my (gloved) hands was extremely moving.

The main building of Greenvale Manor still stands, as does Chowning Ferry Farm; when I was given a tour of the latter by Randy Chowning, I saw a Union cannonball that came from one of several naval bombardments of the area during the war.

Another very valuable book on naval activity in the area was Eric Mills' *Chesapeake Bay in the Civil War,* which I happened to purchase in the White Stone Pharmacy during a trip to the Northern Neck shortly after my wedding in 1992. Mary Miller's *Place Names of the Northern Neck of Virginia* also became indispensable as I learned the paths and byways of what has become an adopted second home for me. I suppose the locals might call me a "come here."

Chapter Sixteen: The Sulphur Spring Academy
Source Notes and Related Commentary

The unindexed pages of *The Southern Churchman* are captured in microfilm, and a careful perusal of these pages revealed the pertinent post-war commentary from Rev. Towles about efforts to re-establish his parish in Prince William County. Articles on "The Future of the Negro" and the debate over religious instruction for Freedmen also came from the *Churchman.* I should mention that the diocesan publication is replete with other fascinating articles, including polemics on topics such as "A word to drinkers," "How people take cold," and "Getting cool too quickly after exercise."

The book "Yesterday's Schools" provided a tantalizing hint as to the origin of the original Sulphur Spring Academy. In an entry entitled "Sulphur Springs (Towles' Gate)/Vancluse/Hazelwood School" the book traces the history of a schoolhouse erected "at Towles' Gate on the corner of Fleetwood Drive and Deepford Lane about one mile east of the old school." The "old school" was said to have been the first school in the southern part of the Brentsville District and was located about a mile southwest of the village of Aden, on Hazelwood Drive. The book reports that this school was likely located in a rented building for its early years (undetermined, but sometime prior to 1877), "taking its name from its location near a branch of Sulphur Springs." The reference to Rev. Towles as the possible originator of the name for the school is noted in a footnote to the entry. The name of the newer school was changed from Vancluse to Hazelwood in 1890, long after Rev. Towles and his family had moved to Maryland. "Vancluse" may be a variation of "Vaucluse," the name of the Towles' Prince William home (see Chapter 1).

Stella L.E. King, mentioned as a contributor to the Sulphur Spring Academy fund mentioned here was the daughter of a Prince William County neighbor of the Towles family. Dr. Edward King, a native of England, had a home called Bushy

Ridge Plantation, near Nokesville, and very near where the Towles family owned property before the war. Dr. King was mentioned in various letters, Robert's diary, and in the book *Autobiography of Arab*. A description of a Prince William County 4th of July celebration, in 1855, when Stella was 17 years old, survives and was published in the Prince William Reliquary, a blog/newsletter that also provided other valuable insights into the Brentsville/Prince William 'scene' for the book.

Finally, to at least partially understand the perspectives of the Virginia Episcopal Diocese regarding slavery, emancipation, and related post-war issues, I referred to various books such as *Religion and the Antebellum Debate Over Slavery*. Suffice to say that the debate was probably much more complex than we can imagine in hindsight.

CHAPTER SEVENTEEN: The sons of Rev. John and Sophronia Towles
Source Notes and Related Commentary

Material on the University of Michigan was obtained primarily through the wonderful Bentley Historical Library on the University's campus in Ann Arbor.

It is unclear as to when exactly Robert's two brothers were disinterred and moved to Louisa, but some light was recently shed on the erection of the obelisk that currently marks their collective graves. A photograph of a similar marker was found in family records, with the notation that the 'sample' was from the Vermont Marble Company. A handwritten notation on the back of the placard (in Ella Towles' handwriting) indicates that this was the monument erected in memory of her brothers. The obelisk is, to quote McDowell and Meyer in "The Revival Styles in American Memorial Art," one of the "most pervasive of all the revival forms" of cemetery art. The obelisk represented a form of Egyptian influence in tomb art that was pervasive for some time after Napoleon's Egyptian campaigns and the discovery of the tombs of the pharaohs—culminating in America's borrowing of the best of ancient cultures. Obelisks were considered to be tasteful, with "pure uplifting lines." The Towles marker was apparently a "vaulted" obelisk, with a capital (or top structure) in the shape of an urn. The capital no longer exists on the monument. The Vermont Marble Company was in existence during the period 1860 to 1913, but the date of its erection in the Louisa cemetery can be further narrowed by a faint, pencil inscription on the placard, indicating the size, the price ($125) and date (March 1888) it was ordered and shipped. Clearly, this was a late addition to honor the memory of the three boys who were buried together at Oakland Cemetery. Ironically, the 1888 date would have placed the monument after the death of John Towles, who passed away in

1885 (see Epilogue). Sophronia lived until 1897. This new insight as to the date of the erection of the monument in no way diminishes the efforts taken after the war to unite the boys' remains in Louisa. Such dedication remains extraordinary.

At least one of the busts of Confederate generals crafted by E.A. Poole survives. Not long ago, an auction listing, along with a photo of a bust of Gen. Joseph E. Johnston, surfaced. Upon inquiry, it was discovered that the bust had been purchased by a member of the Johnston family. A photocopy of a number of quotes from letters regarding the Poole bust series survives in the family archives. Former Confederates such as Charles Marshall, and aide to General Lee, and former Virginia Governor John Letcher congratulated the artist on his work. "The likeness is strikingly accurate, and the execution of your work reflects the highest credit upon you as an artist of merit," wrote Gov. Letcher. Joseph E. Johnston himself noted that he had examined Poole's bust of Robert E. Lee and found it to be an "excellent" likeness "in all respects." Being a great fan of the "Immortal Stonewall," I was perhaps most interested in a somewhat lengthy comment from former Confederate Brigadier General John Imboden concerning the bust of "Stonewall" Jackson. "...in your bust of Jackson, you have given the natural *expression* of his remarkable face, with more success than I have seen it in any other work. I knew Gen. Jackson intimately, and was often struck with the difference between his expression when in repose from that his face assumed when animated by conversation. It was this changeful expression that made it so difficult for any artist to produce what would strike all as a good likeness. I think you have imparted to his face that peculiar smile which always preceded the transition from the sadness of expression in repose, to the lively animation of eye and countenance when he was about to speak. In this respect I regard your work as a very great success. Donovan's bust of the great hero is capital as he appeared in meditation and silent; yours exhibits him to my mind, as he looked when about to speak to a friend." Testimonials such as these were no doubt solicited by the artist, in order to encourage other commissions. While we know now that the Johnston bust survives, no information is currently available as to whether or not the other busts still exist in private collections.

Our extended family possesses a number of E.A. Poole's portraits and landscapes. Two of our favorites are the oil portraits of his inlaws, John and Sophronia Towles, which hang in our living room.

It remains somewhat a family puzzlement as to why youngest son Churchill Towles ended up in Texas. A clue may be in an obscure reference to Rev. John Towles in the parish history of St. Stephen's Church in Goliad, Texas, near San

Antonio. Goliad was the scene of a massacre of "Texian" nationalists by Mexican dictator Santa Anna in 1836, prior to the famous siege of the Alamo. "Remember Goliad" became almost as important as "Remember the Alamo" in the war of Texan independence. According to the archives of the Episcopal Diocese of West Texas, twenty-four years after the massacre, an Episocopal mission was started in Goliad by the Rev. John Towles. "No record is available of his work there. We are told that for music the mission was dependent upon an old-fashioned harmonium that could be folded up and carried under the arm. The player held it in his lap and blew the bellows by rocking it back and forth across his knees. Apparently the music it rendered was not duly appreciated by the boys in town who somewhat irreverently referred to it as the 'Comanche Baby.'" The Church News, in an October 1946 entry, goes on to say that the first service at Goliad was on April 20, 1860, on a visitation of Bishop Gregg, "accompanied by the Rev. John Towles of Virginia, who then returned to Virginia." It isn't known why John Towles went as far afield as Texas in 1860 to help found a mission church, but perhaps he made enough friends there to feel comfortable sending his son there in the lean years following the war.

A February 1894 letter from Churchill Towles to his mother, Sophronia, survives in the family archives. Addressed from Houston, Texas, it enumerated the birthdays (and, in the case of "little Robbie," his death) for all of Churchill's children. The children's names were Bertha ('adopted' according to a notation in Sophronia's hand), Rosalie, John, LeRoy, Vivian, and Claude. Interesting that Churchill chose to name four of his children after his siblings and father. "Give my love to Roy and sister [Ella] when you write her," closed Churchill.

Ella Towles Poole posted a note on the front of what she called "her Mother's book," essentially a scrapbook of Sophronia's most personal and important clippings and transcribed letters. "It must have been very sacred to her, for none of us knew of it 'til after her death," Ella noted.

As for Ella, she was recently honored with a wreath-laying at her grave in the St. Mary's Whitechapel cemetery in the Northern Neck. The local chapter of the United Daughters of the Confederacy, which Ella organized with 16 charter members in July of 1912, honored her leadership, which continued until her death in 1932. Sandra P. Sherrill's manuscript "The Confederate Memorial of Lancaster County, Virginia" notes that "through her efforts… a roster of all Confederate soldiers who served in the War Between the States was secured… a remnant from the past erected with love by the Ladies Memorial Association of Lancaster County." Love does, indeed, make memory eternal.

EPILOGUE: I would not live always
Source Notes and Related Commentary

The description of John Towles' death is found in the Diocesan Convention of Maryland publication.

Much of the genealogical information on the Towles family came from the meticulously researched and prepared applications for the Daughters of the American Revolution and Colonial Dames, in which the women in the family were included due to the family history dating back to pre-Revolutionary times in Virginia. Clearly, over the years, this history has meant a great deal to the family!

Diary.
Kept while a prisoner

Wednesday, Aug 5th 1863 ~
First days experience in
Yankey hands.

For three days I have been
inside a very compact line
of yankey pickets, the enemy
were in line of battle expecting an attack almost
momentarily, and conse-
quently were very vigi-
the whole country all
around with pick-
ets also. For three
I had been trying to
my way through but was unsuccessful each night.
Last night I determine
to try it again in anothe

DIARY
kept while a prisoner
Robert C. Towles
Company A. 4th Virginia Cavalry

"Breathes there a man
with soul so dead,
who never to himself hath said
This is my own
my native Land"

Wednesday Aug. 5th 1863
First days experience in Yankey hands.

For three days I have been inside of a very compact line of yankey pickets, The enemy were in line of battle expecting an attack almost momentarily and consequently very vigilant, and the whole country around covered with pickets and patrols.

For three nights I had been trying to make my way through, but was unsuccessful each night. Last night I determined to try it again, in another place.

A kind Lady friend remonstrated with me, begged me not to go. but I still persisted. She said she was not afraid of my being captured, she was afraid the pickets would halt me, and I would not halt, and they would shoot me. I started about ten o'clock, the moon was full, but it was a little cloudy, so that for a few minutes the light would be obscured, and then for a few minutes bright; this suited me exactly. I got within about two hundred yards of the extreme lines with much difficulty; the line of pickets ran along a lane with cedar trees on each side, the men standing about fifty or a hundred yards apart. I drew my pistol, got on my hands and knees and while the moon was behind a cloud, I crawled up through the high grass until I got in the fence corner, and could see the pickets in the road. Sometimes one would walk not more than six feet from me just on the other side of the fence.

Finding them too close, I crawled back from the fence, and up at another place, and continued to do so trying to find a place where the pickets were far enough apart until three o'clock. Having lost three nights rest, I would sometimes find myself nodding in the fence corner, not twenty feet from a picket.

Finally finding it was almost day, I determined to cross the road in spite of consequences. I got through the fence and stood behind a little cedar, and could see the pickets standing on each side of me, but on account of the peculiar grey I wore they could not see me.

There was wattling on the opposite side of the road, and putting my pistol up, I made two or three huge strides across the road, put my hands on two of the stakes and hopped over as light as a kitten, without being seen or heard. I walked on half bent through the field until I got some hundred yards from the road. then stopped—looked back and found all quiet and undisturbed.

There was yet another difficulty of which I was not aware; a double line of pickets—another about three hundred yards outside the one I had just passed. It was nearly day and I feeling like a bird out of a cage walking on rapidly not dreaming of any more danger, when suddenly and unexpectedly "Halt" said one of Mr. Blinker's largest sized Dutchmen. According to orders I halted. "Who comps deer?" said the before mentioned individual. Friend said I. "Advance friend." His intimate friend. then advanced drawing his pistol. When I got within about twenty yards of him, I asked him if he knew where my company was. he asked what company it was, company I said I, and by this time getting near enough, I caught his gun below the bayonet with my left hand, put my pistol at his head and ordered him to surrender, he having his gun at the position of ready right hand on the lock, and his left hand about half way the barrel, had the advantage of me, and instead of obeying my order, suddenly jerked his gun around, striking the bayonet against the side of my head, and at the same time fired; if he had not had the bayonet on, he would have accomplished his object, for then the muzzle of the gun would have been before my face.

After firing he dropped his end of the gun and ran, I still holding the other end, seeing about a dozen others coming up, I dropped my end of the gun and ran too.

I now found I had many other pickets to pass; some of which I passed in sight of and could see them straining their eyes to see me, but could not on account of the color of my clothes. I finally found myself outside the second line of pickets.

I went about a mile further to Cooper's barn, Day was breaking, I still had cavalry camps and pickets to pass. so I went into the barn expecting to stay only a few minutes, seeing that Cooper was cleaning out wheat, I determined to wait until

Cooper came down, and to find out from him, where the Cavalry were camped, so that I might know what body of woods it would be safest to stay in during the day.

I got in the stable loft and unintentionally went to sleep. I suppose I must have been asleep about a quarter of an hour, when I was awakened by some one opening the door; supposing it was Cooper, I raised up on my arm, when instead, Mr. Dutchman No. 2, gun in hand and wished to be informed who I might be. I replied by snapping my pistol at him, and Mr. Dutchman seeming to be perfectly satisfied as to who I was, ran out and shut the door.

I jumped down into the floor of the barn, ran to the back door and found about twenty infantry—dutch gentlemen—ready for me with their guns at their shoulders. I shut the door, ran to the front where the first one made his appearance and found the front as well guarded as the back. I then climbed up into the loft, got down into the back stable and found about half a dozen at that end. I then got into the loft again, took off one of my pistols, and about a dozen leaves out of my pocketbook and hid them under the wheat.

During this time I could hear the Capt. trying to get his men to come in and get me out; he called about half a dozen names, told them to go in and get him out. They would not do it. then he detailed six others and told them to try it. then I heard the voice of the individual who first made his appearance, bawl out "If any body wants to get his brains blown out just let him put his head inside that door."

I went to the window, put my head out and asked the Capt. how many men he had, he said plenty to take me out, and if I did not come out he would fire on me. I told him I could whip that many easily, simply wishing to annoy him, for I knew I had no chance in the world. He said if I did not come out he would burn the barn down, I told him to burn away, I did not care. He ordered the barn to be burned. Then I concluded to get out.

As I stepped out they raised their guns on me and stepped back, I then threw my pistol down, and they made me step back from it before any of them would venture up to get it. Then such crowing was heard, One would have supposed they had Gen. Lee.

I was now taken to the Col's Head Quarters on Dr. King's farm, the Col. was a good natured fat old Dutchman, and treated me very well. But officers and men made a tremendous fuss over me, making such remarks as "We've got you at last have we? you are the boy we have been after for a long time. I thought we would get you after awhile etc. etc." I then found they had arrested Mr. Cooper; they sent us together guarded by a sergt. and seven men, to the Brig. Gen. at Weaversville, whom I found to be a cross illnatured old fellow. He had me stripped and searched from head to feet. My pocketbook he examined himself, took an exact inventory of its contents and sent it by my guard to the Div. Gen. about a mile distant where I was ushured into the presence of Otto Schurtz Agnt. Gen. whom I immediately recognized having seen him at Dr. King's before I was taken prisoner. Of course he did not recognize me, for he had never seen me, but I knew him as soon as I saw him. He was a very nice man. invited me into his tent, gave me a seat on his bed, and commenced asking me questions, among others my name, I told him, it startled him, and turning suddenly around he looked at me in surprise. I knew then that he knew all about me and I laughed. He asked me if I ever saw him before. O yes said I. where did you see me asked the Col. At Dr. Kings said I. He enjoyed it very much and said that Miss King told him the next day, that while he was there the evening before, I slipped up from the woods and took a good look at him.

The Gen. then came up. The Col. told him that I was the young gentleman who spent the evening with him at Dr. King's.

He came up to me took my hand and shook it tremendously, said How are you Sergt. Towles, I am glad to see you. He treated me more as a guest, than a prisoner. Took me into his tent, talked with me some time, & discontinued the guard, I took dinner with them. and they sent me on to Maj. Gen. Howard at Gibson Catlett's. they also sent my pocketbook by the guard.

I was brought up before the Agnt. Col. A whom I found to be one of the meanest yankeys that ever was. As soon as he found out who I was, he commenced "Oh yes you scoundrel we have got you at last have we? Now I will see if you can't stretch some hemp." All right Col. said I just as you say and laughed at him, which made him furious. "All that I regret sir said he, is that you were taken with your uniform on. I think I will have to hang you any how." I told him if he felt like hanging a prisoner of war, captured with his uniform and arms on, he could proceed.

"You need not say one word in defence of yourself said the Col. I know you of old, I have heard of you for a long time, and have plenty of proof against you to hang you."

Gen. Howard then sent for me, and I was taken up to his tent. I found him like Schurtz an excellent man he is a minister, and has lost his arm in the War which has cooled him down considerably I expect.

He took me into his tent to have a private talk with me; asked me a great many questions about my family. My Father's occupations and so on—all of which I answered candidly and as far as expedient truthfully.

While he was talking he held my pocketbook in his hand; When he had gotten through, I asked him to let me keep it. I told him it was not on account of the value of the book. and that it was not worth much to the United States government; that

I prized it very highly as a trophy as it was Gen. Popes, and that I had captured it in a piece of woods near his [Howard's] headquarters. Certainly said he, you seem to be a very truthful young man, and you shall keep it. said he wished to look at it since it was Pope's. he did not wish to see any thing private whatever. He finished looking at it, shut it up, handed it back to me, and told me to keep it.

He then asked me if I knew Mr. Catlett. I told him I did, and asked how Mr. Catlett & family were, he said they were well, and he went to the door, called Mr. C__ and told him there was one of his acquaintances out there.

Then he told me if I wished to talk with Mr. Catlett I could go with him, stay as long as I chose, and return to him when I had finished, which I did. Then I was sent to the "station" and back again to the camp where I will spend the night. And I expect to sleep very soundly as I have not slept for four nights.

Thursday Aug. 6th

I slept very soundly last night, and breakfasted on pork and crackers this morning. Was hurried off to the station, where we took the cars to Warrenton Junct. then on foot to Germantown Gen. Mead & Gen. Patricks HQ where I went through about the same ordeal that I did yesterday, and was sent to the guardhouse, where I found many fellow soldiers, friends and acquaintances, & among others Mr. Clark of my company, Rev. Mr. Pugh [Presbyterian Minister] of Warrenton, Mr. Conway & Mr. Wallace from Stafford County and several old gray headed citizens from this county. I hope to be sent away in the morning. for this is the hottest and dirtiest place I ever was in.

Friday Aug. 7th

We are still here, and know not when we may leave. I was sent to Head quarters to day, but nothing of importance transpired.

Saturday, Aug. 8th

They are bringing in prisoners, principally Citizens, almost every old gray headed Citizen of Stafford County is here in this miserable guard house. Mr. Stone came up today to see his brother, and brought Miss Bettie with him. I was very glad to see them indeed; and through Miss Bettie I was enabled to send my watch, and love and a great many messages to my friends at T___ and other places.

They marched us all out this morning to send us to the Old Capitol prison, but afterwards the order was countermanded and we were marched back. and about forty of the Citizens were released on parole of honor.

Sunday Aug. 9

This is the fourth day I have been in this miserable guard house. Although some forty Citizens were released yesterday, there are now about a hundred prisoners crowded together here in a space of about forty feet square.

I have just been out in the woods under guard breaking branches from the trees to make a bed. This has been a beautiful Sabbath day, I have passed it very miserably. According to my calculation, I am about four hundred yards from Mrs. Weaver's. They do not know that I am here and I do not wish they should know.

Monday Aug 10th

We still find ourselves here, the day has passed very wearily; with the exception of about one hour this morning in which I enjoyed playing Dominos with a frenchman who would not speak a word of English.

I have met with some very agreeable companions, Sergt. McPherson of the 8th Virginia infantry. Rev. Dr. Packard's son of the 7th Virginia Cavalry. Several Citizens, Mr. Francis of Loudon County.

They have given us our rations this evening, and we expect to start to Washington City tomorrow morning.

Tuesday August 11

We are on the train at last whirlling on our way to the Old Capitol prison. We were formed in line this morning (some seventy five in number) and marched through the hot sun and dust to Warrenton junction, where we were put on the train, and now we are dashing on to an earthly Hades.

We have passed Dr. Shumate's and are whirlling across Cedar Run Bridge, and I call to mind the morning I worked so hard to destroy it. Now I see Mr. Mark's house, and now I get a glimpse of Teneriffe, next we pass the station and a crowd of "blue backs" which article I see all over the fields. Now I have a view of Mr. Catlett's where Gen. Howard's H.Q.s are. Now I see Mr. Stone's & Dr. Edmonds' and on the other side, I see the hill at the edge of the woods where I have so often laid down—where once I lost my hat…

Now I pass the woodyard and now the second woodyard, and I am fast leaving my native haunts, and Oh! well—it would be impossible to describe my feelings, as I sit and grit my teeth, to think of my condition.

Oh for a pistol.

Now we pass Dr. Osmund's, Kettle Run Bridge, Bristoe Station, Broad Run bridge, Manasses, all familiar places. We are now dashing on at almost lightning speed. Union Mills, Sangster's Station, Fairfax Station, Burks Station, Springfield Station. Now we see the Episcopal Theological Seminary, and now we whirl into Alexandria, stop a few minutes, and on again across the Long bridge and into Washington.

And now I am looking through the iron bars of the Old Capitol prison.

We got off the Cars at the Depot and stopped some time under the shade of some trees where the friends of the south flocked around us in spite of the guards, Basket after basket of provisions, and bucket after bucket of water were brought to us, and any thing else that the men needed, was cheerfully given.

I got the name of one family which was particularly kind and I shall not soon forget it.

We were then marched through the City to our present abode where I fear I will be likely to stay for some time.

Wednesday Aug. 12.

I have been fortunate enough to get into one of the most pleasant rooms in the building, in the third story fronting the street. My roommates are a very select class of the nicest young men in the building. The guards and officers seem to be very kind and attentive to us, but our fare is most miserable.

We enjoy ourselves in some way most of the time. In the evening we sit at the window and see the pretty Ladies pass, kiss their hands, and slyly wave their handkerchiefs to us. But my principle enjoyment is in dreaming. I do have some delicious dreams of friends I have left behind me. Sleep soundly, never dream of any situation, never dream to awake to its realization until morning when my dreams are ended. Well, I do a great deal of dreaming too while I am awake.

It is just one week since I was taken prisoner.

Thursday Aug. 13.

I have been amusing myself all day with a little Confederate flag. Waving it to the Ladies as they pass. Some take no notice of it; One shook her head very emphatically while others would smile and kiss their hands so sweetly, or wave their handkerchiefs slyly.

We bought a watermelon today, paid half dollar, rather indifferent it was tho.

Friday Aug. 14th

This is the fourth day of my imprisonment in the old Capitol, and Oh! how sick I am getting. How I do long to see some familiar face. One sweet one, yet I would not wish to see them under existing circumstances for any thing. I have not seen a single acquaintance—at liberty—since I have been here.

Saturday Aug. 15.

I have been quite sick today, had a high fever all night, and my head has been aching dreadfully ever since. I fear I will spend a very disagreeable night.

Sunday Aug 16.

I spent the night much better than I expected, and this morning feel so much better that if I were at home, I would not be sick at all.

Yesterday one of our men had a fracas with the sutler of the prison, in which the sutler cursed the prisoner, the young man retorted & the sutler called the sergt. of the guard, had the young man handcuffed and put in the guard house for three days.

Monday Aug. 17.

There are various reports about Lee's and Mead's armies but we cannot hear the truth. My fever came on again last night, and I have been quite sick all day, today. My friends have been trying to get the Surgeon to come up and see me, but he refuses to do so, says if I am too weak to come down to his office, my friends must bring me. I will try and not trouble him.

Tuesday Aug. 18th

I feel much better than I did yesterday, have been walking about this evening. I have just devoured two delicious peaches, and some delicious pie which I bought of the sutler, which put a good taste in my mouth, and has been instrumental in putting me in good humor. I have not yet seen a single friend.

Wednesday Aug. 19th

I am still improving, but it is very hard for one to improve in this place.

Thursday Aug 20.

I received a letter a few moments ago and have been cutting tremendous "shines" on account of it, but upon opening it, found it was for another man.

I feel almost well today only a little weak.

Friday Aug 21.

Joyful News—Mr. Wood has just called the roll, and notified us that we leave here at seven o'clock in the morning.

The questions still arises, where will they send us? I hope to Dixie. Some say to "Point Lookout" prison. Any where in preference to this place.

Saturday Aug. 22.

The good news is confirmed. We are to go this morning.

We are now in the yard and Mr. Wood is calling the roll in alphabetical order and the men march out as their names are called. All my friends—their names come before mine—threfore they have all gone. But Mr. Wood is calling in the letter T. and I am momentarily looking for my name, but alas! he has finished that letter, and never said Towles once. Now he has finished the roll, folds his paper, slams the gate, and I am still here; yet I know not why.

I also find that three South Carolineans have been kept here as hostages for three negro soldiers captured at Fort Sumpter. Two of them are friends of mine, and have been my roommates ever since I have been here.

I have been removed from my former room to the Barracks in the yard, the worse place in the prison. There are some eight or ten others left on the same footing with myself, but all are strangers to me.

I have just gotten a letter from the Rev. Dr. Dalrymple of Baltimore. He says he will certainly come to see me tomorrow or next day. It will be a very pleasant visit to me indeed.

Sunday Aug. 23.

We had a very good Sermon this evening from a Chaplain of Morgan's command. He is a non-combatant and will be sent through to Dixie.

I feel very lonesome now, but it may be better that I am left here.

Monday Aug. 24.

Received this evening a letter from Dr. Dalrymple enclosing ten dollars—all he was allowed to enclose—which is very acceptable to me. He came over from Baltimore today to see me, but could not get permission to see me. which I very much regretted.

Tuesday Aug. 25.

The whole prison was treated today to watermelons, peaches, tomatos etc. by some Ladies from Georgetown. And this evening I have been put into the same room which I formerly occupied, with four others, the three Carolineans held as hostages for Negroes, and Mr. Horner 6th Va. Cavalry. Mr. White informs me that there is a very serious charge against me, that of being a spy.

Wednesday Aug 26.

More prisoners were brought in last night. Several from the 6th Va. Cavalry.

Thursday Aug. 27.

We are still here awaiting our fate, but very impatiently.

I bought a large watermelon today which we enjoyed very much, as much a(s) our circumstances would admit of.

Friday Aug. 28.

Times are rather dull now, nothing of interest has transpired today, excepting that we had tomatos for dinner, a decided improvement.

We still enjoy the smiles of the pretty Ladies at a distance which no doubt tends to keep our spirits up. I am suffering now with a bad cold and cough.

Saturday Aug. 29.

The day has passed quietly except when some of my roommates getting desperate, yell out and stamp around the floor as if they would tear the house down.

Sunday Aug. 30.

Another Sabbath has passed. We had tomatos for dinner.

Another very fine sermon this evening, by another of Morgan's chaplains. One week today, I will be twenty years old. If I could only get to Dixie, to spend my birthday, but alas! vain hope—I fear.

Monday Aug. 31

Summer is gone, today is the last day, and I am still here. O the peaches, apples and watermelons I am losing: the worse season of the year to be a prisoner. O for wings like a dove.

Tuesday Sept. 1st

The weather is very beautiful, but I cannot enjoy it. I have rubbed the hair off each side of my head, looking through these iron bars. It seems to me that I have been here almost an age.

Wednesday Sept. 2.

I am longing to see some friend, I have friends here, in Alexandria and in Baltimore, and I think it is strange that only one has been to see me and he was not allowed to see me. "Hope on, thy day will come"

Thursday Sept. 3.

I got a letter from Dr. Dalrymple this morning, he anticipates coming to see me again. Says he has notified some of my friends—my Father's friends—that I am here, and I surely expect to hear from some of them.

Friday Sept. 4.

We have had a lively time today, romping, scuffling and cracking jokes to such an extent that Mr. White and the Sergt. of the guard had to come in and complain.

If I could only spend evening where I was just one month ago.

One month ago.

Saturday Sept. 5.

Today is just one month since I was taken prisoner. It seems to me an age, and none know how many weary months may pass, and still find me looking through the bars.

Sunday Sept. 6.

Today is my birthday. I regret exceedingly having to spend it under such unpleasant circumstances; I shall undoubtedly miss my cake, however it cannot be helped. There is no use in grieving over spilt milk. I should be thankful if I do not have to spend another in the same embarassing situation.

I believe that I am destined to see the Elephant in all its various forms, and this may simply be a portion of the exposition which has been decided upon that I shall undergo; Therefore, under the circumstances I shall be compelled quietly to submit.

"Trust to luck. trust to luck. stare fate in the face sure your heart will be easy If it's in the right place."

I think my heart is undoubtedly in the right place—hope so anyhow.

Monday Sept. 7

The fare to day has been intollerable, we have been in the habit of buying butter from the sutler, and in that way make out very well in the eating line. Our fare consists of Coffee, bread and meat. The meat is not fit to eat; with coffee, bread and butter we do very well, but the sutler is out of butter now, and we do miss it considerably.

Tomorrow is reception day—I hope some friend will come and see me. We only receive visitors on Tuesdays and Fridays.

The only familiar face I have seen—at liberty—since I have been here is that of my old sorrel horse—Racer—familiarly named Bones. Who walks majestically past my window every day carrying the worthless carcass of a big yankey sergt.—I think if Bones knew how little his rider became him, he would throw him and break his neck.

Tuesday Sept. 8.

All quiet to day; no news from any source, and the worst is no friend has called to see me as I anticipated. I shall have to wait until Friday.

Wednesday Sept. 9.

I am glad to see they are exchanging prisoners again, from yesterdays paper I see that seven hundred and fifty prisoners were sent on to City Point for exchange. I fear though it will be some time before our time comes if at all; We are near the last that have been captured, and there are a great many ahead of us.

Thursday Sept. 10.

Tomorrow is reception day. I still wait and hope for some friend to come to see me, if what friends I have here are not too strong union to help a poor Rebble.

Friday Sept. 11

Wo! be unto the inhabitants of Washington if ever I come in here with old Stuart for

"I was sick and ye visited me not"

"I was in prison and ye came not unto me"

The day is almost gone and no friend has been to see me, or even send me anything good to eat.

Saturday Sept. 12.

Another long day has passed, since the last prisoners were sent to Point Lookout prison. We have been occasionally reinforced until we now number some forty or fifty, and we have rumors of our being sent off almost every day.

A good many citizens have been sent down from time to time and lodged in the "Carroll prison", among them several acquaintances.

Sunday Sept. 13

Another beautiful Sabbath, and another excellent sermon from one of Morgan's Chaplains.

Monday Sept. 14

I was very sick last night scarcely slept any, but am up again today feel much better. but quite low spirited.

Tuesday Sept. 15.

Some forty prisoners were brought in last night, among them was a Lieut. in the Baltimore Artillery, who was put in our room. he says there were about forty captured with him, and three pieces of Art. About seventy were brought in this evening which were captured later in the day.

Wednesday Sept. 16.

Very important events have transpired today, Mr. White came around and notified me that I was to leave, I got ready, went down into his office and found I was to be sent to the Carroll prison, where I now am. They have positively refused to treat me as a prisoner of War.

No hope for an exchange until I have had a trial. I have met with many friends here—have been put in the room with several who were at Meads Hd.Q. and were brought down on the Cars with me.

Thursday Sept. 17.

I am still in Caroll prison, have been moved twice since I have been here. First I was put in this room with my old friends, then I was put into a small room in another part of the building with three detectives, and to day have been moved back to this first room. South Attic.

The three South Carolinians who were my room-mates in the Old Capitol prison were brought over this morning.

Friday Sept. 18th

I am about as comfortably fixed here, as I was in the Old Capitol, and am among equally as many friends. But we were allowed a few more privileges in the former "Hotel" I had much rather be there than here, do not feel at all safe here.

Saturday Sept. 19th

There were some men from Delaware brought in last night, they were arrested on a vessel, on the Potomac—near Evansport Virginia.

Sunday Sept. 20.

About twenty more Citizens were brought in last night, principally from Culpepper Co. Va. Our particular friends—the "Yankeys", have a peculiar way of arresting every body and everything they see. I heard a man say this morning he had a dog at home that he was very much afraid they would get. The dog had but one eye yet he was afraid they—the yanks—would get him.

Some of my friends seem to think I am held as a hostage—hope not for a Negro.

Monday Sept. 21.

There is considerable excitement on account of a rumored defeat of the army of the Cumberland—Yankey.

Tuesday Sept. 22.

The reports of yesterday, are confirmed in the papers of today. and I think from their own account they have been badly whipped. I earnestly hope so.

Wednesday Sept. 23.

The papers are still full of the news from Tennesee, we have today established a rule which will prove a great comfort and I hope a great benefit to us all. A chapter from the Bible is to be read, and a prayer every night by Rev. Mr. Pugh.

Thursday Sept. 24.

We are daily expecting to hear of a battle on the Rapidan Va—I feel very confidant as to the result.

Friday Sept. 25.

Some eight or ten Citizens were brought in last night. Some from Prince Wm. Va. some prisoners of War were also brought down and put in the old Capitol among them Jimmie Dulin. I understand that the prisoners of War, will be sent to "Point Lookout prison" this morning.

Saturday Sept. 26.

I received another very kind letter from Dr. Dalrymple—as yet my only friend, he urges me to send him a list of what things I need, I have complied with his request, shall expect the articles I mentioned in a few days.

Sunday Sept. 27.

This is only seven Sabbaths I have spent in this place, how many more cannot yet be told.

Monday Sept. 28th

All quiet in Carroll to day. Many rumors of an exchange.

Tuesday Sept. 29.

The Baltimore Gazett publishes a report of a great battle near Chattanoga Tenn. on Thursday.

Wednesday Sept. 30th

Yesterday I was taken down to the Officer and questioned. and to day the officer of the day came into our room and enquired for a rebble Sergt. I told him I was his man, he asked my age, occupation, when & where taken etc. Then, "Do you belong to Mosby's guerillas?" No sir said I. "What guerillas do you belong to?" First regular bushwhackers said I. and amid the cheers of my twenty companions, Mr. Officer of the day withdrew.

Thursday Oct,. 1st

I have a slight presentment, that it will not be long before I leave here; for what place I cannot yet say.

Washington City D.C.
October 2nd

Now I can tell in what way I expected to leave "Mr. Carroll" I am no longer a prisoner. Last night, I took my leave, my flight, by way of a window, and am now at large in the City.

Saturday Oct. 3rd

At home in the woods. I am now in the height of my enjoyment.
King of the Woods
Night before last, a young friend and I got out of the window of the South Attic. the room in which I was confined. and by means of a light pole, which I had previously arranged—by taking a hook from my iron bedstead and driving it into the end of the pole—we climbed to the top of the roof, went along the top some twenty five yards, then fixing the hook, We decended by means of the pole to the attic window of the tenement occupied by the family of Mr. Wood. (the keeper of the prison). We got into the attic which was not occupied, where we remained

some time—until the family were asleep—during which time I occasionally looked down the stairs and could see some one lying & sleeping in bed, the door of the room being open.

About the time we got ready to decend the stairs, another of my roommates came crawling into the window and after waiting a few moments we started down. I at the head of the party armed with a pocket knife and one of my long cavalry boots, We got to the floor of the third story, found the doors open and the sleepers snoring within. We passed on as quietly as three kittens to the second story, found one door open about a foot, a light—Mr. Wood's and other male voices within. Here my comrade's courage failed them, one of them started back up stairs; I beckoned to him to come back, then peeping into the room, found they could not see through the door from where they were sitting, I quietly stepped past the door, and was soon joined by my comrades; then on to the next and last floor, found a gaslight burning in the hall, and a sentinel out at the front door, I went to the back door, found it bolted, I moved the bolt & stepped out into a small back yard and closing the door behind us, we put on our boots. We now had three plank fences to climb; the first some ten feet high and could not be reached from the ground, but from my window I had seen a rick of stove wood stocked against it, and immediately above it hung a tree of peaches; I had told my roommates before leaving them that when I got on that fence, I intended to stop and fill my pockets with peaches, so according to promise when I mounted the fence I reached up for a peach, but just at that moment my friend Tom climbed up on the wood, it rolled down with him, and he being very excitable caught at the top of the fence & struggled to the top making such a tremendous noise that I jumped down on the other side.

We easily climbed the other two fences and I found myself on Pennsylvania Avenue in Confederate uniform. I had taken the precaution to cut the straps off my pants, and put my boots under them, and taking my jacket off, rolled it up—wrong side out—took it under my arm started down the Avenue accompanied by my friend Tom. The third party having started in another direction. We walked about the City some, then went to Dr. ___ s. then to Tom's father's where we remained an hour and where I was furnished with a Citizens coat & pants.

I put the coat on over my jacket took my pants under my arm; then we started out again, went to a stable loft, where we spent the remainder of the night. and the whole day yesterday. Tom's Father sent us something to eat during the day; And last night we started in a most terrible storm to make our way out of the City.

We passed through Georgetown, got supper at an eating house, bought some things that we needed at a store, then we started out on High St. taking the pike to

Rockville. via Tenelly-town where many troops were camped, and guards on the pike to prevent any from passing.

In this however we had been posted, and as soon as we arrived near the edge of the troops, we left the road and crawled under a haystack which Providence placed in our path, we concluded to stop until day. The rain was pouring down in torrents, and I think it was the darkest night I ever saw except one.

We pulled out some dry hay, and lay down under the shelter of the stack until day. In the meantime it cleared off very cold, and "your humble servant" came very near freezing.

At day we arose from our bed of hay and found we were surrounded by camps. Seeing a house not far off, and an old negro man cutting wood we concluded to go and ask him a few questions; the first of which was who lived there. he said Mr. _____ the policeman & looking around I saw a pair of large blood-hounds lying at the door. Thinking this was not the house for us, we declined asking any further questions than the road to Rockville, and started for a small body of woods immediately in front of us which we passed through from the edge of it, we could see a long line of fortifications stretching out on our right and left, a redoubt on either side of us & very near sentinels walking upon them; these we had to pass between, fortunately for us there was a deep ravine immediatley on our left making obliquely towards the Potomac, this we got into and hid by the high weeds and undergrowth, we passed through unnoticed. Thinking we had passed all danger we left the ravine, bearing to the left over the hill we suddenly came upon another redoubt and barracks full of soldiers; here, we turned back to the river again and travelled it until we got entirely outside the fortifications. There were pickets some distance to the front of us on the pike, but I—being a good woodsman—travelled through the woods and fields keeping about a half mile from the pike until we arrived to where we are now, about eight miles from Georgetown.

About a mile further back, we came to a small house, from the outward appearance of which, I felt certain the inmates were Southern. I proposed to Tom that we should stop and get breakfast. We did so, and soon found from the conversation of the Old Lady I was not mistaken. In fact she said she did not know to whom she was talking, and she did not care—that she was not afraid to show her sentiments. etc.

After we had finished our breakfast, I told her we had fortunately met with a southern Lady, and I would tell her a secret, and begging her not to reveal it, I opened my black dress coat and showed her my gray uniform. She turned very pale & came near falling to the floor. I then told her we had made our escape from the

"Carroll prison". She gave us many blessings, cautions, directions, etc.—begged us if we ever came back that way, to come and see her.

As soon as I was put in Carrol prison I saw the chance to make my escape and determined to take advantage of it; but at the time the moon arose about or before sunset and the nights were too bright, I awaited the moon rising later and later each night until the first day of Oct. when it rose about half past ten o'clock. The last roll call was at nine, and I had to make the trip across the roof between these two hours.

I spoke of my intention to several of my most intimate friends and roommates, among them was Mr. Francis from Loudon County. Mr. Pugh—my bedfellow—Mr. Kelly & Mr. Davis from Fauquier Co. who had once belonged to the army, had lost his right leg at the battle of Rich Mountain. They all, with the exception of Mr. Francis opposed it bitterly, their principal arguement was that I knew nothing about the situation of things in Woods part of the house. Here they were mistaken. From my window I could see the top of the entire building—which was originally built by one man Carrol, in six tenements—on three sides of a square—three of these tenements were occupied as a prison, the other three as private residences, Wood, the keeper of the prison occupied one. Clark and Donley the other two. I could see that each tenement was built on the same plan, and by examining the prison carefuly, could tell exactly the situation of every thing in the other tenements; and offered to bet my friends I could tell exactly how many rooms, how many steps in the stairs, and how many boards? there were in the railing in Woods house.

I saw that the window I intended to get into was immediately over a circular stairway, and when I swung down from the window, I knew if I should let go, I would go to the bottom. but knowing where the stairs ought to be, I reached out my foot and struck it exactly.

Sunday Oct. 4.

I am now about six miles from the Potomac River, and two from Rockville. We continued to travel through the woods and fields yesterday until we got in sight of Rockville, knowing the detectives would be on the watchout for us, I did not intend to go through the town, but to leave it to our right and strike the road to the Falls; wishing to go to a man on that road Mr. A____ whose name we had gotten while in prison.

But we found out there was a large Union meeting and Barbecue going on in town, and saw there was an immence crowd in the streets, so we for curiosity sake walked straight through the crowd cheering for President Abe, as bold as any other Union Man. There was about two companies of Cavalry and I did not in the least feel <u>at home</u> rubbing against big blue yankeys with their sabres and pistols buckeled on—pushing shoulder straps out of my way, and taking the Falls road we came on here, and are now in the woods among friends.

We have fortunately fallen in with Mr. A___ and Mr. T___ warm friends not only to us, but to the cause of the South.

We are now waiting for a chance to cross the river, which is very closely watched by Scott's 900.

I slept in a <u>feather bed</u> last night. Mr. A___ & Mr. T___ are doing all they can for us.

Monday Oct. 5

As I have not said much about my friend Tom, I will now endeavor to give a slight history of him.

When I determined to leave Carrol, I could not get one of my roommates to go with me—in fact could not find a man in the prison—excepting Tom—who was willing to undertake it. All were anxious to make their escape, but all thought my plan too dangerous.

I was introduced to Tom by my friend Mr. Jas. Howison—and a near neighbor at home—who recommended him to me. Thomas Thompson is a native of England. Eight years ago when he was about twelve years old, his Father came to America and commenced business in Alexandria, and from thence moved to Washington where the War found him keeping a jewelry store. Tom is a watchmaker. From some cause or other, the whole family turned out strong southern sympathisers. About the first of Feb. Tom left Washington, went to Baltimore under the pretense of fixing some watches or doing something in that line—slipped out into the country with others. made his way to the Potomac, crossed over & went to Richmond carrying some very valuable information to our authorities. He then thought he could recross the river slip back into Washington without any one knowing that he had been farther than Baltimore. He started taking many letters with him from parties in Richmond to parties in Wash. and some important papers. In crossing the Potomac he was captured by a gunboat, taken to Washington where he was recognized, and having positive proof that he was acting in the capacity of a spy, they put him in prison tried & condemned him to be executed. It was said, the sentence was passed the day before we left, He did not know it positively, he knew there was no chance for him, and this moved him to make the attempt.

He has been raised entirely in Cities, never knew anything of the Country; does not know one tree from another, one grass from another, a hare from a squirrel, in fact he is the most perfectly <u>green</u> young man in such matters, I ever saw. Yet he is a smart youth, and has a heart as big as all out of doors. He knows nothing about travelling off the roads, will get lost in the fields, knows very little about doing any thing—yet is willing to undertake anything. He is most grateful to me, says he feels that to me he owes his whole life.

In prison, he occupied a small room in the lower part of the building from which there was no possible chance of escape, and I had to smuggle him up to my room as the crowd came from supper, and hide him under my bed, and got some of his roommates to tell the Sergt. when he came around, that he had gone to get water. He thinks that to me he owes his life. Finis.

Tuesday Oct. 6.

This morning I went with Mr. A___ to the house of a union man, bought a beef, helped him to bring it over and butcher it. The river is too full for us to cross yet.

Wednesday Oct. 7

We took a squirrel hunt to day, killed two.

Thursday Oct. 8.

From information received to day, Mr. A___ thinks we can cross the river Saturday. It is falling slowly, has been quite high.

We killed two more squirrels to day.

Friday Oct. 9.

Mr. T___ has been to the river to day, and he thinks we can cross tomorrow. I would have swam it long ago, but for Tom who cannot swim, and we have to wait until it is sufficiently low for us to cross.

Saturday Oct. 10.

We have been disappointed, the river is still too full for us to cross.

Sunday 11th.

Mr. A__ & Mr. N___ have been down on the river today, and found it very strongly guarded, we will have to wait for a change.

Monday, Oct. 12.

We sat in the woods this morning and saw a gallant charge made by eight of Beekers detectives on Mr. A___'s house, where we have been staying.

The "Washington Star" says the notorious spies Towles and Thompson have made their escape from Carrol prison by way of a lightning rod.

It is reported that Gens. Lee and Mead are fighting.

Tuesday Oct. 13.

We are still waiting and longing for a chance to cross the river. They are enforcing the draft here, and watch the river very closely for men wishing to escape to Dixie, and also for deserters from their army, who are constantly crossing the river, from the other side.

Wednesday Oct. 14.

Fighting has been going on all day in the direction of Bull Run. I hope Lee with his gallant boys may kill and capture Mead's entire army. God grant they may gain a glorious victory.

Thursday Oct. 15.

Mr. A___ went to Washington yesterday; returned today. says he saw several hundred yankey prisoners who had been paroled. and thirteen Confederate prisoners from the 4th Va. Cavalry—my regt. I fear our boys have suffered much.

Friday Oct. 16

We can hear nothing from the fight on Wednesday, from the yanks keeping so very quiet on the subject, I feel certain they have been whipped.

Saturday Oct. 17.

We have at last hit upon a plan of crossing the river and will start in the morning if nothing happens to prevent.

Sunday Oct. 18.

Disappointed again. The wisest and best laid schemes will sometimes fail.

Monday Oct. 19.

We had a slight stampede last night. About nine o'clock we were—fortunately for us—standing out in the yard with Mr. A___ when we heard cavalry coming up the road toward the house; Tom and I immediately started down the hill, at the back of the house, but rallied after running about fifty yards, which we had no sooner done than we were joined by Mr. A____ coat, hat and boots in hand, & stepping at the rate of about "a mile a minute" and at the same rate we saw the yanks dash around each side of the house. Then took place a general stampede down the hill, of a sort of "D___l take the hindmonst"

Tom went at the fence, rolled over in a hurricane like manner, breaking a rail, then almost breaking his neck in the bottom of a deep ditch. Where he laid all night. As for myself, I do not distinctly remember troubling the fence at all, and am very certain that I did not see any ditch.

Mr. A___ and I went to the woods, where we stayed until about four o'clock when Mr. A___ concluded to venture up to the house; he had not been there long before the dog barked and he thinking they were coming again, stampeded the second time, ran into a pile of lumber near the house, made enough noise to be heard a mile, and we have not seen or heard from him since. We have kept in the cool shade of the thickest pines all day, and make a start out this evening or tomorrow morning.

Tuesday Oct. 20.

We slept last night in Mr. T____'s barn. This morning we started out. took a walk of about twenty miles to where we now are, at Mr. H____'s about three miles above Poolesville—we traveled all the way through fields and woods, flanked Poolesville and other places, and are again in the hands of friends, who think there is a much greater chance of our getting across the river her, than there was lower down.

Wednesday Oct. 21.

We started out this morning with Mr. U___ to where we now are a No.1. hiding place, where Mr. U___ left us promising to be back at twelve o'clock.

It is now passed five, and he has not yet made his appearance. He is to let us know if there is any chance for us to get over the river.

Thursday Oct. 22.

We slept in a strawstack last night, got neither dinner nor supper yesterday.

Started this morning to a piece of woods to watch for Mr. U___. met a youth singing the "Bonnie Blue Flag" he passed us then turned and came back to the piece of woods where we were, made himself known to us, took us to his Fathers's house near by, where we made a tremendous breakfast.

We are now in our old hiding place. Mr. U___ failed to find us yesterday but came today and brought us dinner.

Friday Oct. 23.

Mr. R____ has been working hard all day to make some arrangement by which we can get across the river, we hope to make the trip tonight.

Saturday Oct. 24.

Over at last.

About seven o'clock last night Mr. R___ said to us that he was prepared to see us over. We started for the river where we found three ferrymen waiting for us.

The canal was about sixty feet wide and the only means by which we could cross was with a piece of plank about fifteen feet long, 1 inch thick and some six inches wide. This one of the ferrymen got on, and stooping down near the centre paddled quietly across or pushed across with a light pole; then pushing the plank back another followed his example, and so on until all were over. We then had to walk a mile down the canal where we found a boat which had been stolen from some man on the Virginia shore by some yankey deserters, on board of which we embarked and in a short time were on Virginia soil once more.

We landed on the old battle field Balls Bluff. It had been raining all night, and we had a very wet muddy walk of some five miles, where we rested under somebody's straw stack until morning, when we arose from our uneasy bed tired, wet & and feeling about as near frozen as two such youths ever were.

We went to a house near by, got thoroughly warmed, and some hot breakfast, and directions in regard to our route, came on in direction of Union. We spent half an hour examining the Fort on the top of the mountain near Leesburg. Took dinner with a good Southern man, then came on to where we now are, and where we will spend the night, about three miles from Union. It has been raining all day, and we have had a very wet walk.

Sunday Oct. 25.

I am now in the hands of a most excellent friend, Dr. Peyton. His surprise at seeing me can scarcely be imagined.

I parted with Tom this morning at Rectors Xroads, he making on towards Richmond, and I trying to get to Prince Wm. County.

I stopped in Rectortown a short time to see some friends. Met with Mr. Lake a young soldier who was taken to the Old Capitol prison with me, and afterwards sent to Point Lookout where he made his escape.

Dr. Peyton tells me my old friend Julian Lee has gone on to Prince Wm. He left here this morning. I hope to fall in with him.

Monday Oct. 26.

I left the Dr.'s this morning, struck out for the mountains in the direction of New Baltimore, ran into a foraging party of about three or four hundred yankey infantry, which suddenly turned me back. I watched their movements some time. and finding they did not intend to get out of my way, I took another direction and halted at Mr. Robt. Beverleys where I will spend the night.

I fear I will have much difficulty in getting down into Pr. Wm.

Tuesday Oct. 27.

I am now lying in the pines about fifty yards from the pike, (watching for a chance to cross) between Buckland and Gainsville. Where I can see a continual stream of yanks passing. The Pike is very strongly guarded by stationary guards every hundred yards, and by mounted patrol every two hours. On leaving Mr. Beverley's this morning, finding all the Mountain Gaps guarded, I crossed between

Hopewell and the Thoroughfare; had some little difficulty in crossing the M.G. R.R. but at last am here waiting and longing, <u>"Oh that night or Stuart would come".</u>

Wednesday Oct. 28.

I succeeded in crossing the pike last night, went to Dr. Macrae's and fearing he had a guard, I got into the shrubery & crawled up near the porch, found three guards on the porch, one, whisteling "When this Cruel War is Over." & two more in the kitchen. I lay there some time hoping to be able to get some of the family out, but seeing no chance I left waded Broad Run, and came to Mr. Greens, curled up under the calm side of a straw stack and slept until day, when Mr. G came up found me nearly frozen, he took me to the house, gave me some warm breakfast, which was a great help to me, for I had not had a meal since night before last.

After breakfast I travelled on through the pines to Mr. Butlers, & hearing he had a guard, I stopped at the edge of the pines. Soon I succeeded in arresting his attention and getting him to come out. After talking some half hour I left him and came on to Mr. Manuels where I have spent the day in the edge of the pines trying to get him out, but have not yet succeeded. I find the country overrun with yankeys, every body has a guard, and the yanks are prowling through the country in every direction, even through the thickest pines, several have passed very near me today—none have seen me.

Thursday Oct. 29

I find it will be very difficult to cross the R.Road; there is almost a continuous line of encampments from Catletts to Bristoe, Last night wagons were running all night and there being a strong guard with them I could not cross, consequently am here for another day.

I succeeded in getting Mr. M___ out last night. He brought me some supper and some blankets with which I made myself very comfortable by the side of a haystack.

He has been out to see me several times today and brought me something to eat.

Friday Oct. 30.

I crossed the R.Road last night and am largely enjoying the society of my kind friends at the "Grove" I am comparatively out of the yankey range.

Only one Lieut. S___ of the 8th Illinois Reg. has broken in upon my enjoyment. He came in—being acquainted with the family—and I gently subsided into the closet. He took his seat about two feet from me, and commenced a lively conversation with Miss Lou in which he asked her if she knew Sergt. Towles. "O yes said Lou very well indeed."

"He is a very sharp little fellow said the Lieut. We took him up here, last spring, started to camp with him and he got away from us before we got to the camp." Little did he think I was so near him.

Saturday Oct. 31.

I find the picket lines are in the same situation exactly, that they were when I was captured, consequently I have not been able to get to Tennerife from where I started the night before I was captured; but I went last night to the barn at Vaucluse where I hid my pistol, found the wheat had been overhauled, much of it had been taken out—suppose by the yankees—I got into the loft, ran my arm down into the wheat, put my hand on my pistol without the slightest difficulty. The rats had almost eaten the holster up but the pistol has not rusted in the least bit. I took it down on Cedar run to day and although it had been loaded nearly three months, not a barrel snapped.

Sunday Nov. 1st.

What a blessing it is after we have been absent so long from those we love, and after having gone through the troubles, hardships and dangers that I have, to be suddenly ushered into the presence of those friends.

If these miserable yankeys were only away, how much I could enjoy, yet it must not be thought. I allow them to disturb my enjoyment much.

For the last day or two I have been enjoying the society of my old friends, and also taking a quiet good rest which I so much needed. But on account of the yanks, I have not been able to see many of my friends and shall have to pay them all nocturnal visits.

Monday Nov. 2.

I have been wandering through the woods all day, expect to go on a scout tomorrow.

Tuesday Nov. 3rd.

I went last night to Mrs. Howison's, got into the house in spite of three yankey guards, and spent some two hours very pleasantly indeed.

Returned this morning to the Grove. I will try to get to Tennerife to night.

Wednesday Nov. 4.

Once more I press the hands & enjoy the presence of the dear friends I have not seen since the night of August 4th previous to my extensive scout to that far famed city of Washington; Just three months past.

I left the Grove about dark last night, passed Vaucluse two yankey guards there, passed Epsom & the three yankey guards there; then retracing almost exactly my steps of the night previous to my capture, I found myself safely at Tennerife once more. But oh! What a change—not in my friends—no—the same glow of spirits, the same hearty welcome as of old; but I could hardly realize it was the same place.

The fencing gone, the cornfield packed as hard and stripped as clean as any road, and even in the yard there are ditches cut and heaps of stone collected together somewhat in the shape of chimneys, huts, etc. Yet, it is really gratifying to see how well it is all taken. The girls laugh and talk about it as if it were all a good joke, had little anecdotes to tell about the killing of all the poultry etc. The pickets were moved from their old position, and the troops moved from their camps around the house night before last.

Gen. Barney occupied the parlor as his Hd.Quarters. I remained about four hours, being hardly able to tear myself away—and came down to the piece of pines which I now occupy and in which I have spent the day much more agreeably than I had the slightest idea of. Four of my young Lady friends have spent the day with me. I went to Mr. Colvin's this morning and received a hearty welcome and Mrs. Colvin has sent me the greatest profusion of "Commisary stores."

I shall go to T____ again tonight, and from there try to cross the R.Road.

Thursday Nov. 5.

I left my hiding place yesterday evening, as soon as it was dark, went straight to T__ and hearing that the yanks were too thick along the R.R. for me to cross, I stayed all night, I started out about day, and am now at the Grove, where I feel almost as much at ease as if there was no war.

Friday Nov. 6.

I have been resting today. I walked over this evening to find a member of my company for a companion but failed. I shall make another attempt to cross the railroad in a night or two if circumstances permit.

Saturday Nov. 7.

I would have tried crossing the R.R. last night, but my friend Lou most positively decided I should not try it. I think I must be cruel enough not to heed her advice to night.

Sunday Nov. 8.

I made a desperate attempt to cross the R.R. last night, but could not get within fifty yards of it. found guards on it, and many pickets on this side of it, one of which I ran off his post without saying a word to him & without meaning him the slightest harm whatsoever.

I finally concluded that it was not a "very healthy place" for me, and left, came to my old hiding place in the pines, where I was joined this morning by "Cooney" with breakfast.

I slept until one o'clock, then arose, & walked around for a few minutes and soon spied "Mr. Yankey Cavalry man" riding up the road from me and about half a mile ahead of me, and liking his appearance very much at that distance, I started out to flank him, ran about a mile, waded the run and came in on the road ahead of the fresh gentleman in order to gently dismount him. But somehow his horse had thrown him and partly knocked him out of his senses, he had lost his pistol & carbine. I found his carbine but could not find his pistol. He is or was the most splendidly equiped yankey I think I ever saw. he has all a cavalryman could call for, just three days old. I took his horse, equipments and trapings and let him go. he thanked me.

Monday Nov. 9.

After relieving my yankey & as soon as it was dark I started out for the Grove, where I stayed all night. This morning I took leave of them and started down through Stafford Co. for the Army but finding a large force of Yankeys moving down the Marsh road, and thinking that the entire army was on the move to Falmouth, I turned back, and am again at the Grove.

I shall start for the R.R. tonight & try to cross.

Tuesday Nov. 10.

I left the Grove last night as soon as it was dark, came to T___ and stayed until day, then mounted, put my oilcloth around my shoulders, pinned my blue blanket around my body so that it hung down and hid my gray pants; then rode along the R.R. about half a mile & crossed in sight of the guards, came on through the Thoroughfare, and am now at Dr. Peyton's.

Wednesday Nov. 11.

I stopped at a shop and lost about half the day in having my horse shod, am now at the Rock ford on the Rappahannock river where I will spend the night. I have met with two gentlemen who are acquainted with my friends at the Grove.

Thursday Nov. 12.

I have not been able to get to where my reg. is camped to night as I had hoped

Friday Nov. 13.

I am with Gen. Stuart at last. I stopped with my Company a short time today, they were all very much surprised to see me, and all are very anxious for me to stop scouting.

Saturday Nov. 14.

I am still at Gen. Stuarts H.Q.—no furloughs are granted now—but Gen. Stuart has made a special application to Gen. Lee for a furlough for me, and I am waiting its return.

Sunday Nov. 15.

I am with my company today, will remain with them until morning. then return to Gen. Stuart's H.Q.

Monday Nov. 16.

Homeward bound. I came to H.Q.s this morning & got my furlough for fifteen days, and am on the march for Lancaster. Am now at the Wilderness.

Tuesday Nov. 17.

I am on the road again, came through Fredericksburg this morning, found it looking much better than I expected. Crossed the river at Port Royal late this evening, and am now about a mile from Port Conway.

Wednesday Nov. 18.

I have taken a long ride to day, am now only twelve miles from Greenvale— where my parents sister & brothers are—at Mr. McCartys.

I rode up to the gate, asked if I could be accomodated there for the night. Mr. McCarty came out, told me I could & asked me to ride around to the barn with him, which I did, and where I found Father's old carriage, I recognised it as soon as I saw it. Mr. McCarty told me my Cousin Jno. Robt. Chilton had brought it up. He too was surprised to see me.

Thursday Nov. 19.

"Home again".

Home once more

Oh what a joy, what a blessing after being separated so long from Father, Mother, Sister & brothers, to be once more suddenly clasped in their arms. But oh! what change time has made, all have changed so much, I hardly would have known them; and two are no more. two the brightest, two happiest, have gone, gone to their eternal rest. A sister and a brother.

God forbid that I should wish them back to this dark world again.

They are <u>free, forever free</u> from Sin and sorrow, forever free from War and strife, and God grant that though the home circle has been broken on earth, we may be <u>all</u> united in <u>Heaven.</u>

As the duty to which I have been assigned renders it impossible for me to keep a diary, I have concluded to stop it at once.

As soon as my furlough expires I will probably be back in old Pr. Wm. with my friends there, and the Yanks. Finis.

NOTE:

Spellings (and misspellings) in the diary transcription are from the original, as are all punctuation and line spacing.

Timeline of the Civil War

Courtesy of the Smithsonian Institution (www.civilar.si.edu) and other sources.
The "Towles-related" entries are in italics.

1859

OCTOBER 16-18
John Brown, in an attempt to amass arms for a slave insurrection, attacks the Federal armory and arsenal at Harpers Ferry, Virginia.

DECEMBER 2
Brown is hanged for murder and treason at Charles Town, Virginia.

1860

SEPTEMBER
Rev. John Towles resigns as parish Rector and prepares to "refugee" south with his family.

NOVEMBER 6
Abraham Lincoln is elected President.

Virginia militia "Grand Encampment"

DECEMBER 20
As a consequence of Lincoln's election, a special convention of the South Carolina legislature votes to secede from the Union. Eventually 11 southern states secede from the Union. Kentucky and Maryland, slave-holding border states that did not secede, are included in the Confederate flag, with 13 stars.

1861

MARCH 4
Abraham Lincoln is inaugurated as the 16th President of the United States.

APRIL 12-13
Fort Sumter in Charleston is bombarded and surrenders to South Carolina troops led by P.G.T. Beauregard.

JUNE 1
Skirmish at Fairfax Courthouse

JULY 21
First Battle of Bull Run (or Manassas). Confederate General Thomas J. Jackson earns the nickname "Stonewall" for tenacity in battle.

NOVEMBER
George B. McClellan replaces the aging Winfield Scott as general-in-chief of the Union armies.

Julia Ward Howe, inspired by seeing a review of McClellan's army, composes the lyrics to "The Battle Hymn of the Republic."

WINTER 1861-62
"Sitzkrieg": a period of relative inactivity in the Eastern Theater of the war

1862

JUNE 1
Robert E. Lee takes command of the Confederate Army after Joseph E. Johnston is wounded at the Battle of Seven Pines.

JUNE 25-JULY 1
Lee forces McClellan's army to retreat during the Seven Days campaign. McClellan's Army of the Potomac is eventually withdrawn from the Virginia Peninsula to reinforce the newly created Union Army of Virginia.

Lincoln appoints John Pope to command the Union Army of Virginia.

AUGUST 22
J.E.B. Stuart's raid on Catlett's Station

AUGUST 29-30
Confederate victory at the Battle of Second Manassas

SEPTEMBER 17
The Battle of Antietam, Maryland, exacts heavy losses on both sides—the bloodiest single day in the war, with more than 20,000 total casualties.

OCTOBER 31
Rosalie Towles dies of fever in the Northern Neck of Virginia.

DECEMBER 13
Confederate victory at the Battle of Fredericksburg

1863

JANUARY 1
Lincoln issues the Emancipation Proclamation, which declares that slaves in the seceded states are now free.

APRIL
Robert Towles is detached as a "scout for General Stuart" in Prince William County, Virginia.

MAY 1-4
Lee hands the Army of the Potomac another serious loss at the Battle of Chancellorsville. "Stonewall" Jackson is wounded during the battle. He will develop pneumonia and die on May 10.

JULY 1-3
The Battle of Gettysburg is fought in Pennsylvania. General George G. Meade compromises his victory by allowing Lee to retreat South across the Potomac.

JULY 4
After a long siege, Confederates surrender Vicksburg, Mississippi to Ulysses S. Grant, thus securing the Mississippi River for the Union.

July 13-15
Violent riots erupt in New York City in protest of the draft.

August 5
Robert Towles is captured while scouting in Prince William County. He is taken to Old Capitol Prison in Washington City and is eventually transferred to the Carroll Prison annex as a "prisoner of State," or spy.

September 19-20
Confederates under General Braxton Bragg win a great tactical victory at Chickamauga, in the Western Theater of the war.

October 1
Robert Towles escapes from Old Capitol/Carroll Prison.

October 11
Vivian Towles is killed in a skirmish at Raccoon Ford.

November 13
Robert returns to his unit, reports for duty, and is granted a 15-day furlough to visit his family in the Northern Neck.

November 19
Lincoln delivers his Gettysburg Address, in which he reiterates the nation's fundamental principle that all men are created equal.

1864

March 10
Newly-commissioned to the rank of Lieutenant General, Ulysses S. Grant is given official authority to command all of the Union armies.

May 5-6
The Battle of the Wilderness in Virginia is the first of a bloody series of month-long engagements between Grant and Lee.

May 9
Jimmie Towles is killed in a skirmish near Spotsylvania.

JUNE 11-12
Battle of Trevilian Station. Robert Towles is mortally wounded in battle, dies, and is buried near Louisa in Oakland Cemetery.

JUNE 30
Potomac Flotilla seaborne raid on the Northern Neck. Greenvale Manor and surrounding properties are shelled and sacked by Union marines. Sophronia Towles defies the raiders by singing "The Bonnie Blue Flag."

SEPTEMBER 2
After forcing the Confederate army of John Bell Hood out of Atlanta, Georgia, General William Tecumseh Sherman captures the city, a major munitions center for the South.

NOVEMBER 8
Lincoln is re-elected President.

NOVEMBER 16
Sherman leaves Atlanta and begins his "march to the sea," in an attempt to demoralize the South and hasten surrender.

1865

MARCH 4
Lincoln is inaugurated as President for a second term.

MARCH 29
The Appomattox campaign begins, with Grant's move against Lee's defenses at Petersburg, Virginia.

APRIL 2-3
Petersburg falls, and the Confederate government evacuates its nearby capital, Richmond. Union troops occupy Richmond.

APRIL 9
Robert E. Lee surrenders the Army of Northern Virginia to Grant at Appomattox.

APRIL 14
John Wilkes Booth shoots President Lincoln at Ford's Theater.

APRIL 15
Lincoln dies, and Andrew Johnson is inaugurated as President.

APRIL 26
Joseph E. Johnston surrenders to William T. Sherman in North Carolina. John Wilkes Boot is shot in a barn in Virginia and dies.

JUNE 30
All eight conspirators are convicted for the assassination of President Lincoln; four are sentenced to death.

--- 1866 ---

SEPTEMBER
Rev. John Towles returns to Prince William County and seeks to re-establish his parish churches. Unable to do so because of limited resources, he creates a school called the Sulphur Spring Academy, and plans to minister to and educate freed blacks, among others. After warnings, arsonists set fire to the building.

--- 1867 ---

APRIL
Rev. John Towles and his family move to Accokeek, Maryland.

BIBLIOGRAPHY

Primary Sources

Towles, Rev. John C.
Collected letters

Towles, James
Collected letters

Towles, Robert C.
"Diary, Kept While a Prisoner"

Towles, Robert C.
Collected letters

Towles, Sophronia C.
Collected letters

Towles, Vivian
Collected letters

Published Sources

Abel, E. Lawrence. *Singing the New Nation*. Mechanicsville: Stackpole Books, 2000.

Axelrod, Alan. *The War Between the Spies*. New York: Atlantic Monthly Press, 1992.

Ash, Stephen V. *When the Yankees Came*. Chapel Hill: University of North Carolina Press, 1995.

Avary, Myrta Lockett. *A Virginia Girl in the Civil War*. New York: D. Appleton and Co., 1903.

_____. *Dixie After the War*. Boston: Houghton Mifflin Company, 1937.

Bakeless, John. *Spies of the Confederacy*. Philadelphia and New York: J.B. Lippincott Co., 1970.

Baker, La Fayette C. *History of the United States Secret Service*. Philadelphia: L.C. Baker, 1867.

_____. *Spies, Traitors and Conspirators of the Late Civil War*. Philadelphia: J.E. Potter & Co., 1894.

_____. *The United States Secret Service in the Late War*. Philadelphia: J.E. Potter & Co., 1889.

Beale, G.W. *A Lieutenant of Cavalry in Lee's Army*. Boston: The Gorham Press (reprint by Butternut and Blue, Baltimore), 1994.

Beale, R.L.T. *History of the Ninth Virginia Cavalry in the War Between the States*. Richmond: B.F. Johnson Publishing Co., 1899.

Benson, Susan Williams (ed.). *Berry Benson's Civil War Book*. Athens: University of Georgia Press, 1992.

Black, Robert C., III. *Railroads of the Confederacy.* Chapel Hill: University of North Carolina Press, 1952.

Blackford, W.W. *War Years With Jeb Stuart.* New York: Charles Scribner's Sons, 1945.

Boyd, Belle. *Belle Boyd in Camp and Prison.* Baton Rouge: Louisiana State University Press, 1998.

Brooks, Noah. *Washington, D.C. in Lincoln's Time.* New York: The Century Company, 1896.

Brooks, U.R. *Butler and His Cavalry in the War of Secession.* Columbia: The State Company, 1909.

_____. *Stories of the Confederacy.* Columbia: The State Company, 1912.

Brown, George B. *A History of Prince William County.* Historic Prince William, Inc., 1994.

Brown, R. Shepard. *Stringfellow of the Fourth.* New York: Crown Publishers, Inc., 1960.

Butler, Diana H. *Standing Against the Whirlwind: Evangelical Episcopalians in Nineteenth-Century America.* Oxford University Press, 1995.

Campbell, Helen Jones. *Confederate Courier.* New York: St. Martin's Press, 1965.

Carter, Samuel. *The Last Cavaliers.* New York: St. Martin's Press, 1979.

Carter, Lt. Col. William R. (ed. By Walbrook D. Swank). *Sabres, Saddles, and Spurs.* Shappensburg: Burd Street Press, 1998.

Chowning, Larry S. Soldiers at the Doorstep: Civil War Lore. Centreville: Tidewater Publishers, 1999.

Cooke, John Esten. *Wearing of the Gray.* Baton Rouge: Louisiana State University Press, 1997.

Cozzens, Peter and Robert I. Girardi (ed.). *The Military Memoirs of General John Pope.* Chapel Hill: University of North Carolina Press, 1998.

Cutrer, Thomas W. and T. Michael Parris. *Brothers in Gray.* Baton Rouge: Louisiana State University Press, 1997.

Denney, Robert E. *Civil War Prisons and Escapes.* New York: Sterling Publishing Company, Inc., 1993.

Dunaway, Rev. Wayland Fuller. *Reminiscences of a Rebel.* New York: The Neale Publishing Co., 1913.

Ellis, John B. *The Sights and Secrets of the National Capital.* New York: United States Publishing Company, 1869.

Ewell, Alice Maude. *A Virginia Scene or Life in Old Prince William.* Lynchburg: J.P. Bell Company, Inc., 1931.

Faust, Drew Gilpin. *This Republic of Suffering.* New York: Alfred A. Knopf, 2008.

Field, Ron. *Brassey's History of Uniforms: American Civil War Confederate Army.* London: Brassey's (UK), Ltd., 1998.

Fishel, Edwin C. *The Secret War for the Union.* Boston: Houghton Mifflin Co., 1996.

Funk, Joseph. *The Harmonia Sacra.* Intercourse: Good Books, 1993.

Garnett, Theodore Stanford (Robert J. Trout, ed.). *Riding With Stuart.* White Mane Publishing Co., 1994.

Gilmor, Harry. *Four Years in the Saddle.* New York: Harper & Brothers, 1866.

Goodwin, Rev. William A.R. *History of the Theological Seminary in Virginia and Its Historical Background, Vol. II.* Rochester: The DuBois Press, ___.

Griffith, Paddy. *Battle Tactics of the Civil War.* Yale University Press, 1987.

Grimsley, Mark. *The Hard Hand of War.* Cambridge University Press, 1995.

Guelzo, Allen E. *For the Union of Evangelical Christendom: the Irony of the Reformed Episcopalians.* Pennsylvania University Press, 1994.

Hackley, Woodford B. *The Little Fork Rangers: A Sketch of Company "D", Fourth Virginia Cavalry.* Richmond: Dietz Printing Company, 1927.

Hard, Abner, M.D. History of the Eighth Cavalry Regiment Illinois Volunteers During the Great Rebellion. Aurora, 1868.

Harrison, Fairfax. *Landmarks of Old Prince William.* Berryville: Chesapeake Book Co., 1964.

Haynie, Miriam. *The Stronghold: A Story of Historic Northern Neck of Virginia and Its People.* Richmond: The Dietz Press, Inc., 1999.

Haythornthwaite, Philip. *Uniforms of the Civil War.* New York: Sterling Publishing Company, Inc., 1990.

Helm, Lewis Marshall. *Black Horse Cavalry: Defend Our Beloved Country.* Higher Education Publications, 2004.

Henderson, E. Prioleu. *Autobiography of Arab.* Fox Books, 1997.

Hesseltine, William Best. *Civil War Prisons: A Study in War Psychology.* Columbus: Ohio State University Press, 1998.

Holmes, David L. *A Brief History of the Episcopal Church.* Trinity Press International, 1993.

Horowitz, Tony. Midnight Rising: John Brown and the Raid That Sparked the Civil War. New York: Henry Holt & Co., 2011.

Howard, Oliver Otis. *Autobiography of Oliver Otis Howard, Vol. I.* New York: The Baker and Taylor Company, 1907.

Hunton, Eppa. *Autobiography of Eppa Hunton.* Richmond: The William Byrd Press, Inc., 1933.

Jacobs, Lee (comp.). *The Gray Riders: Stories from the Confederate Cavalry.* Shappensburg, 1999.

Jones, Virgil Carrington. *Ranger Mosby.* Chapel Hill: University of North Carolina Press, 1944.

Kane, Harnett T. *The Smiling Rebel.* Garden City: Doubleday and Co., Inc., 1955.

_____. *Spies for the Blue and Gray.* Garden City: Hanover House, 1954.

Katcher, Philip (Martin Windrow, ed.). *American Civil War Armies I, Confederate Troops.* Oxford: Osprey Publishing, 1998.

Kimmel, Stanley Preston. *Mr. Lincoln's Washington.* New York: Coward-McCann, 1957.

Knapp, David. *The Confederate Horsemen.* New York: Vantage Press, 1966.

Krick, Robert K. *Lee's Colonels.* Morningside House, Inc., 1992.

_____. *9ᵗʰ Virginia Cavalry.* Lynchburg: H.E. Howard, Inc., 1982.

Leech, Margaret. *Reveille in Washington 1860-1865.* New York: Tim Inc., 1941.

Longacre, Edward G. *Custer and His Wolverines.* Pennsylvania Combined Publishing, 1997.

_____. *Fitz Lee.* Da Capo Press, 2005.

Lonn, Ella., *Desertion During the Civil War.* Lincoln: University of Nebraska Press, 1998.

Lowry, Thomas P. *Tarnished Eagles.* Mechanicsburg: Stackpole Books, 1997.

Mahony, D.A. *The Prisoner of State.* New York: G.W. Carleton and Co., 1863.

Markle, Donal E. *Spies and Spymasters of the Civil War.* New York: Hippcrene Books, 1994.

Marshall, John A. *American Bastille.* Philadelphia: Thos. W. Hartley, 1872.

Marten, James (Gary Gallagher, ed.). *The Children's Civil War.* Chapel Hill: University of North Carolina Press, 1998.

Matter, William D. *If It Takes All Summer: The Battle of Spotsylvania.* Chapel Hill: University of North Carolina Press, 1988.

McArthur, Judith N. and Orville V. Burton. *A Gentleman and an Officer*. New York: Oxford University Press, 1996.

McClellan, Henry B. *I Rode With Jeb Stuart*. New York: Da Capo Press, 1994.

McKivigan, John R. and Mitchell Snay (ed.). *Religion and the Antebellum Debate Over Slavery*. Athens: University of Georgia Press, 1998.

McPherson, James M. *Battle Cry of Freedom*. New York: Oxford University Press, 1988.

_____. *Drawn With the Sword: Reflections on the Civil War*. New York: Oxford University Press, 1996.

_____. *For Cause and Comrades*. New York: Oxford University Press, 1997.

_____. *What They Fought For*. Baton Rouge: Louisiana State University Press, 1994.

Miller, Mary R. *Place Names of the Northern Neck of Virginia*. Richmond: Virginia State Library, 1983.

Miller, Randall M., H.S. Stout, C.R. Wilson (editors). *Religion and the American Civil War*. New York: Oxford University Press, 1998.

Mills, Eric. *Chesapeake Bay in the Civil War*. Centreville: Tidewater Publishers, 1996.

Mogelever, Jacob. *Death to Traitors: The Story of General Lafayette C. Baker, Lincoln's Forgotten Secret Service Chief*. Garden City: Doubleday & Company, Inc., 1960.

Moore, Henry Woodbury. *Chained to Virginia While Carolina Bleeds*. 1996.

Moore, James. *Kilpatrick and Our Cavalry*. New York: W.J. Middleton, 1865.

Mullin, Robert Bruce. *Episcopal Vision/American Reality: High Church Theology and Social Thought in Evangelical America*. New Haven: Yale University Press, 1986.

Munson, John W. *Reminiscences of a Mosby Guerrilla*. New York: Moffat, Yard and Co., 1906.

O'Connor, Richard. *Sheridan the Inevitable*. Bobbs-Merrill Company, Inc., 1953.

Opie, John N. *A Rebel Cavalryman With Lee, Stuart and Jackson.* Chicago: Morningside, 1997.

Phillips, Philip. *Hallowed Songs.* Cincinnati: Hitchcock and Walden, ___.

Prichard, Robert W. *A History of the Episcopal Church.* Morehouse, 1991.

Rable, George C. *Civil Wars: Women and the Crisis of Southern Nationalism.* Urbana: University of Illinois Press, 1991.

Quaife, M.M. (ed.). *Absalom Grimes, Confederate Mail Runner.* New Haven: Yale University Press, 1926.

Ramage, James A. *Gray Ghost: The Life of Col. John Singleton Mosby.* The University Press of Kentucky, 1999.

Ratcliffe, R. Jackson. *This Was Prince William.* Manassas: REF Typesetting and Publishing, 1978.

Rawlings, Kevin. *We Were Marching on Christmas Day.* Baltimore: Toomey Press, 1995.

Reade, Frank Robertson (Robert J. Trout, ed.). *In the Saddle With Stuart.* Gettysburg: Thomas Publications, 1998.

Rhea, Gordon C. *The Battles for Spotsylvania Court House and the Road to Yellow Tavern.* Baton Rouge: University of Louisiana Press, 1997.

Robertson, James I. *Soldiers Blue and Gray.* Columbia: University of South Carolina Press, 1988.

Robinson, William M. *Justice in Grey: A History of the Judicial System of the Confederate States of America.* New York: Russell & Russell, 1968.

Sangston, Lawrence. *Bastilles of the North, by a Member of the Maryland Legislature.* Baltimore: Kelly, Hedian and Piet, 1863.

Scarborough, Ruth. *Belle Boyd: Siren of the South.* Macon: Mercer University Press, 1997.

Scheel, Eugene M. *Crossroads and Corners.* Historic Prince William, 1996.

Schutz, Wallace J. and W.N. Trenerry. *Abandoned by Lincoln: A Military Biography of General John Pope.* Urbana: University of Illinois Press, 1990.

Sigaud, Louis A. *Belle Boyd: Confederate Spy.* Richmond: The Dietz Press, Inc., 1941.

Simkins, Francis Butler and James Welch Patton. *Women of the Confederacy.* Richmond: Garrett and Massie, Inc., 1936.

Simmons, C. Jackson. *Speaking of the Northern Neck of Virginia.* 1998.

Speer, Lonnie R. *Portals of Hell: Military Prisons of the Civil War.* Mechanicsburg: Stackpole Books, 1997.

Starr, Stephen Z. *The Union Cavalry in the Civil War, Vol. II.* Baton Rouge: Louisiana State University Press, 1981.
Staudenraus, P.J. *Mr. Lincoln's Washington.* New York: Thomas Yoseloff, 1967.

Stiles, Kenneth L. *4th Virginia Cavalry.* Lynchburg: H.E. Howard, Inc., 1985.

Sutherland, Daniel E. (ed.). *Guerrillas, Unionists, and Violence on the Confederate Home Front.* Fayetteville: The University of Arkansas Press, 1999.

Swank, Walbrook Davis. *Battle of Trevilian Station.* 1994.

Tatum, Georgia Lee. *Disloyalty in the Confederacy.* Chapel Hill: University of North Carolina Press, 1934.

Templeton, Eleanor Lee and Nan Netherton. *Northern Virginia Heritage,* 1966.

Thomas, Emory M. *Bold Dragoon.* New York: Harper and Row, 1986.

Thomason, John W. *Jeb Stuart.* Charles Scribner's Sons, 1930.

Tidwell, William A. *Come Retribution.* Jackson: University Press of Mississippi, 1988.

Tighe, Adrian G. *The Bristoe Campaign: General Lee's Last Strategic Offensive with the Army of Northern Virginia, October 1863.* XLibris Corporation, 2011.

Tower, R. Lockwood (ed.). *Lee's Adjutant.* University of South Carolina Press, 1995.

Trout, Robert J. *They Followed the Plume.* Mechanicsburg: Stackpole Books, 1993.

_____. *With Pen and Saber.* Mechanicsburg: Stackpole Books, 1995.

Urwin, Gregory J.W. *Custer Victorious.* Edison: The Blue and Grey Press, 1983.

Von Borcke, Heros and Justus Scheibert. *The Great Cavalry Battle of Brandy Station.* Gettysburg: Olde Soldier Books, Inc., 1976.

Warner, Ezra J. *Generals in Blue.* Baton Rouge: Louisiana State University Press, 1993.

_____. *Generals in Gray.* Baton Rouge: Louisiana State University Press, 1995.

Waugh, Charles G. and M.H. Greenberg. *The Women's War in the South.* Nashville: Cumberland House, 1999.

Wellman, Manly Wade. *The Ghost Battalion.* New York: Ives Washburn, Inc., 1958.
_____. *Giant in Gray.* New York: Charles Scribner's Sons, 1949.

_____. *Ride Rebels!* New York: Ives Washburn, Inc., 1959.

Wells, Edward L. *Hampton and His Cavalry in '64.* Richmond: B.F. Johnson Publishing Company, 1899.

Wert, Jeffrey D. *Mosby's Rangers.* New York: Simon and Schuster, 1990.

_____. *Cavalryman of the Lost Cause: A Biography of J.E.B. Stuart.* New York: Simon & Schuster, 2008.

Whitehorne, Joseph W.A. *The Battle for Baltimore, 1814.* Baltimore: Nautical & Aviation Publishing Co., 1997.

Williamson, James J. *Prison Life in the Old Capitol.* West Orange: Williamson Publishing, 1911.

Wills, Mary Alice. *The Confederate Blockade of Washington, D.C. 1861-1862.* Shappensburg: 1998.

INDEX

Page numbers in *italics* indicate a photo or figure on that page.

About the Author

KEITH KEHLBECK is a writer, historian, and marketing consultant with clients in the hospitality, nonprofit, and publishing sectors. He currently serves as Executive Director for DiRoNA (Distinguished Restaurants of North America). His clients have included the W.K. Kellogg Foundation, Schuler's Restaurant & Pub, *Inns Magazine*, and the Corporation for Public Broadcasting. For eight years, he served as Director of Marketing and Communications and then Executive Director for Select Registry, Distinguished Inns of North America, the premier marketing association for the upscale innkeeping industry. He has served on various boards, including the regional Convention and Visitors Bureau, the local Chamber of Commerce, and the Marshall Historical Society (serving as its Chair).

From the time his family took a cross-country bus trip to visit Gettysburg on vacation when he was ten years old, he has been fascinated by the War Between the States, its personalities, participants, and details. His wife Ali and their daughter Emma share his interest, if not quite his level of passion for the topic. They live in Marshall, Michigan—"the City of Hospitality"—but have a second home in the Northern Neck of Virginia.

CPSIA information can be obtained at www.ICGtesting.com
Printed in the USA
LVOW01*0336261213

366753LV00006B/29/P